Handbook of Practice Management

Ninth Edition

RIBA ⧉ **Publishing**

© RIBA Enterprises Ltd, 2013, reprinted 2016
1st edition published 1965*
2nd edition published 1967*
3rd revised edition published 1973*
4th revised edition published 1980*
5th edition published 1991†
6th edition published 1998†
7th edition published 2001†
8th edition published 2010†
*Under the title RIBA Handbook of Architectural Practice and Management
†Under the title RIBA Architect's Handbook of Practice Management

Published by RIBA Publishing, 76 Portland Place, London W1B 1NT

ISBN 978 1 85946 505 9

Stock code 80465

British Library Cataloguing in Publication Data
A catalogue record for this book is available from the British Library.

Publisher: Steven Cross
Commissioning Editor: Sharla Plant
Project Editor: Alasdair Deas
Designed and typeset by Academic + Technical, Bristol
Printed and bound by Polestar Wheatons, Exeter, UK
Cover image: © iStock / Tony Baggett

RIBA Publishing is part of RIBA Enterprises Ltd.
www.ribaenterprises.com

Contents

Foreword

Since the first edition was published over 50 years ago, the RIBA *Handbook of Practice Management* has become a long-standing companion in the challenges of running and managing an architectural practice.

This ninth edition builds on the developments brought to the previous edition and brings it right up to date, incorporating the new RIBA Plan of Work 2013, additional advice on starting a practice, plus more on IT, sustainability, working collaboratively and BIM as well as other key topics.

The *Handbook* complements the ninth edition of the *RIBA Job Book*, and just as the *Job Book* sets the standard for running an architectural project, so the *Handbook* sets the standard for running the practice as a whole.

Through better management of its finances, its processes, and – that most valuable of assets – its people, any architectural practice can ensure it operates on a more secure, more profitable, and ultimately more creative basis. This is the case whether the practice is new or well established, and whether a sole trader or a large firm; all should make good use of this book.

Stephen R. Hodder MBE
President, RIBA (2013–2015)

Preface

This ninth edition of the *Handbook of Practice Management* was prepared after publication of the ninth edition of the *RIBA Job Book*, and is intended to be complementary to it. The two publications form a dual reference source and practical practice management tool. It can also be read in conjunction with the *RIBA Small Projects Handbook* which provides guidance on managing projects up to one million pounds in value and concise practice management advice specifically aimed at small practices. The *Handbook of Practice Management* covers the wide spectrum of knowledge required for the successful management of an architectural practice, including business and financial management, marketing, communication and information management.

The presentation and content of the book are intended to make the information it contains accessible and relevant to both large and small practices as well as students of architecture. As with the eighth edition, this edition has been written with an emphasis on the practical aspects of working as an architect, with the broad premise that architects are busy people who need to access the information required to undertake a specific task quickly, and need that information to be precise and to the point, providing just what they need to be able to execute the activity in hand, rather than having to trawl through a broad background narrative.

As the *Handbook of Practice Management* is intended as a first port of call, it includes lists of references and suggestions for further reading (located at the end of each chapter) for those wishing to gain a wider understanding of the subject matter and, in Chapter 1, information on key industry bodies, together with their contact details.

There are a number of key changes encompassed by this edition. Revised statistical analysis and broad transformation in the industry – accelerated by the economic downturn – are reflected in Chapter 1: The industry and Chapter 2: The profession, the latter also including advice on equality and diversity in the workforce. Chapter 1 has an updated schedule of the key industry bodies, their functions and contact details. Chapter 2 reflects on the future challenges to the profession associated with an increased focus on providing value and tighter cost management, specialisation, roles for architectural graduates outside of practice and the nature of architectural education. Chapter 3 provides a general update on legislation and, new to this edition, changes with regard to legislation on environmental sustainability. Chapter 4: Setting up a practice, has new advice on business planning and collaborative practices and Chapter 5 now includes advice on the use of social media in marketing. Chapter 8: Office management, has a new section on running a 'green' office, and Chapters 10: Procedures and processes and 12: Computing, CAD, BIM and IT have been updated to reflect revisions to the Uniclass classification system and BIM processes. Last, but not least, the book has been updated to reflect the new RIBA Plan of Work 2013, primarily with regard to Chapter 10.

The book is structured into three broad sections:

- The industry
- Practice management
- Project management.

Each chapter has a brief introduction, and given the close relationship of much of the subject matter, cross-referencing to other parts of the book has been included to aid navigation.

Nigel Ostime

Acknowledgements

The author would like to thank Richard Fairhead for his contribution in updating Chapters 10 and 12 with regard to classification and BIM. Thanks also to David Stanford, Graham Hickson-Smith and John Waddell whose contributions to the previous edition have not been forgotten; to Adrian Dobson and Richard Brindley from the RIBA for their invaluable input and advice; to Jane Duncan for her input on diversity and equality in the profession; to David Gloster for his input on architectural education; to Lynne Sullivan, who wrote *The RIBA Guide to Sustainability in Practice* (2012), used as a source for Chapters 3 and 8; and to Simon Howard of the ARB.

About the author

Nigel Ostime is an architect and Project Delivery Director at Hawkins\ Brown Architects.

He has wide experience in the design and delivery of complex projects, including numerous large-scale developments in aviation, utility infrastructure, commercial offices, high-end residential, retail, town-centre mixed-use and industrial/distribution buildings. He has delivered planning permissions on sensitive sites, both urban and rural, and has expertise in the management and coordination of multidisciplinary consultant teams through all project stages.

He is an active member of the RIBA, currently being a member of the Practice and Profession Committee and also chair of the Client Liaison Group, which provides an interface between the Institute and client bodies. As a member of the Large Practice Group he set up the RIBA Future Leaders initiative, an education programme for business-focused, post-Part 3 skills for architects.

He was editor of the previous edition of this book and the current edition of the *RIBA Job Book*. He is author of the *Small Projects Handbook* (2014) and has developed quality management and briefing/evaluation toolkits for RIBA Chartered Practices.

He lives in north London with his wife, three children and six bicycles.

Part 1
The industry

The construction industry

THIS CHAPTER:

- discusses current issues within the construction industry;
- considers trends within the industry;
- lists the key roles within the construction industry;
- provides a list of useful organisations that offer support and information.

1.1 Introduction

We have undoubtedly witnessed significant change in the construction industry over the past seven years or so in terms of its composition, increased competitiveness, advancing technology and, of course, a reduction in its capacity due to the economic downturn experienced across much of the globe.

Architectural practices have needed to respond to these changes to remain in business by being flexible in their business planning and project execution. This has been a difficult transition, but there are many positives to be taken from it, including:

- the need to focus on design quality while maintaining tight control on costs – both of the construction and of design development;
- the need to embrace emerging information technology and building information modelling (BIM);
- the benefits of collaboration, facilitated by the RIBA Plan of Work 2013.

The European economy remains fragile and the key issue in the UK construction industry will remain a financial one for some time to come, with continuing public spending cuts and restricted lending for private development. Some sectors have shown signs of recovery, and there is still an enormous demand for housing, particularly in London and the South East. Large public infrastructure projects have helped limit the deficit of construction activity, but a return to pre-recession levels of activity is some way off.

Sustainability has taken something of a back seat and targets for improvement have been eroded. Framework agreements have diminished, at least in the private sector if not in the public sector. BIM has had greater uptake in the private sector, despite government dictates on public sector procurement. Payment conditions are often poor, with the public sector being better than the private, where sub-contractors and consultants complain bitterly about delays in payment causing a strain on cash flow.

According to the *Building* White Paper *Client Intelligence 2013*, of approximately £100 billion of capital expenditure in UK construction in 2012, around 14% was public spending, including 4% on housing. Of the 86% private sector spend, offices accounted for 5%, retail 6%, industrial 3% and leisure/other 10%. Infrastructure, including airports, other transport, energy, water and so on, accounted for 11%. Private housing accounted for 17% of spend. Repairs and maintenance was 35%, of which 16% was for housing.

There is a continuing trend for construction companies to look to international markets, with South Asia and Middle East/North Africa (MENA) being seen as the most significant. Political and social factors are having a significant effect on the MENA region though.

The construction industry remains a large and dynamic one, made up of a diverse collection of companies and organisations with a broad skills base and with a vitality and energy that make it a unique and stimulating environment in which to work.

It is important for architects to understand the scope of the industry and their relationship to the key parties involved:

- employers/clients;
- contractors and sub-contractors;
- suppliers of building materials and products;
- consultants.

1.2   Contracting and procurement

The RIBA Plan of Work 2013 (see Chapter 10) focuses on the benefits of collaboration and BIM-enabled procurement, reflecting the drive by both public and private sector clients to find further efficiencies, increase value and improve quality in construction output. Time will tell what impact this will have on procurement, alongside the other factors that influence how project teams and construction supply chains are engaged, not least of which is cost.

Construction is underpinned by the different methods of contracting used to procure building and engineering projects. There are many standard forms of construction contract, although the essential principles remain the same.

Building procurement methods are founded on the allocation of risk between employer and contractor – and on down the supply chain to the contractor's sub-contractors and suppliers. Somewhere in the middle

1

are the construction professions, who have traditionally protected the employers but who also have a contractual relationship with and liability to them – adding a layer of commercial tension.

The differing forms of construction contract either place more risk on the contractor or allow the employer to retain a degree of the risk – for a reduced price. As well as proportioning risk, the different forms of contract provide differing degrees of control over the three key performance indicators for building work:

- cost
- programme
- quality.

In any single project the correct balance between these three – to some extent competing – performance targets needs to be found, in order to best meet the requirements and expectations of the client. The various building procurement methods each place different emphasis on the relative importance of these targets, and as trends have changed – generally with changes in the economy – the differing methods have in turn shaped the direction, structure and organisation of the construction industry at any given time.

Consultants have traditionally acted to represent the interests of the employer, but today often work as a service provider to contractors as well. The fact that consultants are increasingly working for contractors when they take on design responsibilities complicates matters further. This change has required architects to adapt to a differing role and a different sort of client. Data from the RIBA Business Benchmarking Survey 2012/13 indicates that 19% of architects' fees now come from contractor clients.

The contractual arrangements between the key parties in the industry are increasingly complex and their roles overlap to a greater degree. Some contractors are becoming developers and also, increasingly, are taking on projects before the design is complete, allowing employers to transfer more of the risk to them.

Over the past 15 years the industry has experimented with partnering arrangements of different types with varying degrees of success, but partly as a result of economic forces there has recently been renewed interest in more traditional methods of competitive tendering and building procurement as well as design and build procurement. Partnering has been a positive response to the frequently adversarial nature of construction contracts, and the inherent waste and inefficiency of the resultant conflict.

Partnering involves the sharing of risk, and an emphasis on longer term relationships for repeat commissions, knowledge-sharing and continuous improvement. However, there is also a perception that it can carry with it higher costs, and may lead to complacency – as opposed to the cut and thrust of competitive tendering. The truth is no doubt somewhere in the middle. Regardless of this, it is generally recognised that collaboration within the design team and the wider supply chain (particularly when aligned to BIM technology) can bring significant efficiencies and improved quality to the project and the RIBA Plan of Work 2013 facilitates this.

Design and build favours delivery time and cost; traditional single-stage tendering tends to result in longer programme timescales but gives closer control – in theory at least – to cost and quality; construction management gives programme benefits, and two-stage tendering provides a halfway position – reducing programme but with a potential uplift in cost.

Whole-life contracts, with design-construct-operate agreements, such as PFI, continue to be used for public works and on commercial projects. Design and build is the norm when the type of project is appropriate – and sometimes when it isn't. Construction management is used less than it was 10–15 years ago, and this may be indicative of the increasing importance of cost certainty. Employers naturally look for a guaranteed maximum price, and margins are getting ever tighter, for consultants as well as contractors. This tightening of profit is forcing consultants to find more efficient ways of producing design and, encouraged – or perhaps coerced – by the insurance industry, place a greater emphasis on managing their risk (see Chapter 11).

For many larger projects the architect's traditional role of lead consultant has been reduced, and although the team may be led by architects, frequently this will not be case. The RIBA Plan of Work 2013 adopts the terms 'project lead' and 'lead designer' for the individual or practice that performs these functions on projects of any size.

The project may be procured through a core relationship between consultant and 'constructors', possibly through the use of design and build or construction management procurement, or through the use of traditional procurement coupled with a partnering charter, or through the use of a multi-party partnering contract. Although these arrangements will generally be confined to larger projects, and the role of the 'general practitioner' architect will undoubtedly continue, even smaller practices may find themselves asked to participate in partnering arrangements or to join consortia. It is essential that architects take a proactive role in managing their response to these new arrangements, and seize new opportunities where they arise.

1

1.3   Future trends

So where is the industry heading and what are the key issues facing it today? The past few years have seen a continued increase in:

- the importance of equality and diversity in the workforce;
- the importance of managing risk;
- technological advances;
- reliance on electronic means of communication;
- consolidation of businesses; and
- globalisation.

Sadly, to this list one could add increasing insolvencies. This has led to clients taking a keener interest in the financial health of their teams, although unfortunately it has not resulted in improved payment conditions, which are still poor in some areas. Consequently, stability is currently one of the three most important criteria for selection of a contractor, the other two being price and quality.

One could also add that while the need for sustainable design solutions and construction methods is acknowledged, there has been a deceleration in regulatory reform and clients are putting far less emphasis on it than on commercial criteria. Interestingly though, BIM comes lower on the list of priorities, for contractors at least.

Innovation remains important in selecting the team, particularly where it can bring commercial advantage, and site safety continues to be taken seriously, although accidents and fatalities remain too high.

Sustainability has regrettably become a lower priority for clients as a result of tightening financial constraints, although the need for a sustainable approach is unabated. Construction continues to have a major part to play, with the built environment being responsible for around 45% of carbon emissions. (It should, however, be noted that new buildings account for just 1% of the total stock.) Legislation on the environment continues to evolve; see Chapter 3 for further guidance.

New buildings and refurbishment of the existing building stock still have to meet the challenges of the UK's drive to cut emissions by 34% by 2020 – the first step towards an 80% reduction by 2050, in line with the Climate Change Act 2008. In addition, in 2009, the UK Government committed the country to sourcing 15% of its energy from renewable sources by 2020. A significant amount of legislation and many policies have been enacted that impact significantly on the construction industry and practices will need to keep abreast of this increasingly complex and changing environment. Refer to Section 3.7 for legislation related to environmental sustainability.

The RIBA provides a freely available range of climate change toolkits for architects, which provide an overview and introduction to particular areas of professional knowledge, with detailed guides to further sources of authoritative information. Advice can also be sought from organisations such as the BRE (see Section 1.5), which has developed a range of sustainability standards, codes and methodologies (such as BREEAM) for buildings, homes and communities. For more information, go to the BRE website (www.bre.co.uk) or refer to the RIBA website.

There have been significant changes to the town planning system, with the advent of the National Planning Policy Framework, and at the same time a diminished role for (Design Council) CABE, which has been a victim of government cuts, reducing its capacity to act as an advocate for the value of design and the promotion of design standards.

1.3.1   Equality and diversity in the workforce

Equality and diversity are important matters for the profession: around half of Part 1 graduates are female, but women only make up 25% of fee earners and just 12% of equity partners and shareholder directors (RIBA Business Benchmarking Survey 2012/13). This points to a case for some reform of architectural education and more flexibility in routes to qualification.

Diversity is important. We live in a world of social, economic and demographic changes – increases in minority ethnic population, globalisation and diversity of workforce – and there is an expectation for employers to accommodate the resultant needs, through approach, flexible working and 'work-life balance'. Tomorrow's markets will be characterised by diversity and not uniformity, thus diversity in the workforce is an important business strategy.

There are benefits to diversity, including:

- a wider talent base;
- employees feeling respected, valued and engaged in their work, providing enhanced creativity and innovation;
- reduced costs of staff turnover and absenteeism;
- improved knowledge of different cultures and with different clients;
- enhancing the practice's reputation; and
- creating opportunities for disadvantaged groups and building social cohesion.

The Equality Act 2010 (see Chapter 3) simplified equal opportunities law. It is unlawful to discriminate against an individual or group based on any

1

one of the following characteristics:

- age
- disability
- gender reassignment
- marriage and civil partnership
- pregnancy and maternity
- race
- religion and belief
- sex or gender
- sexual orientation.

It is interesting to note the following statistics:

• The UK's population is becoming older	• So, on average, are architects
• The UK is becoming more ethnically diverse	• 94% of architects are white (in 2012)
• Ethnic minority and cultural groups make up 13% of the UK population	• Only 6% of architects are from ethnic minority and cultural groups
• 10 million adults have a disability (19% of the working population)	• No statistics for architects
• 48% of employees are women	• 20% of registered architects and 16% of RIBA members are women
• One-third of the workforce work flexible hours	• Architecture's culture is of long and inflexible hours

The RIBA and Fees Bureau's 2012 Employment and Earnings Survey findings show that the ethnicity of architects is predominantly white: 94% of the UK's architects are white. This indicates that the issue of diversity is not firmly on the profession's radar.

So what can we do to improve this situation?

- Consider whether your staff reflect your locality and your clients.
- Introduce mentoring schemes to encourage and support all staff members.
- Move the culture of your business away from being dominated by how many hours employees work in the office.
- Make flexible working available for all as a default. Do not make it women/carer-centric, as this can lead to resentment.
- Offer work experience or paid holiday jobs to people from diverse backgrounds, to allow them to gain experience and dispel any myths they might have about the work involved.

- Make diversity an integral part of your business, not just an HR function. When the practice takes ownership of the need for diversity and diversity is central to all of its systems, it ceases to be a 'nice-to-have' option.
- Adopt fairness, inclusion and respect.

1.3.2   Risk management

As noted above, risk is a key factor in the construction industry and, in a climate of increasing recourse to legal remedy and a tightening of financial margins, risk management is more important than ever (see Section 2.2). This subject is also covered in detail in Chapter 11.

1.3.3   Health and safety

There has been a good deal of debate over the past decade or so with regard to providing a safer working environment on construction sites, resulting in higher standards being expected by clients and required by law. Designers are in a unique position to reduce the health risks that arise from construction work, and have an important role in helping to protect workers. Early design decisions and assumptions can affect health and safety through the choice of materials and construction methods, and the health of the workers who will either construct or maintain a building.

By identifying and assessing health risks, then taking action to eliminate hazards, reduce risks, and share information, health risks to workers can – and should – be reduced.

Although there has been some improvement over the past decade, the rates of injury in the construction industry are still too high and considerable further improvement is needed.

1.3.4   Technological advances

Rapid technological advances have resulted in increasing specialisation in the industry. Projects have become more sophisticated in terms of the design and construction expertise required and processes have become more demanding in terms of information flow, coordination and programming.

Within this context the roles of all professionals within the industry, including that of the architect, have needed to evolve to meet new expectations. Traditionally, the architect has been the client's first point of contact, and design has been largely in the hands of the architect and other construction consultants. With traditional procurement the activities of design and production have been carried out by separate organisations. However, increasing specialisation has meant that a great deal of technical and design expertise has developed in what had traditionally been thought of as the 'supply side', i.e. within contractors, specialist sub-contractors and manufacturers.

Building information modelling (BIM) and digital, single project models are becoming increasingly standardised across the industry and thereby having greater uptake. Investment in BIM and associated technologies can be challenging for small practices in this difficult economic climate and advice on effective implementation can be found in Chapter 12. Chapter 10 outlines the RIBA Plan of Work 2013, which facilitates collaborative working.

1.3.5   Electronic communication

Following an exponential increase in its use, electronic communication has become ubiquitous and Chapter 12: Computing, CAD, BIM and IT provides some key advice on this area.

1.3.6   Consolidation

Another trend is the amalgamation and consolidation of consultancies – particularly in engineering – and the formation of large, multi-disciplinary organisations. The middle ground is diminishing and the gap between the small, local service provider and large corporations is growing. A similar trend can be seen in construction companies. Despite this the UK construction industry remains fragmented. Most companies in the industry are small and domestically owned, with localised operations, but further consolidation is anticipated over the next few years.

1.3.7   The global context

Over the past decade or so international markets in both goods and services have become more interdependent and the term 'globalisation' has become synonymous with the associated increase in trade around the world. Architects' services have experienced this phenomenon in a number of ways, including increased international work for signature architects, internationally branded practices and architects with world-class specialist skills, and the emergence of outsourcing of more routine elements of architectural service provision to lower-cost economies. Developments in CAD/BIM, single project models and e-communication technologies have accelerated these trends.

The RIBA Business Benchmarking Survey 2012/13 found that 36% of the fee income of large UK practices (those employing 50 or more staff) was from overseas projects. Important markets for UK practices include Western

Europe, the Middle East, Eastern Europe, Russia, India and China. The RIBA Business Benchmarking Survey 2012/13 data indicated that overseas projects represented some 20% of the workload by value of the UK architectural sector as a whole.

While many western economies are only slowly emerging from the recession – and some will continue to experience difficulty for years to come – other areas of the world have bucked the trend throughout this period and have experienced growth in construction. There will continue to be demand for UK architects' services to support investment in these growing economies. UK architects are seen to have strong credentials in areas such as sustainable design, master planning, regeneration and conservation, and the UK model for architectural education is perceived to produce architects with a high level of design creativity. Fast-emerging markets such as India and South America, which are relatively unfamiliar to UK architects, may present some exciting opportunities.

The RIBA has produced a reference handbook, called *Working Internationally*, which has valuable content for practices wishing to explore working in overseas markets. This includes information on cultural awareness, business issues, the role of the architect, international contracts, finding international partners, sourcing work and marketing internationally as well as references to further sources of help. The *Working Internationally* handbook can be downloaded from the RIBA's website (www.architecture.com/RIBA/Working%20internationally/Workinginternationally.aspx).

UK Trade & Investment (UKTI) provides expert trade advice and practical support to UK-based companies wishing to grow their business overseas. Their services include participation at selected trade fairs, facilitation of outward trade missions, and the provision of bespoke market intelligence and information on overseas regulations and business practice. Further detail on UKTI services is available at www.gov.uk/government/organisations/uk-trade-investment.

The European Union now effectively represents the 'home' market for UK architects, and much regulation that affects the work of architects and the procurement of buildings is derived from key EU directives, including:

- Directive on Recognition of Professional Qualifications
- Services in the Internal Market Directive
- Procurement Directives.

A significant amount of UK building regulation, health and safety and environmental regulation is now also EU based. The Architects' Council of Europe (ACE), of which both the ARB and the RIBA are members, represents architects in Europe. The principal function of the ACE is to monitor developments at EU level, seeking to influence those areas of EU policy and legislation that have an impact on architectural practice and on the overall quality and sustainability of the built environment in Europe.

1.4   Key roles in the construction industry

The construction industry is engaged in a wide variety of activities, including not only the design and erection of building and civil engineering projects, but also related activities, such as the design and manufacture of special components and equipment, and the maintenance of buildings and other structures. It is characterised by the fact that most work consists of unique physical projects that are site-specific, in contrast to, say, 'consumer goods' industries, where products are manufactured en masse rather than commissioned. The products are generally one-off designs; very few sectors of the construction industry include any standardisation, with the exception perhaps of the house-building sector.

> Information published by the Government Office for National Statistics for September 2013 noted that construction contributes approximately 6.8% to the UK's GDP.

A key characteristic of the industry is the wide range of project values, from minor works – frequently either domestic projects or maintenance work costing a few thousand pounds or less – through to major infrastructure projects with budgets of several billions of pounds. Clearly there are enormous differences in the skills, knowledge and resources needed to execute projects of such differing size, and this is reflected in the differences in scale to be found within the industry. Most sectors comprise a small number of large companies and a great many medium-sized and smaller firms and sole traders.

In the architects' profession there are a few major practices with several hundred employees. According to RIBA Chartered Practice data, the total large practice sector (defined by the RIBA as practices employing 50 or more staff) represents only 3% of firms, but employs one-fifth of RIBA chartered members in private practice. Conversely, the small practice sector (defined by the RIBA as practices employing ten or fewer staff) makes up nearly 80% of practices and employs 44% of the chartered architects working in private practice.

Roles in the design team have been re-examined with the advent of the RIBA Plan of Work 2013. There is now a greater emphasis on collaboration and BIM processes. There is also a greater emphasis on post-completion activities and how these can feed into the initial stages of future projects.

The roles listed in the RIBA Plan of Work 2013 are:

- client (see 1.4.1)
- client adviser
- project lead
- lead designer
- architect (see 1.4.4)
- cost consultant (see 1.4.5)
- civil and structural engineer (see 1.4.6)
- building services engineer (see 1.4.7)
- construction lead
- contract administrator
- health and safety adviser.

In addition to these core roles, specialist input may be required in relation to design or information management, masterplanning, sustainability, landscaping, planning, fire engineering, external lighting, acoustics, interior design, catering or other specialist support roles. Refer to the RIBA publication *Assembling a Collaborative Project Team* (2013) for advice on how to successfully incorporate these specialist advisers into the project team.

1.4.1   Client/employer

The person or organisation that commissions the project is generally, although not necessarily, the owner of the site and the eventual owner of the building. Clients range from individuals having work done on a house, to government bodies or multinational corporations. Increasingly, contractors are employing architects, either as employees or by commissioning practices to undertake production information and construction stage services, either directly or following novation of the architect's appointment at a particular stage in the project.

With the growing variety of work and potential areas of specialisation open to architects, it is important for them to identify what areas they want to target. Chapter 5: Marketing and business development gives some guidance on this.

As clients are such an integral part of an architect's working life, there are many references within this book to the architect–client relationship and what it entails:

- Chapter 2 – The profession (Sections 2.1, 2.2, 2.5–2.9, 2.11, 2.12)
- Chapter 3 – The law (Sections 3.2, 3.5, 3.6)
- Chapter 4 – Setting up a practice (Sections 4.2, 4.3, 4.5)
- Chapter 5 – Marketing and business development (Sections 5.1, 5.3–5.5)

- Chapter 6 – People management (Sections 6.2, 6.3)
- Chapter 7 – Financial management (Sections 7.1, 7.4, 7.5)
- Chapter 8 – Office management (Sections 8.1, 8.2, 8.6, 8.7)
- Chapter 9 – The architect's appointment (Sections 9.1–9.4)
- Chapter 10 – Procedures and processes (Sections 10.1, 10.3–10.5, 10.7, 10.8)
- Chapter 11 – Risk management and insurance (Sections 11.1–11.3)
- Chapter 12 – Computing, CAD, BIM and IT (Sections 12.3, 12.5)
- Chapter 13 – Knowledge management (Sections 13.4, 13.5)

1.4.2 Contractor

A main or principal contractor will usually be appointed as the constructor of the building. In practice, most of the actual work will be sub-contracted. Contractors vary in size from small firms with only a few permanently employed staff and close links with other small firms and self-employed tradesmen, to large organisations with a head office, permanent staff and often regional and possibly international offices. Most firms practice as limited companies, with some of the larger ones being public limited companies.

Main contractors are now typically referred to as Tier 1 contractors in many public sector and leading private sector projects. 'Tier 1' refers to their position in the supply chain – that is, the direct contractual relationship with the client.

1.4.3 Sub-contractor

Sub-contractors are companies to whom work is sub-let by contractors. They range from firms who provide relatively unskilled labour for general construction work through to firms providing highly specialised elements of the building such as internal fit-out or IT installations and firms who provide, in addition to the workforce needed to carry out a task, highly technical expertise which contributes to the design of a project, for example piling or cladding manufacturers. Generally the choice of sub-contractor is left to the contractor and their performance is entirely the contractor's responsibility. Sometimes, however, the client or designers may choose the subcontractor, particularly where specialist design input is needed.

Sub-contractors are now more closely defined as specialist and specialist engineering contractors, and are known within the supply chain as Tier 2, 3, 4, etc. contractors, depending on the number of levels they are away from the Tier 1 relationship. If a Tier 1 contractor lets a contract to a supplier who lets a contract to another, who contracts a sole trader heating engineer to do the work on site, this last would be a Tier 4 contractor.

Developer clients

Property developers form an important group among an architect's clients. Essentially a property developer is someone who facilitates change to a piece of land or real estate, with the aim of generating an increase in value. The variety and scale of development is great, from building a single dwelling on a piece of land to master planning a city. Property development is entrepreneurial by nature, with the developer usually taking the greatest financial risk but also realising the greatest reward on success. The property developer initiates the project, raises finance for it and coordinates the activities required to realise the development. This includes land acquisition, through planning, design, construction, finding end-users and perhaps even managing and maintaining the asset following completion.

Developers have differing fields of specialisation:

- **Trader developers** buy and sell, sometimes without doing any development as such, buying at below market value, holding the property for a while, then selling on at a higher price.

- **Investor developers** are property companies or individuals who basically buy an income, and therefore the buildings they purchase will usually be let, yielding a return for them on their investment every year. They will tend to hold property in the longer term where the lessee's covenant is often as important as the income itself.

- **Asset managers** manage real estate for institutions or private individuals against a set of predetermined business objectives. The activities they undertake might include lease compliance, landlord and tenant issues, planned maintenance, credit control, benchmarked rent collection, service charge budgeting and reconciliation, financial management and accounting, procurement and contract management, and health and safety. An asset manager should always seek to ensure that the maximum possible income is gained from a property.

- **An institution**, often referred to in terms of an institutional investor, is an organisation charged with investing a sufficiently large amount of money, frequently on behalf of a group of individuals. Examples of institutional investors include pension funds, insurance companies, banks, foundations and endowments, hedge funds and mutual funds. They will own, invest and hold property assets as part of a balanced portfolio of products that yield a return for their clients or themselves.

1.4.4　Architect

Architects form a relatively small but influential group among the large number of qualified professionals working within the construction industry. Architects are regulated under the Architects Act 1997, although this legislation protects the title rather than the role – there is no requirement under the law for the designer of any building to be an architect. In practice it is normally the architect's responsibility to facilitate the coordination and integration of the work of other designers and specialists into the overall design. The architect has traditionally also acted as the overall lead consultant and administrator of the building contract, although this is not always the case on many large projects, where a project manager or other consultant may take this role. Architects are, however, increasingly being called on to provide a single point of contact to the client for design services, sometimes sub-contracting structural and mechanical and electrical (M&E) engineering and other design services.

With the advent of BIM-enabled projects, a new area is open to architects: that of information management. Under the RIBA Plan of Work 2013 (see Chapter 10), Stages 0 and 7 provide the opportunity for architects to extend their service after the building has been completed. In Stage 7 the building is managed – throughout its life up to its eventual demolition. A BIM model can be used to assist in this and architects should seek opportunities to perform this service for their clients. Traditionally, once a building has been completed the architect has had little involvement in managing it as an asset or a facility, but this could change, with consequent benefits to the profession and the industry. As buildings become 'smarter' they also require greater technical understanding to run them efficiently and information technology can play a key part in this.

1.4.5　Cost consultant

Traditionally the role of the cost consultant (or quantity surveyor) was limited to preparing bills of quantities for tendering purposes but this expanded over time to include the preparation of valuations and final accounts. The role is now broader, and related to the financial management of a project. The cost consultant can analyse cost information on other similar projects, local levels of building costs and cost trends, etc. and can judge whether the client's budget is realistic and compatible with other stated requirements. The cost consultant can prepare the financial appraisal for the feasibility report. They will also advise on procurement and tendering processes, on contract documentation, on cash flow forecasting, financial reports and interim payments, and on the final account.

Titles such as cost consultant are now frequently used in preference to quantity surveyor, reflecting the changed nature of the role to include managing the cost of the project rather than purely measuring it.

1.4.6   Structural engineer

The structural engineer advises on and prepares the structural design for the project, including the foundation design. They can advise the architect on local conditions relevant to the site, such as soil and geotechnical factors, roads, sewers, water supply, etc. They can identify hazards and hazardous substances, arrange for site, structural and drainage surveys, advise on alternative structural solutions, prepare design criteria and calculations and advise on structural aspects of party walls, temporary structures and demolition work.

1.4.7   Building services engineer

The M&E engineers will advise on and prepare designs for the various service systems in the building. They will advise on climatic conditions, energy use and conservation, emission problems, etc. and will consult relevant authorities as necessary. M&E engineers can prepare feasibility studies, estimates, forecasts and maintenance cost options; prepare energy management studies; and report and prepare design criteria and calculations.

Increasingly they play a role in delivering environmentally sustainable solutions and undertaking sustainable design audits. From this point of view it is important that they are involved early in the design process, when key decisions on sustainability have to be made.

1.5   Key representative bodies

CLIENT ORGANISATIONS

British Property Federation (BPF)

The BPF is a membership organisation devoted to representing the interests of all those involved in property ownership and investment. It aims to create conditions in which the commercial property industry can grow and thrive, for the benefit of its members and of the economy as a whole. Its objectives are:

- to raise further the profile of the property industry with political stakeholders, the media, and the public;
- to obtain for the industry legislative, fiscal and regulatory conditions that maximise its success and so enhance the benefits the industry can bring to the UK;
- to encourage best practice within the industry as a means of increasing long-term value and improving stakeholder perception.

The BPF works closely with other representative organisations where there are advantages to be gained from pooling resources or from lobbying in a collective, coordinated way. The property assets of members total over £100 billion.

Membership includes property developers, housing associations, banks, insurers and professionals, including architects. The BPF is a member of JCT Ltd.

www.bpf.org.uk

Local Government Association (LGA)

Established in 1997 and based in Westminster, the LGA is a voluntary lobbying organisation acting as the voice of the local government sector, and an authoritative and effective advocate on its behalf. It targets its efforts on the issues that matter most to councils, working with and on behalf of their membership to deliver their shared vision of an independent and confident local government sector, where local priorities drive public service improvement in every city, town and village and every councillor acts as a champion for their ward and for the people they represent.

Membership comprises all local authorities (nearly 500 in total). The LGA is a member of JCT Ltd.

www.local.gov.uk/

Constructing Excellence (CE)

Constructing Excellence is charged with driving the change agenda in construction and exists to improve industry performance in order to produce a better built environment. It is a cross-sector, cross-supply chain, member-led organisation operating for the good of industry and its stakeholders.

In the mid-1990s a wide spread recognition arose of the need for the construction industry to improve the service it provided to its clients while also ensuring future viability for the wide range of organisations that operated in the industry. In response to Sir Michael Latham's 1994 report 'Constructing the Team' and Sir John Egan's 1998 report 'Rethinking Construction' a number of cross industry bodies were formed to drive change. Significant progress has been made in driving these initiatives into the practicing industry with many examples of projects that have been run in accordance with the fundamental principles. In order to streamline the effort involved, the cross industry bodies were united as Constructing Excellence in 2003 to form a voice for improvement in the built environment sector.

constructingexcellence.org.uk

CONTRACTOR ORGANISATIONS

Civil Engineering Contractors Association (CECA)

CECA is the representative organisation for the UK's civil engineering contractors.

www.ceca.co.uk

Federation of Master Builders (FMB)

The FMB is the UK's largest trade association in the building industry, with national offices in England, Northern Ireland, Scotland and Wales, supported by additional regional offices. Established in 1941 to protect the interests of small and medium-sized building firms, the FMB is independent and non-profit-making, lobbying continuously for members' interests at both national and local levels. The FMB is a source of knowledge, professional advice and support for building firms right across the UK. The FMB also offers practical advice and support to the general public on choosing and working with the right builder.

www.fmb.org.uk

National Federation of Builders (NFB)

The NBF provides business and policy support to builders, contractors and house builders across England and Wales. It aims to promote the building profession and influence the business environment to provide optimum conditions for successful building.

www.builders.org.uk

Contractors Legal Group (CLG)

The CLG was set up in 2009. It works in partnership with the National Federation of Builders, the UK Contractors Group, the Civil Engineering Contractors Association and the Scottish Building Federation to provide a unified voice representing the legal affairs of main contractors in the supply chain.

The CLG represents the main contractors within the construction industry in negotiations concerning legal affairs with government and other industry groups. It is a member of JCT Ltd.

www.builders.org.uk/nfb11/about_us/Working_with_us/Contactors%20Legal%20 Group.eb

At the supply chain level there are two main umbrella bodies:

Build UK

Build UK provides a collective voice for the contracting supply chain in construction and brings together 27 of the industry's largest main contractors and 40 leading trade associations representing over 11,500 Specialist Contractors. The organisation focuses on key industry issues that can deliver change and enable the contracting supply chain to improve the efficiency and delivery of construction projects to the benefit of the industry's clients.

Build UK was created as a result of a merger between the National Specialist Contractors' Council (NSCC) and UK Contractors Group (UKCG) in 2015.

www.builduk.org

Specialist Engineering Contractors (SEC) Group

The SEC Group exists to raise awareness, especially among clients and their professional advisers, of the importance of specialist engineering to the overall construction industry.

www.secgroup.org.uk

PROFESSIONAL ORGANISATIONS

Architects' Council of Europe (ACE)

The ACE represents the architectural profession at European level, with a headquarters and secretariat in Brussels. Its growing membership consists of member organisations that are the nationally representative regulatory and professional bodies of all EU member states, accession states, Switzerland and Norway. Through them, it represents the interests of about 480,000 architects.

The principal function of the ACE is to monitor developments at EU level, seeking to influence those areas of EU policy and legislation that have an impact on architectural practice and on the overall quality and sustainability of the built environment.

www.ace-cae.eu

Architects Registration Board (ARB) (see also sections 2.3–2.6)

The ARB is the UK's statutory regulator of architects. It keeps a public register of around 33,000 architects, which is searchable online. Every architect on its register has met the standards it sets for education, training and practice. The ARB was established by Parliament in 1997 to regulate the architects' profession in the UK. It is an independent, public interest body and its work in regulating architects ensures that good standards within the profession are consistently maintained for the benefit of the public and architects alike.

Its duties are contained in the Architects Act 1997, and cover five main areas:

- prescribing – or 'recognising' – the qualifications needed to become an architect;
- keeping the UK Register of Architects;
- ensuring that architects meet its standards for conduct and practice;
- investigating complaints about an architect's conduct or competence;
- making sure that only people on its register offer their services as an architect in the UK.

www.arb.org.uk

Chartered Association of Building Engineers (CABE)

Formed in 1925 as the Incorporated Association of Architects and Surveyors, the Chartered Association of Building Engineers (CABE) is a leading body for professionals specialising in the design, construction, evaluation and maintenance of buildings.

Its members practise across the United Kingdom, mainland Europe and around the World, and work in both the private and public sectors. The CABE provides the prime qualification of Building Engineer, a title that exactly reflects the professional expertise of members.

The Association was founded with the principal objectives to:

- promote and advance the knowledge, study and practice of each and all of the arts and sciences concerned with building technology, planning, design, construction, maintenance and repair of the built environment and the creation and maintenance of a high standard of professional qualification, conduct and practice;
- encourage and facilitate co-operation between the construction professions.

The Association was granted its Royal Charter in 2013.

www.cbuilde.com/home/

Association of Consultant Architects (ACA)

The ACA is the national professional body representing architects in private practice – consultant architects – throughout the UK. Founded in 1973, it now represents some of the country's leading practices, ranging in size from one-person firms to very large international organisations.

www.acarchitects.co.uk

Association for Consultancy and Engineering (ACE)

The ACE represents the business interests of its members and the consultancy and engineering industry in the UK. It has approximately 550 firms as its members, which range from small to large and operate across many different disciplines. ACE promotes the contribution that consultants and engineers working in the built and natural environment make to the nation's developing infrastructure and represents their interests to decision-makers and key stakeholders in government, client organisations and the media. It gives its members access to services including regular industry intelligence; debate and networking opportunities; free legal, financial and insurance advice; and a representative voice.

www.acenet.co.uk

Association for Project Safety (APS)

APS aims to continuously improve and promote the professional practice of design and construction health and safety risk management. It plays a leading role in helping the industry meet the challenges of implementing CDM2015 effectively and proportionately, and driving the new focus on health. It provides training, education and support for clients and designers. APS works with other professional bodies, and supports key organisations that are driving the industry forward. From experienced industry professionals to students and graduates, it comprises over 5,000 individual members.

www.aps.org.uk

Association for Project Management (APM)

The Association for Project Management develops and promotes project and programme management. The association is a registered charity with over 20,000 individual and 500 corporate members, making it the largest professional body of its kind in Europe. As part of its strategy to raise awareness and standards in the profession it is currently in the process of applying for a Royal Charter.

APM's mission statement is: 'To provide leadership to the movement of committed organisations and individuals who share our passion for improving project outcomes'.

www.apm.org.uk

Commonwealth Association of Architects (CAA)

The CAA is a membership organisation for institutes representing architects in Commonwealth countries. Formed at the RIBA in 1965 to promote cooperation for 'the advancement of architecture in the Commonwealth', and particularly to share and increase architectural knowledge, it currently has 34 members.

Under the umbrella of the Commonwealth, the CAA subscribes to its core values, in particular offering developmental support to the smaller and younger members. The Commonwealth network is increasingly valued as a means of accelerating improvement in the world's living conditions and ensuring a sustainable future for the planet.

www.comarchitect.org

Institute of Clerks of Works and Construction Inspectorate of Great Britain (ICWCI)

The ICWCI is the professional body that supports quality construction through inspection. As a membership organisation it provides a support network of meeting centres, technical advice, publications and events to help keep members up to date with the ever-changing construction industry.

Founded in 1882, it runs examinations for clerks of works and publishes guidance including a manual for clerks of works. Member of the CIC.

www.icwgb.org

Institution of Civil Engineers (ICE)

The ICE is a registered charity that strives to promote and progress civil engineering. It is a qualifying body, a centre for the exchange of specialist knowledge, and a provider of resources to encourage innovation and excellence in the profession worldwide. Founded in 1818, the ICE represents nearly 80,000 members worldwide.

www.ice.org.uk

Institution of Structural Engineers (IStructE)

The IStructE is the world's largest membership organisation dedicated to structural engineering. It has over 23,000 members working in 105 countries around the world and is an internationally recognised source of expertise and information concerning all issues that involve structural engineering and public safety within the built environment.

The core work of the IStructE is supporting and protecting the profession of structural engineering by upholding professional standards and acting as an international voice on behalf of structural engineers.

www.istructe.org.uk

International Union of Architects (UIA)

The UIA is a non-governmental organisation, a global federation of national associations of architects, that are its members. The UIA's goal is to unite the architects of the world without any form of discrimination. From the 27 delegations present at the founding assembly in Lausanne, Switzerland, in 1948, the UIA has grown to encompass the key professional organisations of architects in 124 countries and territories, and now represents, through these organisations, close to 1,300,000 architects worldwide.

www.uia.archi/

Landscape Institute (LI)

The LI is an educational charity and chartered body responsible for protecting, conserving and enhancing the natural and built environment. It champions well-designed and well-managed urban and rural landscapes. The LI's accreditation and professional procedures ensure that the designers, managers and scientists who make up the landscape architecture profession work to the highest standards. Its advocacy and education programmes promote the landscape architecture profession as one that focuses on design, environment and community in order to inspire great places where people want to live, work and visit.

The LI represents 6,000 members, including chartered landscape architects, academics, scientists and students who work for organisations such as local authorities and government agencies and in private practice and are involved in a broad range of tasks including master planning, environmental assessment, public consultation and design.

The LI provides member services including support and promotion of the work of landscape architects; information and guidance to the public and industry about the specific expertise offered by those in the profession; and training and educational advice to students and professionals looking to build upon their experience.

www.landscapeinstitute.org

Royal Town Planning Institute (RTPI)

Founded in 1914, the RTPI is the UK's leading planning body specialising in spatial, sustainable, integrative and inclusive planning.

As a membership organisation it represents and assists its 23,000 members by: promoting planning as a profession; providing information and guidance to policy makers; funding and undertaking research; and supporting members throughout their professional career. It has both regional and interest-group networks.

www.rtpi.org.uk

Royal Institution of Chartered Surveyors (RICS)

The RICS has 110,000 members and 18 faculties, including diverse fields such as antiques and fine art, facilities management, mineral and waste management and project management. Activities include library services, awards and competitions, conferences, CPD and publishing.

Member of the CIC and of JCT Ltd.

www.rics.org

Royal Institute of British Architects (RIBA)
(see also Sections 2.7–2.13)

The RIBA is the UK-based professional body for architecture. It provides support for its 40,000 plus members (comprising chartered, associate, student and affiliate members) through advice, training, technical and business services, and the setting of standards for the education of architects, both in the UK and internationally.

www.architecture.com

Royal Society of Architects in Wales (RSAW)

The Royal Society of Architects in Wales/Cymdeithas Frenhinol Penseiri yng Nghymru (RSAW) is the voice of the RIBA in Wales. As part of the Royal Institute of British Architects (RIBA), the RSAW champions better buildings, communities and the environment through architecture and our members.

Covering a large geographic area from its base in Cardiff, RSAW provides support for members through CPD, Spring School and our annual conference. It recognises outstanding architecture through the RIBA Awards and the Welsh Architecture Awards and supports the National Eisteddfod of Wales with the delivery of the Eisteddfod Architecture Medal and student scholarship.

Its core programme is complemented by local events organised by volunteer members in branches throughout Wales.

www.architecture.com (and search RSAW)

Royal Incorporation of Architects in Scotland (RIAS)

The RIAS was founded in 1916 as the professional body for all chartered architects in Scotland, and is the foremost architectural professional institute in the country dealing with architecture and the built environment.

The RIAS has charitable status, and offers a wide range of services and products for architects, students of architecture, construction industry professionals, and all those with an interest in the built environment and the design process.

The RIAS and the RIBA have an agreement on joint chartered membership; it allows registered architects born in Scotland or educated at a Scottish School of Architecture to be eligible for joint chartered membership of both the RIAS and the RIBA.

www.rias.org.uk

Royal Society of Ulster Architects (RSUA)

The RSUA is the professional body for chartered architects in Northern Ireland, with approximately 900 members.

It was established in 1901 and a direct alliance was formed with the RIBA in 1925. The RSUA continues to act for the RIBA in Northern Ireland.

www.rsua.org.uk

Royal Institute of the Architects of Ireland (RIAI)

The RIAI is the regulatory and support body for architects in Ireland and its role encompasses promoting architecture, supporting architects and architectural technicians, regulating architects and protecting the consumer. The RIAI carries out a statutory function as the registration body and competent authority for architects in Ireland. It also provides support services for architectural technicians.

www.riai.ie

INDUSTRY ORGANISATIONS

British Board of Agrément (BBA)

The BBA works in conjunction with the European Organisation for Technical Approvals, and is responsible for assessing new building products and issuing related certificates, including European Technical Approvals and Agreement Certificates.

www.bbacerts.co.uk

British Standards Institution (BSI)

The BSI is the authority responsible for the preparation and review of national standards covering a wide range of matters such as definitions, dimensions, preferred testing methods and performance, and for the preparation of codes of practice. Many of these standards and codes apply to the construction industry. The organisation must also publish British versions of European standards, and withdraw any conflicting national standards.

www.bsigroup.com

Building Cost Information Service (BCIS)

BCIS publishes and distributes up-to-date cost information including indices, trends and market conditions.

www.rics.org/uk/knowledge/bcis/

Building Research Establishment (BRE)

BRE undertakes research and publishes reports on building materials and various aspects of construction technology. Provides consultancy, testing and information services. Member of the CIC.

www.bre.co.uk

Building Services Research and Information Association (BSRIA)

BSRIA undertakes research and publishes reports on various aspects of building services. It provides consultancy, testing, information and market research services and runs an on-line bookshop. Member of the CIC.

www.bsria.co.uk

Construction Industry Council (CIC)

Established by the Government in 1988, the CIC is the largest pan-industry forum representing all aspects of the built environment, including most of the professional bodies, most research organisations and many of the specialist trade associations. It carries out quarterly surveys of construction industry activities. The RIBA is represented on several of its committees and working parties.

www.cic.org.uk

Construction Industry Research and Information Association (CIRIA)

Funds and coordinates research activities, although it has no laboratories or testing facilities of its own. It is funded by government grants and research contracts from industry. It publishes a newsletter and reports, disseminating the research it has funded.

www.ciria.org

CITB – Construction Skills

This was established under the Industrial Training Act 1964 as the Construction Industry Training Board (CITB), with its remit to improve training so that there would be an adequate supply of suitably qualified people to work at all levels of the construction industry. It runs courses at its training centres, works with colleges of technology, and gives grants to employers who undertake its courses.

www.citb.co.uk

Joint Contracts Tribunal Limited (JCT)

The JCT publishes and reviews the standard forms of building contract and sub-contract generally used throughout the building industry. It also publishes guidance related to these forms as Practice Notes, and funds and publishes research. The RIBA is a shareholder in the JCT and is represented on the JCT Board through its membership of the Consultants' College. It thereby has a voice in influencing the content of JCT contracts and endorses their use.

www.jctltd.co.uk

National House-Building Council (NHBC)

The NHBC is an independent regulating body for the UK house-building industry. It maintains a register of 18,000 house builders who construct 85% of new houses in the UK. It sets technical standards for construction of new homes, with the aim of reducing defects. It also offers warranty and insurance services that house builders can pass on to home buyers. Member of the CIC.

www.nhbc.co.uk

Timber Research and Development Association (TRADA)

TRADA is an international centre for specification and use of timber and wood products. It undertakes research and publishes reports, books and other guidance information and runs an on-line bookshop. Member of the CIC.

www.trada.co.uk

References and further reading

The Future of Building: Perspectives. Methods, Objectives, Prospects (Munich: DETAIL, 2012).

Building. White Paper 13: Client Intelligence 2013 (London, 2013).

Pelsmakers, S., *The Environmental Design Pocketbook* (London: RIBA Publishing, 2012).

Sinclair, D., *Guide to Using the RIBA Plan of Work 2013* (London: RIBA Publishing, 2013).

Sinclair, D., *Assembling a Collaborative Project Team* (London: RIBA Publishing, 2013).

The profession

THIS CHAPTER:

- outlines the guiding principles of the profession of architecture, and considers potential future trends and challenges;
- looks at the statutory regulations governing the practice of architects;
- describes the role of the ARB, and its code of conduct and disciplinary procedures;
- explains the structure and governance of the RIBA, and its purpose;
- discusses the membership benefits and entry requirements of the RIBA, current thinking on education and the role of CPD.

2.1   Introduction

The RIBA/CABE publication *The Professionals' Choice* sets out four guiding principles of the professions:

- formal association;
- trustworthiness;
- observing the public interest;
- maintaining and developing a body of knowledge.

The professions need formal means to control membership, and they do this by requiring a level of proficiency for entry and by being able to exclude those who do not practise within their rules. These standards need to be set at a level such that members have appropriate knowledge and expertise, and exercise reasonable skill and care, but not be so high as to make fees uncompetitive. Members of the architects' profession operate in a broadly free market for the provision of architectural services, albeit with protection of the title 'architect' through the Architects Act 1997, and have to be able to provide value compared with non-members offering a similar service.

Professions must also be trustworthy, and not use their knowledge to gain undue commercial advantage over their clients: this is increasingly achieved through regulation and the law, and through auditing, both internally, and by external, client-appointed consultants. They should be independent of the purely commercial interests in their industry, and balance the needs of their members against those of the public. Architects traditionally act as an independent agent between their client and the contractor while balancing the interests of the client with those of the wider community and the environment. However, with the growth in Design and Build procurement, architects also increasingly find themselves employed directly by the contractor, and this presents new challenges in meeting their wider responsibilities.

Architects are creative designers as well as project managers and contract administrators, and this will always make them unique among other construction professionals. Critically, however, this creativity is combined with experience and knowledge that is gained through experience and not easily found through reference. It is becoming increasingly important for architects to manage their knowledge for commercial advantage (see Chapter 13).

A professional body, then, can be defined as a formal association of specifically educated members that assures their ability through examination and certification, and their trustworthiness through regulation, and provides support and advice to achieve those aims.

In most countries throughout the world there is generally some regulation of function or, at the least, protection of title for architects. Successive UK governments have been keen to ensure free competition for architectural services and have shown no appetite for regulation of function, perceiving that the industry is sufficiently regulated through planning, building control and health and safety legislation. They have been prepared to accept the argument for continuing protection of title, provided it is self-funded by the profession through a body such as the Architects Registration Board (ARB). The question could be asked, though: Is protection of title really of benefit to the public or the profession, or does it simply restrict the development of more flexible services?

2.2   Future challenges

2.2.1   Adaptability and specialisation

There is no such thing as a job for life anymore, particularly in architecture and the broader construction industry. Construction has always been susceptible to the vagaries of the economy, but with greater complexity and the advent of a truly global marketplace, what might have been considered a difficulty can instead be viewed as an opportunity. Architects will increasingly need to be adaptable and prepared to turn their hand to new tasks and to undertake further training where necessary, especially in the fields of technology and electronic information and communication.

There is, however, an opposing requirement to specialise in order to compete against other specialists. An area of specialisation may be a sector type, such as workplace, retail or airports, or it may be a technical

2

or a conceptual emphasis or a specific understanding of green buildings – this last example being an area that will surely become more prevalent with escalating fuel prices (as well as a continuing change in our climate). Adaptability can be just within the chosen field, although clearly if the specialisation is in a single sector then some degree of cross-fertilisation is a good thing, at least within a practice if not in one individual. There is always an amount of work to be found in every field and, whatever the area, excellence will always be in demand.

2.2.2 Ownership of the BIM model

The advent of building information modelling (BIM) and the potential emergence of an information manager role provides a whole field of specialisation in itself. Architects must rise to the challenge and not let this role, or the building information model, be owned by other (or new) professions in the way cost management and project management have. The RIBA Plan of Work 2013 is leading the way and provides a framework for extending the architect's role into the building's use, refurbishment, alteration and potential re-use. Architects could again become architect 'to' a building as well as 'of' it, as has happened with the maintenance of historic buildings and estates.

2.2.3 Client focus

Architects must always take trouble to understand their clients and understand where value lies. (Value is providing what the client needs – not what the architect determines as being required, independently of the client conversation.) The profession needs to ask questions (of clients and other stakeholders) and listen to the answers. The best architects already do this, but it is far from a universal trait. Architects are not just providers of a service; they also have responsibilities to society and must take responsibility for their actions. Individuals make up the profession and it is up to all of us, not just the institutes that represent us, to improve the built environment and the conditions for enabling this.

2.2.4   An increased range

There can be a tendency to describe architectural graduates who do not continue to complete their professional qualifications as having 'dropped out'. However, the skills in design (problem-solving) and leadership which these graduates have gained through the unique education provided in UK architecture schools can be used to good effect in related construction professions and other industries. Many architects who do complete their final professional qualifications go on to perform senior roles in construction outside of architectural practice and the profession should aim to maintain their association of both these groups rather than lose them to other institutional bodies.

There is currently a focus on the nature and content of architectural education, with consideration both of the (low) percentage of graduates who continue on to professional qualification and practice and the (typically poor) level of remuneration practising architects receive. One consequence of low pay for practitioners may be an increase in architects working as employees for their clients rather than as agents. Architectural education is more or less the same across all UK schools of architecture. The time may be right for some to provide more specialisation in certain fields or to prepare their alumni for work outside of practising as an architect in private practice. We might ask: What is architectural training for – just to create architects or also creative thinkers who can make a contribution to a broader field? If the latter, should architectural education be changed to reflect this? Should it include entrepreneurial skills as well as design? The answers to such questions will ultimately be reflected in the direction the profession takes in future years.

In the modern era architects have focused on creative design and problem-solving as their key differentiator, but this has come with a corresponding diminution of responsibility for project management, so that the project team comprises cost and project managers as separate professions. For architects to retake the centre ground, and move upstream in meeting their clients' needs, they will need to reinforce the value of their core creative skills, but also accept the need to undertake the more routine project management processes. This will be helped by improvements in digital technology (see Section 12.3 on BIM), and such a move would be accelerated if the current trend for architects to provide a multidisciplinary role continues, employing other designers as sub-consultants or working as the lead in a multi-disciplinary service provider. A parallel scenario is that design and build contractors move further upstream, employing the design team at an earlier stage and providing a complete turnkey service.

There is an increasing emphasis on tightening financial margins, which can be at odds with the architect's desire to deliver the highest quality, sustainable design solutions. The market is starting to demand sustainable buildings, but this is inhibited to some extent by the economy and a focus on capital cost. The drive to reduce price has led to an increased requirement for tendering work between consultants, moving away from the traditional direct appointment with fees being linked to building cost. Some clients now require consultants to tender for each stage of the design process (i.e. strategic definition/preparation and brief/concept design/developed

2

design/technical design/construction) with the aim of further cutting cost. Whether this process adds value is questionable, but it seems to have momentum.

There has been an increase in the importance of risk management, encouraged by the insurance industry (see Chapter 11), and this can be viewed as being in opposition to the need for creativity and innovation. There has been a tendency for increased resource to be applied to auditing the design and recording the design process, as opposed to the act of designing itself. There has also been increased pressure to find less bespoke, more repeatable building solutions. Influenced by the manufacturing industries, and particularly the motor industry, there has been a trend towards better understanding of the supply chain and 'design for manufacture', so that the design enables efficiencies in the construction process.

2.2.5   Professional fees

In an increasingly global and competitive marketplace for building design services, it seems likely that fees will increasingly be linked to value rather than to the cost of the building. Architects will need to have greater regard for the commercial drivers of the industry than they traditionally have, in order to develop their field of influence and safeguard – or increase – their market share. They will also need to find ways to increase the financial reward that architects achieve, to attract the best recruits and thereby enable continuous improvement and growth. Failure to do this may lead to a diminishing role in the industry, and a shift away from the traditional differentiators of the profession. The profession needs to understand better what the public and clients value them for, and deliver their services accordingly, while retaining their role as guardians of the environment.

Architects will need to demonstrate that their independence and creativity provide value. As the profession that most directly influences the quality of our built environment they need to persuade the public that this is worth investing in. If this aim is supported, the profession can lead the cause and in doing so reinforce its core purpose.

2.3   Practising as an architect

In the UK a person cannot practise or carry on a business under any name, style or title containing the word 'architect' unless they are registered with the Architects Registration Board (ARB). The ARB was established by Parliament in 1997 to regulate the architects' profession in the UK, to ensure that good standards within the profession are maintained for the benefit of the public and architects alike.

In addition to becoming registered, most architects also join a professional body. The largest UK membership body for architects is the Royal Institute of British Architects (RIBA). Founded in 1834, and awarded its Royal Charter in 1837, the RIBA is the UK's charter body for architecture. The RIBA champions better buildings, communities and the environment through architecture and its members. Its mission is to advance architecture by demonstrating benefit to society and promoting excellence in the profession. Chartered members of the RIBA are entitled to describe themselves as chartered architects, and to use the post-nominal letters RIBA.

Both the ARB and the RIBA publish codes of professional conduct, and operate complaints and professional conduct investigation systems. Both bodies may impose sanctions when an architect fails to meet the codes' standards. The RIBA's primary role is the promotion of architecture, as discussed further in Section 2.8, whereas the role of the ARB is defined by statute and is aimed principally at consumer protection. The ARB has a statutory duty to allow onto its register EU architects who have the qualifications and training, recognised under the EU Professional Qualifications Directive, as well as UK qualified architects who have the prescribed qualifications of the UK, which are the RIBA Parts 1, 2 and 3 qualifications. The ARB does this through a process of course and qualification prescription in the UK. The RIBA carries out a robust validation system of all schools of architecture which provide RIBA Parts 1, 2 or 3 courses by a visiting board system. The ARB and RIBA have successfully collaborated in the development of commonly held validation criteria and the Quality Assurance Agency benchmark statement for architecture.

Changes with regard to the requirements of architectural education across the EU are currently being planned following review of the EU Professional Qualifications Directive and a fundamental review of architectural education is being undertaken by the RIBA in response to this.

Origins of the profession

In the 19th century, the construction industry underwent radical change. Master craftsmen were overtaken by firms of building contractors, headed by people whose aims were profit-oriented and sometimes speculative. Professionalism as applied to architecture was formalised and consolidated. Practitioners with a common, professed interest banded together, in part for protection and so as to be able to present a unified approach when tackling injustices, in part for promotional reasons. Architects looked to provide a uniquely impartial and independent service. The newly emergent professions developed the following characteristics:

- an intellectual basis – principles, theories and concepts capable of testing and implementation;
- independence of practice – integrity and impartiality in services, personal attention, reward by fee;
- a consultancy role – advice, skills, resources, defined liabilities;
- established practices – conduct, conditions, procedures, performance standards;
- a representative institute – protection of interests for members and clients, corporate voice and lobby, learned society role, advancement of knowledge and expertise.

The RIBA was founded in 1834 (at that time without its Royal Charter), and during its first 50 years it set up in embryo form many of the activities that characterise its work today. During its first decade of existence a register of architects seeking work was instituted, and in 1837 the first Royal Charter was granted by William IV. The first board of examiners was set up in 1862, and the first voluntary architectural examinations were held in 1863. The Supplemental Charter of 1887 made the examination in architecture compulsory for associate membership of the RIBA, and made provisions for regulations to govern exclusion or suspension from membership. The first RIBA Code of Professional Conduct was published in 1900.

The Architects (Registration) Act came into force in 1931 and with it the Architects' Registration Council of the United Kingdom (ARCUK). Registration was a voluntary matter, but by the Architects (Registration) Act 1938 use of the word 'architect' in any business style or title was restricted to those who were registered (with some exceptions, e.g. landscape architects or golf course architects).

Under the Housing Grants, Construction and Regeneration Act 1996 ARCUK was replaced by a new Architects Registration Board (ARB), with powers to maintain a register of architects, and discipline them for breaches of its code. All the provisions concerning the registration of architects are now to be found in the Architects Act 1997. The changes to the Act clarify the different roles of the professional institute, which is to promote professional knowledge, and the registration body, which regulates the use of the title 'architect' in the public interest.

A watershed study, *The Architect and his Office*, was undertaken by the RIBA in 1962, and this brought to light the need for increased awareness of, and skill in, the business side of architectural practice. As a result, the RIBA published the first *Handbook of Practice and Management* and the *Job Book*.

2.3.1   Statutory regulation

The ARB is an independent statutory regulator, funded entirely by the registration fees that architects pay to register/remain on the Register. Its overall role is to protect the consumer, support architects through registration and deliver the Architects Act 1997 – in other words, to ensure that those practising under the title 'architect' are competent to do so. The key functions of the ARB are to:

- prescribe the qualifications needed to become an architect;
- keep the UK Register of Architects;
- ensure that architects meet its standards for conduct and practice;
- investigate complaints about an architect's conduct or competence in respect of its Architects Code;
- make sure that only people on its Register offer their services as an architect in the UK.

Sanctions can be imposed against ARB registered persons found guilty of unacceptable professional conduct or serious professional incompetence. They include reprimands, fines, suspensions or even erasures from the Register. Issues of competence can relate to the way in which business is carried out as well as to the service provided. The ultimate control in reaching professional conduct decisions rests with the Professional Conduct Committee which has a voting majority of non-architects.

2.4   The role of the ARB

The Architects Registration Board consists of seven elected architect members (elected by ballot from among registered persons) and eight appointed lay members (appointed by the Privy Council, but not registered persons). The Board members elect their own Chair and Vice-Chair from among themselves. The duties of the ARB include the following:

- to appoint the Registrar of Architects;
- to publish an annual Register of Architects;
- to issue a code laying down standards of professional conduct and practice expected of registered persons;
- to establish a Professional Conduct Committee (PCC) that will impose disciplinary sanctions where investigations show that a registered architect is guilty of unacceptable professional conduct or serious professional incompetence;
- to establish other committees as may be necessary to discharge its functions under the Architects Act 1997;
- to prosecute people using the title 'architect' who are not on the Register;
- to rule on various matters concerning registration;

- to set the educational and professional practice standards to qualify for admission to the Register.

The Registrar of Architects is appointed by the Board, and their duties include:

- maintaining the Register of Architects;
- carrying out various prescribed functions concerned with registration;
- maintaining a list of visiting EEA architects (i.e. from European Economic Area states).

The PCC consists of seven members of the Board (three architects and four lay persons), six appointed persons (three architect and three lay), and three legally qualified persons nominated by the Law Society. A voting majority on both the Board and the PCC therefore lies with non-registered persons (i.e. outside the architectural profession).

The ARB operates a number of routes to registration as an architect in the UK. The three principal routes are as follows.

UK qualifications:

- Completion of UK prescribed qualifications at Part 1, Part 2 and Part 3 levels, including a minimum period of two years' practical training as required by the ARB General Rules.

European qualifications:

- Completion of EEA qualifications covered by the Professional Qualifications Directive (2005/36/EC), followed by securing access to the profession of architect in the state of qualification. (Special provisions are available for persons who have qualified in Switzerland under 'saved' legislation.)

Other recognised qualifications, including overseas, are:

- completion of qualifications in architecture that are not within either the UK or European routes above, but which after consideration through the ARB Prescribed Examination are found to be equivalent to prescribed UK qualifications; followed by
- completion of a UK prescribed qualification at Part 3 level, including a minimum period of two years' practical training as required by the ARB General Rules.

Anyone wishing to apply for registration should contact the ARB for details of the specific procedures relevant to their professional circumstances.

Only persons who are registered may practise or carry on business using a name, style or title containing the word 'architect'. Any contravention will be a breach of Section 20 of the Architects Act, and may lead to a fine of up to £2,500 if convicted at the Magistrates' Court.

Where a company is being registered whose title includes the word 'architect', the application may be referred to the ARB by Companies House. The ARB will grant permission for the name to be used only where the architectural work of the company is under the control and management of a registered person.

To remain registered, a person must:

- pay the annual retention fee at the appropriate time;
- notify the ARB of any change of business address;
- not be subject to a disciplinary order imposed by the PCC that amounts to suspension or erasure;
- maintain competence to practise.

If an architect is off the Register for more than two years, he or she has to satisfy the Board of their competence to practise in order to be re-admitted. This is to prevent architects who have not practised for many years having an automatic right to be reinstated on the Register as 'qualified', as after such a length of time they may be out of touch with current practice.

2.5   The ARB Code

The ARB Code is currently published under the title *Architects Code: Standards of Conduct and Practice* (2010). It consists of an introduction, 12 standards and general guidance. Note that the full title includes the words *conduct* and *practice*, understandable in view of the emphasis given in the Architects Act 1997 to rejecting both unacceptable professional conduct and serious professional incompetence. As with the RIBA Code of Professional Conduct, it states that not every breach of the Code will necessarily result in proceedings, but that the spirit of the Code must be observed at all times.

Employer architects and employee architects are equally bound to respect and observe the Code obligations. UK-registered architects are still subject to the ARB Code when they practise abroad, unless it can be shown that compliance would be inconsistent with local law and customs. The standards incorporated in the *ARB Architects Code: Standards of Conduct and Practice* (2010) are shown in the following box.

2

Standard 1 – Be honest and act with integrity

1. You are expected at all times to act with honesty and integrity and to avoid any actions or situations which are inconsistent with your professional obligations. This standard underpins the Code and will be taken to be required in any consideration of your conduct under any of the other standards.
2. You should not make any statement which is contrary to your professional opinion or which you know to be misleading, unfair to others or discreditable to the profession.
3. Where a conflict of interest arises you are expected to disclose it in writing and manage it to the satisfaction of all affected parties. You should seek written confirmation that all parties involved give their informed consent to your continuing to act. Where this consent is not received you should cease acting for one or more of the parties.
4. Where you make or receive any payment or other inducement for the introduction or referral of work, you should disclose the arrangement to the client or prospective client at the outset.

Standard 2 – Be competent

1. You are expected to be competent to carry out the professional work you undertake to do, and if you engage others to do that work you should ensure that they are competent and adequately supervised.
2. You are expected to make appropriate arrangements for your professional work in the event of incapacity, death, absence from, or inability to, work.
3. You are expected to ensure that the necessary communication skills and local knowledge are available to you to discharge your responsibilities.
4. You are expected to keep your knowledge and skills relevant to your professional work up to date and be aware of the content of any guidelines issued by the Board from time to time.

Standard 3 – Promote your services honestly and responsibly

1. You are expected to promote your professional services in a truthful and responsible manner.
2. In advertising and promoting your professional services you should comply with the codes and principles applying to advertising generally. These include those of the Advertising Standards Authority or any other body having oversight of advertising standards in various media.
3. The business style of a practice should not be misleading.

4. If you are a principal in a practice you are expected to ensure that all architectural work is under the control and management of one or more architects, and that their names are made known to clients and any relevant third party. You should notify your client promptly of any change in the architect responsible for the work.

Standard 4 – Manage your business competently

1. You are expected to have effective systems in place to ensure that your practice is run professionally and that projects are regularly monitored and reviewed.
2. You should ensure that you are able to provide adequate professional, financial and technical resources when entering into a contract and throughout its duration. You should also, where appropriate, ensure you have sufficient suitably qualified and supervised staff to provide an effective and efficient service to clients.
3. You should ensure that adequate security is in place to safeguard both paper and electronic records for your clients, taking full account of data protection legislation, and that clients' confidential information is safeguarded.
4. You are expected to ensure that before you undertake any professional work you have entered into a written agreement with the client which adequately covers:

   - the contracting parties;
   - the scope of the work:
   - the fee or method of calculating it;
   - who will be responsible for what;
   - any constraints or limitations on the responsibilities of the parties
   - the provisions for suspension or termination of the agreement;
   - a statement that you have adequate and appropriate insurance cover as specified by the Board;
   - your complaints-handling procedure (see Standard 10), including details of any special arrangements for resolving disputes (e.g. arbitration).

5. Any agreed variations to the written agreement should be recorded in writing.
6. You are expected to ensure that your client agreements record that you are registered with the Architects Registration Board and that you are subject to this Code; and that the client can refer a complaint to the Board if your conduct or competence appears to fall short of the standards in the Code.

7. You should make clear to the client the extent to which any of your architectural services are being subcontracted.
8. At the end of a contract (if requested) or otherwise upon reasonable demand you should promptly return to a client any papers, plans or property to which the client is legally entitled.

Standard 5 – Consider the wider impact of your work

1. Whilst your primary responsibility is to your clients, you should take into account the environmental impact of your professional activities.

Standard 6 – Carry out your work faithfully and conscientiously

1. You are expected to carry out your work promptly and with skill and care and in accordance with the terms of your engagement.
2. You should carry out your professional work without undue delay and, so far as is reasonably practicable, in accordance with any timescale and cost limits agreed with your client.
3. You are expected to keep your client informed of the progress of work undertaken on their behalf and of any issue which may significantly affect its quality or cost.
4. You should, when acting between parties or giving advice, exercise impartial and independent professional judgment. If you are to act as both architect and contractor you should make it clear in writing that your advice will no longer be impartial.

Standard 7 – Be trustworthy and look after your clients' money properly

1. You are expected to keep proper records of all money held by you which belongs to a client or other third party, and to account for it at all times.
2. You should keep such money in a designated interest-bearing bank account, called a 'client account' which is separate from any personal or business account.
3. You are expected to instruct the bank in writing and ensure that all money in the client account is held as clients' money, and that the bank cannot combine it with any other account, or exercise any right of set-off or counterclaim against it.
4. You should ensure that money is not withdrawn from a client account to make a payment unless it is made to or on behalf of a client on the client's specific written instructions
5. Unless otherwise agreed by the client, you should arrange for any interest (or other benefit) accruing from a client account to be paid to the client.

Standard 8 – Have appropriate insurance arrangements

1. You are expected to have adequate and appropriate insurance cover for you, your practice and your employees. You should ensure that your insurance is adequate to meet a claim, whenever it is made. You are expected to maintain a minimum level of cover, including run-off cover, in accordance with the Board's guidance.
2. The need for cover extends to professional work undertaken outside your main practice or employment.
3. If you are an employed architect you should, as far as possible, ensure that insurance cover and/or other appropriate indemnity arrangements are provided by your employer.
4. You are expected to provide evidence that you have met the standards expected of this Standard in such form as the Board may require.

Standard 9 – Maintain the reputation of architects

1. You should ensure that your professional finances are managed responsibly.
2. You are expected to conduct yourself in a way which does not bring either yourself or the profession into disrepute. If you find yourself in a position where you know that you have fallen short of these standards, or that your conduct could reflect badly on the profession, you are expected to report the matter to the Board. For example, you should notify the Registrar within 28 days if you:

   - are convicted of a criminal offence;
   - are made the subject of a court order disqualifying you from acting as a company director;
   - are made the subject of a bankruptcy order;
   - are a director of a company which is wound up (other than for amalgamation or reconstruction purposes);
   - make an accommodation with creditors (including a voluntary arrangement);
   - fail to pay a judgment debt.

   The above are examples of acts which may be examined in order to ascertain whether they disclose a wilful disregard of your responsibilities or a lack of integrity, however this list is not exhaustive.

3. In appropriate circumstances, you should report to the Board and/or other public authority another architect whose conduct falls significantly short of the expected standards. If you are in doubt as to whether such a report is required, you should consult the Board for guidance.

2

4. Standard 9.3 may not apply to the contents of privileged information given to you when acting as an arbitrator, adjudicator, mediator, conciliator or expert witness.
5. You should not enter into any contract (other than in a settlement of a dispute) the terms of which would prevent any party from reporting an apparent breach of the Code to the Board.
6. If you are subject to an investigation by the Board you are expected to use your best endeavours to assist in that investigation.

Standard 10 – Deal with disputes or complaints appropriately

1. You are expected to have a written procedure for prompt and courteous handling of complaints which will be in accordance with the Code and provide this to clients. This should include the name of the architect who will respond to complaints.
2. Complaints should be handled courteously and promptly at every stage; and as far as practicable in accordance with the following timescales:

   a. an acknowledgement within ten working days from the receipt of a complaint; and
   b. a response addressing the issues raised in the initial letter of complaint within 30 working days from its receipt.

3. If appropriate, you should encourage alternative methods of dispute resolution, such as mediation or conciliation.

Standard 11 – Cooperate with regulatory requirements and investigations

1. You are expected to cooperate fully and promptly with the Board, and within any specified timescale, if it asks you to provide information which it needs to carry out its statutory duties, including evidence that you are complying with these Standards.
2. You should notify the Board promptly and in writing of any changes in the details held about you on the Register, including your address. Under the Act, architects who do not tell the Board of a change of address may be removed from the Register.

Standard 12 – Have respect for others

1. You should treat everyone fairly and in line with the law. You should not discriminate because of disability, age, gender, sexual orientation, ethnicity, or any other inappropriate consideration.

2.6   ARB disciplinary procedures

When a complaint is made the Board will consider it in detail through one of its Investigations Panels, which may appoint an inquirer (from a panel of experienced registered architects) to advise on aspects of the case. The architect in question is always contacted, given full details of the complaint made, and invited to respond. If the Panel decides there is a case to answer, the complaint is referred to the PCC for a public hearing and decision. (Full details of the procedure can be found in the Investigations Rules and the PCC Rules, which are set out on the ARB website: www.arb.org.uk.) The PCC's decisions are final, but are subject to appeal to the High Court in England and Wales and the Court of Session in Scotland. If the Investigations Panel does not consider the complaint serious enough to warrant a PCC hearing, but nevertheless has concerns about the conduct of the architect, it may issue the architect with a warning letter as to his or her future conduct.

Complaints must fall under one of the two disciplinary headings in the Architects Act 1997: serious professional incompetence or unacceptable professional conduct.

Serious professional incompetence has been defined as 'a service which falls short of the standards required of a registered person'. This could be interpreted as a failure to demonstrate the reasonable skill and care of a competent architect in carrying out the services undertaken, for example in giving advice, preparing designs and technical information, and in managing a project or administering a contract. The failure would need to be significant to rank as 'serious', and could comprise one major error or a series of less major errors, the cumulative effect of which causes considerable problems for the client or for third parties.

Unacceptable professional conduct has been defined as 'conduct which falls short of the standard required of a registered person'. This is normally understood to relate to matters of ethics. It therefore goes further than the making of errors or the demonstration of poor judgement. It should involve a moral or ethical element, such as deception of any sort, misappropriation of the client's funds, failure to deal openly with the client, or breach of any of the detailed parts of the Code that relate to such matters. This could include such matters as conflicts of interest, not having the appropriate PI insurance cover, and breaching client confidentiality.

Following the hearing, the PCC is empowered to make a disciplinary order, which can be:

- a reprimand;

- a penalty order (this means paying a specified sum based on the standard scale of fines for summary offences, currently to a maximum of £2,500 for each charge); in the event of non-payment, a name can be removed from the Register;
- a suspension order (this means removal of a person's name from the Register, with re-entry when the suspension period, not exceeding two years, is over);
- an erasure order (this means removal of a person's name from the Register); it will not be re-entered unless the ARB so directs.

The PCC can also find the architect not guilty of the charge(s).

2.7 Structure and governance of the RIBA

The RIBA has around 40,000 members, including UK chartered, international chartered, retired chartered, student, associate and affiliate members. The RIBA is a professional body with a Royal Charter (controlled by the Privy Council) and also a registered charity (controlled by the Charity Commission).

The RIBA Council is the head of the Royal Charter body, and is ultimately responsible for the policy and development of the Institute. It comprises 60 members, elected by ballot to ensure national and regional representation. The Council determines major issues of policy, and appoints the members of the RIBA Board, which comprises 15 non-executive Trustees. The RIBA Council delegates fiduciary responsibilities and direction of the RIBA's business to the RIBA Board. The RIBA President is elected for a two-year term and chairs the RIBA Council and the RIBA Board. This is an honorary office, and the Charter allows for 'such other Honorary Officers to be elected as the Bylaws prescribe'. At present these include Vice Presidents, an Honorary Secretary and an Honorary Treasurer who are also ex-officio trustees on the RIBA Board.

The executive is led by the Chief Executive and Group Executive team. The RIBA Board is the group board, responsible for directing the overall business of the RIBA. It operates under the overall authority and policy of the elected Council, and coordinates the operations of the whole of the RIBA and its subsidiary companies, such as RIBA Enterprises.

The committees advise on the formulation of policy and strategy relevant to their areas, recommending priorities for the business plan and budget (both income and expenditure). They also review the implementation of Council policies and the progress of work against agreed objectives. They appoint task groups and specialist advisers for relevant projects and subjects.

The RIBA is an institute that functions internationally but with a UK focus. It is a considerable global force and has a great international reputation for championing architecture and maintaining excellence in the architects' profession. For RIBA members, contact with the Institute is likely to be through specific activities, regional offices and branches. All RIBA members are allocated to membership of a branch, of which there are about 60. Most members belong to the branch in which they live or work, but the choice of branch is the prerogative of the individual. Each region has its own office, with a Director and staff. This is the vital grassroots part of the network, responsible for organising regional awards, seminars, courses, lectures, exhibitions and visits. This is where local practice contacts and support can flourish, and where problems can be tackled at a personal level. The network also provides members with an opportunity to exercise considerable influence over RIBA affairs.

The traditional organisational framework of the RIBA is both geographic and knowledge-based. The network of regional offices is overlaid by a pattern of committees, specialist groups and knowledge communities concerned with broad issues such as practice, education, planning and sustainability. There has been a lively debate within the RIBA membership about the role that specialist accreditation for architects may have to play in this, and the RIBA has established two such specialist registers, one for RIBA Client Advisers and the other for RIBA Conservation Architects.

For further details about the RIBA go to www.architecture.com.

2.8   The purpose of the RIBA

The RIBA Supplemental Charter 1971 states in paragraph 2.1 that 'the objects of the Royal Institute are the advancement of Architecture and the promotion of the acquirement of the knowledge of the Arts and Sciences connected therewith'. Ever since the original Charter, overall primacy has been given to the advancement of architecture, not to the advancement of architects.

Currently the RIBA's efforts to advance the cause of architecture are expressed in many ways:

- by raising environmental and ecological concerns and seeking to influence government and public opinion;
- by facing the challenges to architectural quality in times of changing building procurement and technology;
- by providing support services for practitioners;
- by striving to improve the status and competence of architects through continuing professional education and research;

2

- by engaging in consultation on the legal, technical and financial controls and constraints within which architecture is now practised;
- by maintaining the architect's professed concept of providing a unique design service.

From a list of support services now offered by the RIBA to members, the following are likely to be of particular interest to practitioners:

- RIBA Chartered Practice accreditation and Register (details of all accredited RIBA Chartered Practices published annually and accessible to clients online through www.architecture.com);
- RIBA Client Services (matching of suitable practices with client enquiries by the Clients Advisory Services team);
- RIBA Information Centre (professional library help service responding to most kinds of architectural queries);
- RIBA Specialist Practice Consultants (telephone guidance on practice matters, including legal, contractual and regulatory matters);
- RIBA Toolkits (quality management, environmental policy, health and safety);
- RIBA Collections (photographs, drawings, record documents);
- RIBA Dispute Resolution Service (for resolving disputes between architects and clients and clients and contractors);
- RIBA Insurance Agency (RIBA-approved policies for professional indemnity cover).

In addition, the following services are offered through RIBA Enterprises:

- RIBA Appointments (for members looking for work or seeking to recruit staff);
- NBS (a range of specification and information products for the construction industry);
- RIBA Bookshops (including an online shop, www.ribabookshops.com);
- RIBA Publishing (providing information, books and documents for architects and other built environment professionals).

As befits a learned society, the RIBA also demonstrates through its journal, e-bulletins, sessional programmes, education policy, library and drawings collections its right to be seen as a centre of knowledge upon which the practice of architecture is based. Through its Code of Professional Conduct, its admission standards, appointment documents, and range of other publications, the Institute is able to assure the public of the standards of integrity and competence of its members. The RIBA is affiliated to, and represented on, various associations of direct relevance to architects, including the Association of Consultant Architects, the Society of Chief Architects in Local Authorities, Architects in Industry and Commerce,

Architects in Agriculture and the Countryside, the Commonwealth Association of Architects, the Association for Consultancy and Engineering, and the International Union of Architects (UIA).

Of particular concern to members in practice, the RIBA has direct representation on many bodies that, although outside the immediate profession, are prominent in the construction industry, including the Joint Contracts Tribunal (through the Consultants' College), the Construction Industry Council, the National House-Building Council (NHBC) and the Architects' Council of Europe (ACE). The RIBA is also actively represented on various bodies that are principally concerned with environmental matters, including urban and building conservation.

2.9   Membership benefits of the RIBA

2.9.1   RIBA services

RIBA Chartered Members receive a wide range of benefits and services, including:

- **Knowledge, research and information**

  - Free specialist guidance on architectural practice, business matters, history, and the work of the RIBA through the RIBA Information Centre.
  - Access to information and discussions on specialist topics of interest with those who work in the architectural and wider construction profession through the RIBA Knowledge Communities.
  - Free subscription to the *RIBA Journal*.
  - Up-to-date news on practice, international and CPD matters through the RIBA Member Update (weekly e-newsletter).
  - Debate on the issues of the day with fellow RIBA members and staff through the online discussion forum (RIBAnet).
  - Access to an extensive collection of books, journals, drawings and photographs on architecture, the built environment and landscape design from the British Architectural Library and online library.
  - Exchange of information and inspiration on topics relating to architecture through the RIBA online community wiki (RIBApedia).
  - Preferential rates for lectures, seminars and other RIBA Trust events.
  - Access to an extensive resource of relevant products and services through the RIBA Product Selector Directory.

- **Business support services**

  - Access to legal, technical and regulatory guidance through free telephone consultation with over 20 specialist practice consultants or RIBA staff with specialist knowledge on a range of topics.

- Insurance guidance, free legal helpline, advice on warranties and appointment documents through the RIBA Insurance Agency.

- **Association with the internationally respected RIBA brand**

  - Use of the 'RIBA' affix and the title 'Chartered Architect' (for work carried out in the UK, any person using the affix and/or title in a business context must be registered with the ARB).
  - Use of the RIBA crest on personal stationery.
  - Entry into the online RIBA Chartered Members directory.

- **Personal and career development**

  - Free access to the RIBA's CPD recording system.
  - Opportunity to apply for specialist accreditation as an RIBA Client Adviser or via the RIBA Conservation Register.
  - Free CPD provision through the RIBA CPD Providers Network directory, office-based seminars, and CPD Providers Network regional road shows.
  - Access to tips, advice and exclusive downloads via the online RIBA CPD section.

2.9.2   The RIBA Chartered Practice scheme

RIBA Chartered Practice accreditation provides a gold standard of quality assurance to potential clients and the wider construction industry. Chartered Practices are committed to excellence in design and service delivery.

In order to qualify as an RIBA Chartered Practice, each separate office within a practice (or each definable architectural practice business unit within a multi-functional organisation) that wishes to register must supply evidence of its compliance with the following criteria:

1. At least one of the full-time principals (Director or Partner) in the practice must be a Chartered Member of the RIBA. For all UK-based practices that Chartered Member must also be registered with the ARB.
2. All architectural work must be under the supervision of a Chartered Member of the RIBA (who must also be registered with the ARB for all UK-based work).
3. At least one in eight of all staff employed in the practice must be a Registered Architect (on the ARB Register) or an Associate Member of the RIBA or a Chartered Architectural Technologist (CIAT member) with RIBA Affiliate Membership.
4. At least one in ten of all staff employed in the practice must be a Chartered Architect (i.e. RIBA Chartered Member).
5. The practice must have a current PI insurance policy appropriate for the work undertaken.

6. The practice must operate an appropriate quality management system.
7. The practice must operate an appropriate health and safety policy.
8. The practice must operate an employment policy that addresses the principles of the RIBA policy statement on employment.
9. The practice must have an appropriate CPD framework in place.
10. The practice must operate an appropriate environmental management policy.
11. The practice must commit to paying at least the statutory minimum wage to architecture students working within the practice. These students must be undertaking experience that complies with the RIBA's practical training rule, and should be completing appropriate records on the RIBA's PEDR website as part of the accreditation criteria.
12. The practice must undertake to make an annual return to the RIBA Business Benchmarking Survey.

The following exclusive benefits and services are available to RIBA Chartered Practices:

- **Promotion and marketing**

  - RIBA Chartered Practices are the only architectural practices endorsed and promoted by the RIBA.
  - RIBA Client Services nominations – a free, unbiased and personalised nomination service, used by over 4,000 clients each year.
  - Promotion at major exhibitions and conferences attended by around 150,000 visitors each year.
  - Entry in the RIBA Directory of Chartered Practices, distributed free to over 3,500 targeted key clients.
  - Free entry in the online RIBA Directory of Chartered Practices on www.architecture.com, which is fully searchable by name, location and/or areas of expertise, with links to the practice's own website, and receives over 4,000 visitors per day.
  - Entitlement to use the RIBA Chartered Practice insignia on letterheads and other promotional materials.
  - Entitlement to use the RIBA Chartered Practice site signboards.
  - RIBA Chartered Practice certificate and registration number.
  - Free entry into relevant RIBA Sector Reviews, published annually, covering nine key sectors of the construction industry and distributed to over 30,000 key clients.
  - Discounts on RIBA corporate adverts in Yellow Pages.

- **Business effectiveness and performance**

  - RIBA Quality Management Toolkit.
  - RIBA Employment Policy and model employment contracts.

- RIBA Health and Safety Policy Template – a generic policy document based on the general needs of a typical architects' practice.
  - RIBA Environmental Policy – sample templates for devising a policy for the practice with valuable background and guidance notes.
  - RIBA Business Benchmarking Service – a business management and development tool, as well as the definitive benchmarking database for the UK architectural profession, providing the opportunity for a practice to assess its business performance against recommended benchmarks devised by Colander and strategic business information indicators, tailored practice benchmark reports and an annual summary report, presenting the key overall findings from the RIBA Business Benchmarking Survey, providing insights into the current business environment for the architects' profession.
  - RIBA Business Support Helpline and RIBA online Business Service provided by Croner – guidance and sample policies, letters, forms and checklists on employment, health and safety, tax, VAT, payroll and other commercial legal issues.
  - Financial planning and debt recovery service provided by Croner – advice for RIBA Chartered Practices on debt recovery, including legal processes, procedures and administration.

- **Preferential business services**

  - RIBA Appointments – discounted fees for recruitment and online recruitment advertising.
  - RIBA Insurance Agency – professional indemnity insurance and range of other insurance policies and services designed to meet practices' needs; cover available includes employer's liability, public liability, cyber risk, household (includes cover for home offices and architectural plans at home), travel, motor, private medical, personal accident, income protection.
  - RIBA Insurance Agency – legal helpline and financial planning (through independent financial advisers AWD).
  - RIBA Microsites – preferential rates on flexible website development and maintenance service offered to RIBA Chartered Practices through partner supplier Acefolio, which allows practices to build and maintain an effective website, and to exploit their portfolio online in more proactive ways.

2.10   Control over entry to the RIBA

Education has always been central to the RIBA, and parallel to the practice of architecture is the centrepiece of the original 1837 Royal Charter. RIBA examinations in architecture were established in 1863; in 1882, successful completion of these became compulsory for those seeking membership of the Institute. Responding to requests from schools of architecture – and as an alternative route to membership – the RIBA developed systems for recognising courses that achieved the standard for exemption from the Institute's examinations. In 1924, RIBA visiting boards were established to evaluate courses and examinations preparing students for professional practice. These visiting boards are the foundation of the current RIBA validation system.

The RIBA wishes to encourage a dialogue supporting and promoting a diverse, engaging, rigorous and intelligent raft of schools of architecture, each clearly distinguished from the other by defined academic objectives and a sense of the individual identity of their courses and qualifications. The RIBA further seeks to enhance the quality of architecture education by recognising and applauding experimentation, innovation and professional relevance in course delivery, teaching methodology and academic outcomes.

RIBA validation is an evidence-based, peer review system. It works internationally as a critical friend to schools of architecture, monitoring courses to improve median achievement, encourage the excellent and ensure a positive student experience. Since the last review of RIBA validation criteria and procedures, the number of schools with RIBA recognised courses in architecture has increased significantly. The criteria and procedures introduced in September 2011 provide an important opportunity for schools to review their course content and define distinctive academic agendas responding to a highly competitive educational environment.

The intention is that schools will:

- state clear academic objectives, distinguishing their offer from competitor courses and highlighting specific areas of excellence;
- avoid prescriptive compliance with the criteria in favour of an interpretation encouraging students to creatively develop all aspects of their professional skills;
- contribute to graduate employability by ensuring that students' skills in digital and analogue media, structured written work and the exploration of design ideas through making are thoroughly represented in all academic portfolios;
- provide courses where at least 50% of all assessed work at Part 1 and at Part 2 is undertaken as design studio projects; and
- provide courses at Part 2 that clearly differ in substance and content from those offered at first degree level and reflect the standards expected of graduates undertaking sustained, specialised postgraduate study.

The RIBA Education department wishes to contribute to realising worthwhile academic objectives throughout all RIBA recognised schools, and to establish a global benchmark for standards in architecture education. Through the system of quinquennial education review known as validation, RIBA visiting boards to schools of architecture will:

- acknowledge experimentation, innovation and professional relevance in course delivery, teaching methodology and academic outcomes, emphasising the distinctive qualities of a school in its written report;
- place emphasis on schools providing the means for students to meet the graduate attributes stated for each award level; and
- use the criteria as diagnostic tools to consider where any shortfall in meeting graduate attributes is apparent.

RIBA validation considers students' work as the primary evidence to decide whether a course or examination in architecture meets, *and exceeds*, academic standards defined by the RIBA validation criteria. These criteria (and the Graduate Attributes at Part 1 and Part 2) are held in common with the Architects Registration Board, and together with the procedures for validation they form the key documents used to consider courses for RIBA validation or revalidation.

Most professional institutions lay down specific standards for entry, and ask that members adhere to codes of professional conduct. The RIBA takes a keen interest in architecture education and, through its validation procedures, closely monitors academic standards in university schools of architecture. It currently reviews courses and examinations in schools of architecture on a four-year cycle; continued recognition depends on standards being maintained and developed.

Many people have their first glimpse of a career in architecture through periods of work experience in an architect's office. This may be initiated by careers advisers in secondary schools, although it is more likely that personal initiative will help develop contacts with sympathetic practices. These arrangements often bring mutual benefits, and provide an important insight into the different types of professional activity.

Practitioners may be asked about suitable courses and entry requirements for those interested in pursuing a career in architecture. Information is available in the booklet *Think Architecture* (also downloadable from the RIBA website, www.architecture.com), and through enquiries to the RIBA Education Department.

2.10.1   Entry requirements

The RIBA is committed to a diverse and inclusive profession, and encourages schools of architecture to adopt admissions policies reflecting this aspiration. Specific admissions criteria are set by the universities, although applicants are advised to have undertaken Art at either GCSE or A2 level to demonstrate visual acuity at an admissions interview.

Generally speaking, a broad mix of subjects at secondary school is desirable for entry to an architecture course, although the idea that mathematics and physics will inevitably be required is inaccurate. Architects do need good writing skills, however, and it is important that this is realised at an early stage – some applicants presume drawing to be the sole requirement, rather than a more balanced mix of communication skills.

Although traditional craft subjects may not be sufficient in themselves for a career in architecture, many schools will, quite rightly, accept these as contributing significantly to the design and problem-solving skills taught and assessed on architecture courses.

2.10.2   Schools of architecture

There are currently 43 schools of architecture and three examination centres in the UK, with both full- and part-time courses recognised by the RIBA.

A full list of the UK Schools of Architecture with courses validated by the RIBA can be found at www.architecture.com.

Academic education is complemented by a minimum of 24 months' practical training under the supervision of a construction professional. This practical training, along with holding Part 1, Part 2 and Part 3 ARB-prescribed qualifications, is an essential prerequisite for those intending to register as an architect; work in practice is logged on the RIBA's Professional Education and Development Record (PEDR) and discussed with a university Professional Studies Advisor (PSA) to ensure the appropriate range of professional skills is acquired.

Unqualified (or part-qualified) employees in an architect's practice may also acquire Part 1 and Part 2 by taking the RIBA's own exam, the Examination in Architecture for Office-Based Candidates. This external route is the only practical option for some candidates, but is demanding. The RIBA franchises this exam to Oxford Brookes University, which also offers enrolled candidates support in the form of workshops and seminars. Anyone seeking to qualify by this route must be based in practice and must meet defined practical experience requirements.

2

The Part 3 Professional Practice Examination is the final element in the education of a student of architecture; success in this, as well as holding Part 1 and Part 2 ARB-prescribed qualifications, allows an individual to register as an architect in the UK and legally use the title 'architect'.

Part-time Part 1 and Part 2 courses are offered at some universities; generally speaking, these add up to a further three years of study over the full-time route, although part-time students can of course subsidise their studies through work in practice (details of universities offering part-time study are also available on www.architecture.com).

Most schools of architecture also offer higher degrees and doctoral programmes in architecture; this field is always changing, and prospective candidates are advised to contact institutions directly.

2.10.3 Practical experience

Practical training is seen by the RIBA to be an integral part of an architect's education, and evaluation of this experience forms an essential component of the RIBA Part 3 Professional Practice Examination. Full details of the RIBA requirements for practical experience are set out in the RIBA online Professional Experience and Development Record (PEDR), which can be viewed at www.pedr.co.uk.

With some variations to this pattern, the first period of a year in practice usually starts at the end of the first three years of the academic course (RIBA Part 1). The second period generally starts on completion of a further two years' academic study (RIBA Part 2).

Each school of architecture offering a Part 3 programme has a Professional Studies Advisor (PSA) responsible for liaison with employers to ensure the optimum training for Part 1 and Part 2 graduates. Advisors welcome details of likely vacancies in practice, and pass these on to interested graduates. During practical training, the status of an architectural assistant is that of employee first and student second. Most PSAs have other responsibilities in their schools, and are unable to visit graduates' offices, especially in the era of the globalised construction economy. Advice given to graduates by a PSA is impartial, but ultimately geared to success in the Part 3 examination.

During either year of practical training, graduates often attend practice and management seminars back at their host school. Employers should expect confirmation that any activity requiring formal leave of absence is of educational importance. Ideally, the practice should arrange a programme of complementary activities such as site visits, participating in client and contractor/sub-contractor meetings, attending planning enquiries, observing specialist construction work, and accompanying clerks of works, and quantity surveyors on their inspections.

Employment mentor

The Part 1 or Part 2 graduate should ensure that one person in their practice acts as an employment mentor, responsible for overseeing their educational and professional development in the workplace. Ideally, the employment mentor's responsibilities should include:

- establishing a framework that will facilitate the provision of high-quality professional experience;
- ensuring the student is not charged with responsibilities inappropriate to their experience;
- discussing work objectives and learning opportunities at the start of each three-month period of experience;
- signing, dating and commenting in the PEDR on the graduate's progress for each eligible period of experience.

2.10.4 The RIBA Part 3 Examination in Professional Practice and Management

Both the RIBA Office-Based Examination and recognised Part 1 and Part 2 courses in schools of architecture contain a strong element of practice, management and law. The Professional Practice Examination is the final means for benchmarking standards of entry to the profession. Each provider defines its own requirements for assessment, but this would typically consist of the following:

- a professional CV;
- a professional development evaluation prepared by the candidate;
- a case study of a project the candidate has had detailed involvement with;
- written examinations, assessed course work, scenario-based essays and reports; and
- a record of professional experience recording the development of competences achieved through practical experience over a minimum period of 24 months.

2.10.5 The oral examination

As the final part of the Professional Practice Examination, candidates are interviewed by experienced examiners to review their knowledge, skills and judgement against the Part 3 criteria for validation.

2

This qualifying examination is intended to establish a high baseline of competence for registration and membership of the RIBA, although candidates should also demonstrate the potential for continuing professional development. Although 24 months of practical training is the mandatory minimum for taking the Part 3 examination, the range and quality of experience that candidates are expected to demonstrate may have to be acquired with further years of experience.

2.11 Control over the professional conduct of members

The latest version of the RIBA Code of Professional Conduct came into effect on 1 January 2005. The object of the Code is to promote the standard of professional conduct, or self-discipline, required of members of the RIBA in the interests of the public. All members, including student and affiliate members, are required to uphold this standard, and their conduct is governed by the Code.

The Code comprises three principles that are of universal application, dealing with integrity, competence and relationships:

Principle 1: Integrity

Members shall act with honesty and integrity at all times.

Principle 2: Competence

In the performance of their work Members shall act competently, conscientiously and responsibly. Members must be able to provide the knowledge, the ability and the financial and technical resources appropriate for their work.

Principle 3: Relationships

Members shall respect the relevant rights and interests of others.

In addition, the Code is supported by a series of professional values (see box below), which in turn are supported by a set of nine more detailed Guidance Notes.

The wording used in the principles is pre-eminent, but members must at all times be guided by the spirit of the Code and not just the words.

Members are governed by the RIBA Charter, Byelaws and Regulations in addition to the Code. Disciplinary measures are provided for under the Byelaws. The RIBA can hold a member personally accountable when acting through a corporate or unincorporated body, and members will not be able to evade this by pleading a higher obligation.

The values associated with each of the three principles

1. **Principle 1 – Honesty and Integrity**

1.1 The Royal Institute expects its Members to act with impartiality, responsibility and truthfulness at all times in their professional and business activities.

1.2 Members should not allow themselves to be improperly influenced either by their own, or others', self-interest.

1.3 Members should not be a party to any statement which they know to be untrue, misleading, unfair to others or contrary to their own professional knowledge.

1.4 Members should avoid conflicts of interest. If a conflict arises, they should declare it to those parties affected and either remove its cause, or withdraw from that situation.

1.5 Members should respect confidentiality and the privacy of others.

1.6 Members should not offer or take bribes in connection with their professional work.

2. **Principle 2 – Competence**

2.1 Members are expected to apply high standards of skill, knowledge and care in all their work. They must also apply their informed and impartial judgment in reaching any decisions, which may require members having to balance differing and sometimes opposing demands (for example, the stakeholders' interests with the community's and the project's capital costs with its overall performance).

2.2 Members should realistically appraise their ability to undertake and achieve any proposed work. They should also make their clients aware of the likelihood of achieving the client's requirements and aspirations. If members feel they are unable to comply with this, they should not quote for, or accept, the work.

2.3 Members should ensure that their terms of appointment, the scope of their work and the essential project requirements are clear and recorded in writing. They should explain to their clients the implications of any conditions of engagement and how their fees are to be calculated and charged. Members should maintain appropriate records throughout their engagement.

2.4 Members should keep their clients informed of the progress of a project and of the key decisions made on the client's behalf.

2.5 Members are expected to use their best endeavours to meet the client's agreed time, cost and quality requirements for the project.

3. Principle 3 – Relationships

3.1 Members should respect the beliefs and opinions of other people, recognise social diversity and treat everyone fairly. They should also have a proper concern and due regard for the effect that their work may have on its users and the local community.

3.2 Members should be aware of the environmental impact of their work.

3.3 Members are expected to comply with good employment practice and the RIBA Employment Policy, in their capacity as an employer or an employee.

3.4 Where members are engaged in any form of competition to win work or awards, they should act fairly and honestly with potential clients and competitors. Any competition process in which they are participating must be known to be reasonable, transparent and impartial. If members find this not to be the case, they should endeavour to rectify the competition process or withdraw.

3.5 Members are expected to have in place (or have access to) effective procedures for dealing promptly and appropriately with disputes or complaints.

Revisions to the Code, and relevant practice notes, may appear in the *RIBA Journal* from time to time. Members will be expected to be familiar with any new provisions right from the date of their introduction, and to comply with them. Ignorance will be no defence.

The Guidance Notes to the Code deal with the following matters:

1. Integrity, conflicts of interest, confidentiality and privacy, corruption and bribery
2. Competition
3. Advertising
4. Appointments
5. Insurance
6. CPD
7. Relationships
8. Employment and equal opportunities
9. Complaints and dispute.

2.12 Enforcing the Code

Where an allegation of a breach of the Code is made against a member, RIBA Byelaw 4 allows for a set of disciplinary processes to deal with it. The processes are designed with the aim of allowing for resolution of disputes between complainant and member, but also for formal investigation and appraisal, where appropriate, by a team of appraisers made up of both RIBA members and other co-professionals. Where an appraisal team considers a complaint to have merit, the member may be called before a hearing panel made up of non-members. Byelaw 4 gives a hearing panel the power to decide upon a sanction where appropriate. The available sanctions are private reprimand, public reprimand, suspension or expulsion.

The procedures allow for independent review of the decisions of the appraisal teams and the hearing panels.

Full details of the Code of Conduct, Guidance Notes, and information on the disciplinary procedures can be obtained from the RIBA website or from the RIBA Professional Standards office.

2.13   Continuing professional development

The term 'continuing professional development' (CPD) is used by the profession to describe those activities that constitute part of the learning process which should continue throughout an architect's professional career. CPD is a matter both for individuals and collectively for offices and departments. It implies the need to formulate a positive plan of action rather than perfunctory attendance at a given number of random events.

The RIBA's CPD rules include the minimum steps members must take to maintain competence. The minimum requirements for Chartered Members are:

- to carry out at least 35 hours of CPD each year, and build up at least 100 learning points to the CPD carried out;
- to gain at least 20 hours of CPD each year from the RIBA CPD Core Curriculum syllabus – the other 15 hours can be done from selected relevant subjects;
- where possible, to gain at least half of CPD from structured learning;
- to record CPD online using the RIBA CPD recording manager;
- to plan CPD as much as possible.

The ten topics covered in the RIBA CPD Core Curriculum are:

- Being safe – health and safety
- Climate – sustainable architecture
- External management – clients, users and delivery of services
- Internal management – professionalism, practice, business and management
- Compliance – legal, regulatory and statutory framework and processes
- Procurement and contracts

2

- Designing and building it – structural design, construction, technology and engineering
- Where people live – communities, urban and rural design and the planning process
- Context – the historic environment and its setting
- Access for all – universal or inclusive design.

CPD is an individual obligation. However, people work in architectural practices and other businesses, and it is therefore also sensible for the business to think about and account for CPD. If the practice is registered with the RIBA, it will have signed a declaration that it has a CPD management system in place. Many businesses will also have appraisal systems in place, at which development and training are planned in accordance with individual and business needs.

Properly planned and implemented, a CPD system in the practice will help to:

- develop both staff and the business;
- keep everyone up to date and competent;
- help the practice's clients;
- take individual staff development needs into account;
- take the general business needs into account;
- help to plan learning and development;
- be flexible enough to take last minute needs into account.

To achieve this, the following are issues to consider in putting together a practice programme:

- What knowledge do you need to meet your current business needs?
- What is your available budget?
- How much will individuals be expected to do on their own?
- How much time can you devote?
- Have you thought about using Investors in People or QA as a tool to help with planning CPD?
- Do you have yearly appraisals at which you plan training for individuals based on the business's needs and individual development?
- Do you actively encourage the RIBA members and other professionals in the practice to undertake their obligations – both on their own and as part of the team?
- What level of knowledge or achievement is sought: general, detailed or advanced?
- What are the individual learning styles of your staff?
- What are the current technical needs for the practice and any projects you have on or are planning?

- The practicalities of running the business – what business, management, financial and marketing knowledge do you need to make it happen?
- Future projects, planned or desired – what skills do you need to acquire to make them happen?
- What specialisms and new skills do you and your staff have, and which do you want to acquire or develop?

Refer also to Chapter 13: Knowledge management.

Given below are a few examples of how 35 hours' worth of CPD might be implemented in a practice:

- **Structured CPD**

  - RIBA CPD Providers Network events and materials – in-house or other
  - RIBA regional CPD
  - Online learning
  - Distance learning
  - Allied construction institutions' CPD events
  - CPD clubs and self-help groups
  - Courses, seminars, workshops and conferences, from the RIBA or others
  - In-house organised lectures, seminars or workshops
  - Diploma courses
  - Certificated courses (e.g. access consultancy, project management)
  - Part-time university courses: either as individual modules or leading to an advanced degree.

- **Informal CPD**

  - Informal in-house CPD presentations
  - RIBA branch events
  - Reading, taking reference notes and in-depth project research
  - Reading the construction press and weekly emails
  - Research
  - Relevant blogs, podcasts, social networking sites
  - Shadowing and mentoring
  - Study tours: UK and abroad
  - Visits to sites other than your own
  - Visits to relevant exhibitions
  - Outreach to schools
  - Relevant voluntary activity (Article 25, Architecture sans Frontières, Business in the Community, Architect in the House, CRASH).

References and further reading

Chappell, D. and Willis, A., *The Architect in Practice*, 10th edn (Oxford: Wiley-Blackwell, 2010).

Foxell, S., *The Professionals' Choice: The Future of the Built Environment Professions* (London: Building Futures, 2003. Update available online at www.buildingfutures.org.uk/projects/building-futures/practice-futures).

Hays, D. L., *(Non-)Essential Knowledge for (New) Architecture* (New York: Princeton Architectural Press, 2013).

Lewis, Roger K., *Architect?: A Candid Guide to the Profession* (Cambridge, MA: MIT Press, 2013).

Architects Registration Board publications

You and Your Architect
Architects Code: Standards of Conduct and Practice, 2010 Version
Dealing with a Complaint
Professional Indemnity Insurance
What we do to regulate use of the title 'architect'

(These leaflets, and others, can be downloaded at www.arb.org.uk)

RIBA publications

A Client's Guide to Engaging an Architect (2013 edition) (London: RIBA Publishing, 2013).

Guidance on Hiring an Architect for your Project (London: RIBA Publishing, 2013).

RIBA Code of Professional Conduct and Standard of Professional Performance (London: RIBA, 2005).

Brookhouse, S., *Part 3 Handbook (3rd edition)*, (London: RIBA Publishing, 2014)

See also www.pedr.co.uk for advice on Part 3 studies.

2

The law

THIS CHAPTER:

- describes the core principles of contract law;
- examines how claims against professionals might arise;
- lists the legislation most relevant to architects, including that pertaining to environmental sustainability;
- provides some sources of further information.

3.1 Introduction

Law pervades the practice of architecture, whether through common law, legislation, or the laws of contract and tort. Of these, contract law will be of most concern to architects on a daily basis, as it underpins:

- employee contracts
- the architect's appointment
- the administration of construction contracts, and
- the architect's role as a member of the design team delivering a project.

It is therefore particularly important for architects to have a solid grasp of the core principles of contract law and to know in detail the standard form contracts they work with.

Beyond contracts, architects also need to have a broad understanding of other areas of legislation including:

- health and safety
- planning law
- property law
- other areas such as human rights, the supply of goods and services, etc.

Several parts of this book cover legal matters specific to their subject and for these matters the reader is directed to the following sections:

- 5.5.2 Data Protection Act
- 6.2   Legal and contractual aspects
- 8.2   The office
- 8.6   Insurance
- 8.7   Health and safety requirements
- 9   The architect's appointment.

3

While the detail of construction contracts is outside the scope of this book (the reader should refer to publications such as the *RIBA Job Book, Which Contract?* and *Law in Practice: The RIBA Legal Handbook*), a broad summary of contract law and its relevance to architects is set out below. Contract administration is central to achieving the appropriate level of quality on site and it is critical that architects have a firm understanding of the standard contract forms (see 'References and further reading') as well as the principles of contract law and building procurement.

Regrettably the construction industry is a litigious one and although attempts have been made to mitigate this in the area of procurement, construction contracts and architects' appointments continue to be areas where great care and attention are required. All those involved in formulating briefs, writing specifications, reporting on the state or potential of land or buildings, designing, inspecting work and administering building contracts, etc. could at some time or other be faced with a reference to adjudication, arbitration or litigation. Sometimes the architect may be forced into the position of claimant, or become caught up as a witness of fact, or be joined as co-defendant in proceedings, or have to face allegations of breach of contract or negligence.

The best defence is risk management. As noted in Section 2.2, architects need to address risk management more rigorously than ever before: Chapter 11 gives some practical advice on this.

3.2   Claims in contract

Claims against professionals may arise in contract or in tort and sometimes in both, but there are important differences. Of the two, contract is by far the more usual.

Definition

A **contract** is an agreement enforceable in law, for a breach of which the law will provide a remedy – usually monetary compensation or damages. Contractual obligations can arise from express or implied terms, the latter usually because of trade custom, or because they are necessary to make the contract workable or most likely because they are implied by statute and cannot readily be excluded. Only the parties to a contract are bound by its terms, and the obligations which it gives rise to are therefore relatively controllable. By and large, the parties are free to agree whatever bargain they wish, and the courts will not be concerned about its fairness, only that it is workable and not contrary to public morality and the law.

There are several matters to be aware of. Where a contractual obligation is not met, an action for breach of contract may be brought and damages claimed in respect of the losses suffered. An architect liable for breach of contract will often be in breach of an express or implied term to exercise that degree of skill and care expected of an ordinary, competent architect. However, if the contractual duty is a strict liability one, i.e. to achieve a particular result, as for example with a 'fitness for purpose' warranty, then it will not be necessary to rely on a lack of skill and care. (It is worth highlighting here the dangers of expressions such as 'fit for purpose', which should be deleted from the wording of any appointment agreement before it is signed.) The fact of failure will, of itself, be sufficient to establish breach of contract. Contract law puts no restrictions on the kind of losses that are recoverable in damages, and economic losses are freely recoverable so long as they arise directly from the breach and it may be supposed that they could reasonably have been within the contemplation of the parties at the time they entered into the contract.

A critical decision facing any employer is the form of procurement for construction of the building, and therefore which form of contract to use, and the architect will usually be called upon for advice on this. It is important to note that if the architect is to be the contract administrator, then they will also have a duty to advise the client on the powers and duties of each of the parties under the chosen contract. In particular they have a duty to advise on the contractual provisions arising from or in place of relevant legislation. The RIBA publication *Which Contract?* provides detailed information on this issue.

It is essential that appointment contracts for professional services are in writing, and that the obligations of the parties are set out in clear and precise terms (see Chapter 9). Wherever possible the suite of RIBA standard forms should be used.

On very small projects many architects prefer to formalise their appointment by means of a letter rather than lengthier standard forms of agreements. There are inherent risks in doing this, and it is a matter for the architect to balance the convenience of appointing by letter against the increased risk. The RIBA publication *A Guide to Letter Contracts for Very Small Projects, Surveys and Reports* provides a safe way to word a letter contract for particular circumstances and points out the risks and pitfalls to avoid. It is recommended that anyone wishing to contract by letter refers to this publication first.

Another critical issue is the recognition of consumer rights in building contracts and contracts for professional services. Failure to explain the consequences of using unamended standard contracts might make an architect liable to the consumer client for damages and/or might lose the protection of the contract in a dispute. Any contract with a consumer must be negotiated in good faith. The RIBA Agreements 2010 include guidance notes on negotiating appointment contracts with a consumer client.

3.3   Claims in tort

> **Definition**
>
> **Tort** is a civil wrong outside contract, although a tortious duty may exist in parallel with a contractual one. Many kinds of tort are relevant to the practice of architecture (for example, trespass, libel, nuisance), but actions in tort against architects are usually for alleged negligence.

There are three essentials for a claim in tort to be established:

- there must be a duty of care owed to the plaintiff by the defendant. For a professional person this will usually be a duty to use reasonable care and skill to the standard of the ordinary skilled man or woman exercising and professing to have that special professional skill;
- the duty of care must have been breached by carelessness, to an extent which in law amounts to negligence; and
- damage must have resulted from that breach.

Often the plaintiff will have no contract with the defendant, and therefore of necessity any claim has to be founded in tort. However, even where there is a contract, the courts may still find that a duty in tort also exists.

Third parties such as funders, lessees, subsequent purchasers, etc. who were not involved with the original contract and who would otherwise have to rely mainly on tort, usually try to establish contractual relationships by seeking collateral agreements or warranties. These should never be entered into if the terms are more onerous than the original contracts, but even so the additional contractual relationships can only increase liability. Legal advice should always be sought before entering into such a warranty (see Chapter 9).

3.4   Legislation

Legislation imposes conditions on the practising architect's work, and is increasingly used to reformulate areas of law that have become unwieldy. It is also used to introduce new areas of law, many of which are the result of complying with European Directives.

Circulars or guidance notes are often published to accompany pieces of legislation. They are written in plain English and are an invaluable aid to a better understanding of legislation, sometimes giving a clear indication of what Parliament intended. However, they are not part of the law, unlike Approved Documents or Approved Codes of Practice, which often have legal standing to the extent that they describe minimum acceptable standards.

3.4.1   European law

European law has been a major influence on English legislation for some time. Both the Council of Ministers and the European Commission can make 'Regulations'. These are directly applicable in all Member States and are published in the *Official Journal of the European Community*. In other cases they may issue 'Directives' or 'Decisions', which are usually also published in the *Official Journal*. Directives, usually the most relevant for architects, are binding in substance on Member States, but the UK Parliament must then implement them in whatever form it chooses. Decisions are binding in their entirety on those to whom they are directed, and are enforceable in national courts. Mere recommendations and opinions have no binding force.

3.5   Some key statutes

An outline of some of the more important Acts is given below.

Town and Country Planning Act 1990

The purpose of the planning system is to regulate the use, siting and appearance of buildings and to protect the environment and public amenity. All developments require planning permission from the local planning authority, except for internal changes to homes and certain small domestic extensions within strict criteria, which may be covered by 'permitted development rights'. Statements on such things as design and access, flood risk, biodiversity and geological conservation may be required with the application together with the appropriate fee. Internal or external alterations or extensions that would affect the character of a listed building of historical or architectural interest require two separate applications, one for listed building consent and one for planning permission. For further information, see the UK Government website www.planningportal.gov.uk.

Human Rights Act 1998

This Act is particularly relevant to issues such as planning application procedures and dispute resolution. Public authorities are forbidden to act in a way that is incompatible with the Human Rights Convention; if they do so the injured party may proceed directly against the authority concerned in the courts.

The effect of the Act is to strengthen the influence of 'proportionality' (that is, the balance between interference with a landowner's rights and the wider public issues such as harm to the environment) as a factor to be taken into account by the decision-maker. The European Court of Human Rights has accepted the principle that a 'margin of appreciation' should be allowed in a State's favour.

Building Act 1984 and Building Regulations 2010

Building Regulations have been devolved to Wales, Scotland and Northern Ireland. The Regulations aim to secure standards of: health and safety for people in and around buildings; energy conservation; and the welfare and convenience of disabled people. The Building Regulations apply to all new building work and impose duties covering the design and construction of buildings, their services, fittings and equipment. 'Approved documents', which set out the requirements and give practical and technical guidance on compliance with the Regulations, cover structure; fire safety; site preparation, contaminants and resistance to moisture; toxic substances; sound transmission; ventilation; hygiene; drainage and waste disposal; heating appliances; protection from falling; conservation of fuel and power; access and facilities for disabled people; glazing; and electrical safety. The local authority or approved building inspector must be given notice, accompanied by a fee, before work commences. Building control inspectors will make independent checks on compliance and issue a final certificate on satisfactory completion. For further information, see the UK Government website www.planningportal.gov.uk or www.legislation.gov.uk.

Construction (Design and Management) Regulations 2015 (CDM)

The CDM Regulations were amended in 2015 and now provide for a role of Principal Designer to replace the role of CDM Coordinator. The Regulations relate to the design, construction, use, maintenance, cleaning, repair and demolition of buildings and structures. They seek to eliminate potential hazards and minimise by careful design and management those that cannot be eliminated; they impose statutory duties on designers and contractors on all projects. They also impose statutory duties on clients, unless the project relates to a single residence for the client's own use with a single contractor. Architects are frequently in the most appropriate position to perform the role of Principal Designer but this should be a separate appointment from that as architect. For further information refer to the HSE website: www. hse.gov.uk/construction/cdm/2015/index.htm.

Party Wall etc. Act 1996

A notice must be served by or on behalf of the building owner notifying the owner and occupiers of the adjoining land if:

- a party wall is to be demolished, rebuilt, extended or repaired;
- a new building is to be constructed near the boundary;
- a new party fence is to be built;
- a new wall is to be built up to the boundary line.

A dispute may arise if the adjoining owner does not consent to the works; the Act sets out a procedure for resolving any such disputes.

Equality Act 2010

The Equality Act replaced previous anti-discrimination laws with a single Act to make the law simpler and to remove inconsistencies. This makes the law easier for people to understand and comply with. The Act also strengthened protection in some situations, and covers nine protected characteristics that cannot be used as a reason to treat people unfairly. The protected characteristics are: age, disability, gender reassignment, marriage and civil partnership, pregnancy and maternity, race, religion or belief, sex and sexual orientation.

The Equality Act sets out the different ways in which it is unlawful to treat someone, such as direct and indirect discrimination, harassment, victimisation and failing to make a reasonable adjustment for a disabled person.

The Act prohibits unfair treatment in the workplace; when providing goods, facilities and services; when exercising public functions; and when buying or renting property.

3.5.1 Site activities

Site Waste Management Plan Regulations 2008

These Regulations require that any person intending to carry out a construction project with an estimated cost greater than £300,000 prepares and maintains a waste management plan.

Defective Premises Act 1972

This Act applies where work is carried out in connection with a dwelling, including design work. It states that 'a person taking on work in connection with the provision of a dwelling owes a duty to see that the work which he takes on is done in a workmanlike or, as the case may be, professional manner, with proper materials and so that as regards that work the dwelling will be fit for habitation when completed' (section 1(1)). This appears to be a strict liability, and is owed to anyone acquiring an interest in the dwelling.

3.5.2   Contracts/payment

Housing Grants, Construction and Regeneration Act 1996

This requires that all construction contracts falling within the definition of the Act, including client–architect professional services agreements, contain certain provisions including the right to stage payments, the right to notice of the amount to be paid, the right to suspend work for non-payment, and the right to take any dispute arising out of the contract to adjudication. If the parties fail to include these provisions in their contract, the Act will imply terms to provide these rights (section 114) by means of the Scheme for Construction Contracts (England and Wales) Regulations 1998. The Act's definition of 'construction contract' includes the appointment of a professional. The Act is of broad application, but with one important exception in the context of minor works – it does not apply to a 'construction contract' with a residential occupier. This means an appointment relating to operations on a dwelling which the client occupies or intends to occupy (section 106). However, work on other residential properties, for example for landlords, local authorities or housing associations, will usually be covered by the Act.

Part III of the Act relating to architects' registration has been repealed and re-enacted as the Architects Act 1997, under the Parliamentary rules for consolidating Acts.

Supply of Goods and Services Act 1982

This statute covers contracts for work and materials, contracts for the hire of goods, and contracts for services. Most construction contracts come under the category of 'work and materials'. For these contracts the Act implies terms regarding care and skill, time of performance and consideration. For example, section 14 implies a term that where the supplier is acting in the course of business, the supplier will carry out the services within a reasonable time, provided of course the parties have not agreed terms regarding time themselves.

These provisions would come into play if the terms of a contract do not provide the relevant detail regarding the programme for completion.

Unfair Contract Terms Act 1977

This regulates contracts by restricting the operation and legality of certain contract terms. A key function of the Act is to limit the applicability of disclaimers of liability. It has the effect of rendering various exclusion clauses void, including:

- any clauses excluding liability for death or personal injury resulting from negligence;
- any clauses attempting to exclude liability for Sale of Goods Act 1979 section 12 obligations (and the equivalent under the Supply of Goods and Services Act);
- any clauses attempting to exclude liability for Sale of Goods Act 1979 sections 13, 14 or 15 obligations (and the equivalent under the Supply of Goods and Services Act) where they are operating against any person dealing as consumer.

It also renders certain other exclusion clauses void insofar as they fail to satisfy a test of reasonableness, e.g. liability for negligence other than liability for death or personal injury, and liability for breach of sections 13, 14 and 15 obligations in contracts that do not involve a consumer.

Unfair Terms in Consumer Contracts Regulations 1999

These only apply to terms in contracts between a seller of goods or supplier of goods and services and a consumer, and where the terms have not been individually negotiated (this would generally include all standard forms).

A consumer is defined as a person who, in making a contract, is acting 'for purposes which are outside his business'. An 'unfair term' is any term which causes a significant imbalance in the parties' rights to the detriment of the consumer, and the Regulations state that any such term will not be binding on the consumer. An indicative list of terms is given in Schedule 2 and includes, for example 'any term excluding or hindering the consumer's right to take legal action … particularly by requiring the consumer to take the dispute to arbitration …. It is important, therefore, that if the arbitration option is selected, or if any other amendments are made which could be seen as limiting the employer's rights, that these have been explained and discussed, in order that they can be considered to have been individually negotiated.

In the RIBA standard conditions of appointment, it advises that the following provisions require such individual negotiation, if they are to be used with a consumer client:

- payment and payment notices (clauses 5.1 to 5.15);
- the right of set-off (clause 5.16);

- the right of joint and several liability (as in the net contribution clause 7.3);
- the provisions for dispute resolution (clause 9);
- the right to cancel the Agreement (clause 10).

In the RIBA domestic conditions of appointment, designed specifically for use with a consumer client, the following items still require individual negotiation:

- the provisions for payment (condition 5);
- liability (condition 7);
- dispute resolution (condition 9);
- the right to cancel the Agreement (condition 10).

Contracts (Rights of Third Parties) Act 1999

This Act provides that where a term of contract expressly confers, or purports to confer, a right on a person who is not a party to that contract, the party has the right to enforce that term. It is possible to exclude this right, and all Conditions of Appointment published by the RIBA contain an exclusion clause, to prevent third parties bringing claims against the architect. As an alternative, the option in the RIBA Standard Conditions for a Third Party Schedule could be adopted. Otherwise, architects should ensure that an exclusion clause is included in any non-standard terms to which they agree.

Late Payment of Commercial Debts (Interest) Act 1998, as amended and supplemented by the Late Payment of Commercial Debts Regulations 2002

This Act implies a term into any contract to which the Act applies between businesses (but not with a consumer) that any qualifying debt created by the contract carries simple interest in accordance with the Act. The contract may avoid the provisions of the Act being implied if it includes terms that give a 'substantial remedy' of interest on any late payment of an amount due. The contracts to which the Act applies would include most forms of construction contract or professional appointment. A debt could be created by the obligation to pay a certified amount or fee, and interest will start to run the day after the debt becomes due. The Secretary of State has the power to set the rate of interest due (see http://webarchive.nationalarchives. gov.uk/20090609003228/http://www.berr.gov.uk/files/file37581.pdf).

Cancellation of Contracts made in a Consumer's Home or Place of Work etc. Regulations 2008

These Regulations establish the right of a consumer to cancel a contract within seven days of them signing it during a visit, such as by an architect or contractor, to the consumer's home or place of work.

Provision of Services Regulations 2009

These are dealt with in Section 9.2.4.

3.6   Relevant texts and sources of information

Architects need to be aware of the legislation that applies to particular situations and have a working knowledge of the consequences of its application. When clients pay for independent and skilled advice, they are entitled to just that. For example, an architect should not simply accept without question the view or opinions of a planning officer of a local authority in the event that the officer is operating a policy that is wrong in law. Architects are not expected to have an expert knowledge of the legislation, but they need to know what is required in terms of compliance, and what procedures need to be adopted.

Architects should have acquired a basic understanding of those areas of law generally relevant to the practice of architecture in order to satisfy the requirements for registration. As a refresher to this knowledge, it may be useful to read books such as *Learning the Law* by Glanville Williams and *Law in Practice*: *The RIBA Legal Handbook*.

For more detailed information about law relevant to specific areas or for situations that arise in practice, the following advice may be useful.

- Refer to books written by lawyers with architect readers in mind. The RIBA *List of Recommended Books* (see www.pedr.co.uk) is published annually and includes selected titles on practice and legal matters, e.g. procurement, design liability, building contracts, contract administration, arbitration, etc. A law dictionary such as *Osborn's Concise Law Dictionary* will also be useful.
- Subscribe to, or make arrangements to access, case law reports and other authoritative texts, e.g. *Building Law Reports*, *Construction Law Reports*, *Construction Law Digest*, *Construction Industry Law Letter*, etc. These are often available for reference at libraries in universities with architecture or law departments.
- Refer to authoritative and up-to-date annotated legislation such as that found in *Halsbury's Statutes*, *Current Law Statutes*, or *Statutes in Force*. Such reference works are usually available at university law libraries.
- Databases such as LexisLibrary by LexisNexis, which holds all reported recent case law, may also be available, but a charge will normally be made for this kind of service.
- Use the RIBA Library's Information Centre or the members' information line (tel: 020 7307 3600). For specific enquiries, the Information Centre may also refer you to the RIBA Practice Department, or to RIBA specialist

3

practice consultants, who can provide help and guidance on a range of practice issues, including legal and contractual problems, debt recovery, taxation, building regulations, party wall matters and planning.

- Keep up to date on developments in the law relevant to practice by reading the technical press and perhaps compiling a file of articles from, for example, the *RIBA Journal*, *Architects' Journal*, and the legal sections from *Building*. Attend CPD events and seminars which feature practice issues and often include legal topics.

The RIBA is represented on the Liability Panel of the Construction Industry Council, which is a construction industry forum for knowledge sharing on contracts, insurance and legal liability issues. The CIC Liability Panel regularly produces liability briefings that can be downloaded from the CIC website (www.cic.org.uk).

The text of UK Acts and Statutory Instruments (covering Regulations) can be found at www.legislation.gov.uk/.

If the name of the legal case is known, the judgment may be found at www.bailii.org.

Some architects may wish to develop their expertise further and perform associated roles such as:

- Adjudicator: the RIBA is a nominating body for qualified persons to act under the adjudication provisions of section 108 of the Housing Grants, Construction and Regeneration Act 1996.
- Arbitrator: the RIBA President is an appointer in cases of disputes to be determined by an arbitrator.
- Mediation: on application, and with the agreement of both parties, the RIBA can appoint a trained mediator from the RIBA Mediation Panel to help parties reach a negotiated settlement.
- Expert: this is where the architect acts as an expert to determine disputes (although not as an arbitrator), or acts as an expert witness, a quite different role.

Membership of one or more of the specialist professional groups, some of which are listed below, also offers the chance to join like-minded architects.

- **Society of Construction Law (SCL)**

  www.scl.org.uk

  Formed in 1983 to enable those interested in construction law to meet and discuss matters of common interest, it provides a forum for lawyers and non-lawyers alike, and meets on a regular basis, usually at King's College, London.

- **Chartered Institute of Arbitrators (CIArb)**

www.ciarb.org

Founded in 1915, this is a multi-disciplinary organisation with worldwide membership, whose primary objective is to promote and facilitate the determination of disputes by arbitration, but which is also active in promoting other means of dispute resolution. CIArb publishes a quarterly journal, *Arbitration*, and organises a wide range of activities nationally, internationally, and locally through its branch network. Further information may be obtained from The Secretary General, Chartered Institute of Arbitrators, International Arbitration Centre, 12 Bloomsbury Square, London WC1A 2LP.

Architects with a sufficient grasp of legal considerations should be able to recognise possible hazards, legal or otherwise, and the likely consequences if the right kind of professional advice is not sought at the appropriate time. They should be able to recognise the nature of the legal problems entailed, and seek appropriate legal advice.

Many architects enjoy long and mutually beneficial association with solicitors; sound legal advice can save a great deal of money and worry in the long term. Information on suitable firms of solicitors currently in practice, together with particulars of their expertise, may be obtained from The Law Society, or by referring to a recent edition of *Waterlow's Solicitors' and Barristers' Directory* (www.waterlowlegal.com), or similar.

3.7   Legislation related to environmental sustainability

In the area of climate change policy, where there is no international accord, often the European Union drives change at UK level. The UK has also developed some of its own ambitious policies leading the way on sustainable development.

3.7.1   EU legislation

EU '20-20-20' targets

In 2007 EU leaders agreed demanding climate and energy targets, to be met by 2020. These are commonly referred to as the '20-20-20' targets:

- a reduction in EU greenhouse gas emissions of at least 20% below 1990 levels;
- 20% of EU energy consumption to come from renewable resources;

- a 20% reduction in primary energy use compared with projected levels, to be achieved by improving energy efficiency.

Different EU countries have different targets to meet in these areas and the UK must achieve 15% renewables by 2020. It has, however, been assessed that the European Union is only on track to achieve around half the desired improvement in energy efficiency.

The Energy Efficiency Directive 2012 (EED) introduced binding measures for energy efficiency on the public sector and industry and EU Member States have to implement it by June 2014. It requires the establishment of a long-term strategy for investment in the renovation of residential and commercial buildings with the aim of improving their energy efficiency. Public bodies are obliged to lead by example and must renovate 3% of the total floor area of central government buildings each year to meet minimum energy performance requirements.

Other measures include Member States setting up an energy efficiency scheme for energy distributors and retail energy sales companies; all large enterprises being subject to independent energy audits (small and medium-sized enterprises and enterprises implementing an energy or environmental management system will be exempt) and by 2015 carrying out a comprehensive assessment of the potential for the joint generation of electricity and useful heat and efficient district heating and cooling. They will be required to implement policies that encourage taking into account at both local and regional levels the potential for efficient heating and cooling systems, to take steps to ensure development of such infrastructure and to undertake a cost–benefit analysis to identify the most resource- and cost-efficient solutions to meet heating and cooling needs.

These measures will lead not only to an increased focus on energy efficiency, but also to additional compliance costs for businesses and a potential impact on the value of inefficient buildings, so consideration of energy efficiency by building owners should be a priority.

Energy Performance of Buildings Directive (EPBD)

The first EPBD in 2002 mandated the requirements that led to Part L of the Building Regulations. Other familiar UK requirements which stem from the EPBD include the requirement for certain public buildings to declare their energy performance through Display Energy Certification, and the requirements for Energy Performance Certificates. The 2010 recast of the EPBD set a target for all new buildings to be 'nearly zero-energy buildings' by 2020, including existing buildings undergoing 'major renovation' (see 'Building Regulations' below).

3.7.2   UK legislation

The Department for Environment, Food and Rural Affairs (DEFRA) is leading the government's sustainable development agenda, but various other departments originate policy in this area. These include the Department of Energy and Climate Change (DECC) and the Department for Communities and Local Government (CLG).

Climate Change Act 2008

The Climate Change Act 2008 commits the UK to reducing greenhouse gas emissions by at least 80% from 1990 levels by 2050, requiring legally binding carbon budgets for five-year periods.

www.legislation.gov.uk/ukpga/2008/27/contents

Carbon Reduction Commitment Energy Efficiency Scheme (CRC)

The CRC requires many companies to audit and report on their annual emissions related to energy use. A sufficient number of emissions allowances must be purchased to cancel these out. Performance of all those companies included in the CRC is published which, along with the cost of emissions allowances, provides a driver to reduce energy use.

www.gov.uk/crc-energy-efficiency-scheme

Carbon Plan 2011

The first Low Carbon Transition Plan for the UK was published in 2009 and included emissions reductions targets that applied to workplaces, homes and communities. The subsequent Carbon Plan 2011 sets out the actions and milestones for achieving the government's carbon dioxide reduction targets.

https://www.gov.uk/government/publications/the-carbon-plan-reducing-greenhouse-gas-emissions--2

Building Regulations

The Building Regulations for England and Wales have increasingly stringent targets for conservation of fuel and power (Part L) and reduction of water consumption (Part G). There are also requirements for other aspects of buildings that affect health and safety, for example:

- toxic substances (Part D);
- ventilation (Part F).

3

Part L carbon reduction targets are currently driven by a stated policy to achieve zero carbon in new domestic buildings by 2016 and in non-domestic buildings by 2019, in line with the Carbon Plan 2011 (see 'Energy Performance of Buildings Directive' above).

Energy Act 2011

The Energy Act 2011, as well as creating the Green Deal (see below), provides the powers to ensure that, as from April 2018, it will be unlawful to rent out residential or business premises that do not reach a minimum energy efficiency standard.

www.legislation.gov.uk/ukpga/2011/16/contents/enacted

Around 40% of commercial buildings in the UK could start to rapidly lose value as these future energy standards approach, unless improvement works are undertaken.

Around 70% of buildings that will be in use in the mid-21st century already exist, and the Committee on Climate Change's first report in 2008, *Building a Low Carbon Economy*, acknowledged that upgrading the energy efficiency of our existing stock, especially in the residential sector, is the most cost-effective way to reduce carbon dioxide emissions.

www.theccc.org.uk/publications

The Green Deal – upgrading existing stock

The Energy Act 2011 includes provisions to create a new financing framework, called the 'Green Deal', to enable energy efficiency improvements to be carried out on households and non-domestic properties. The upfront cost of the improvements, generally the biggest barrier to uptake, will be paid for by a loan. These loans will be paid back over time through a regular charge placed on the property's energy bill. The idea is that the energy bill should be lower after the improvements, so even with the charge added, money should still be saved. The Green Deal was launched in October 2012.

The Energy Act also includes provisions to ensure that from April 2016 private residential landlords will be unable to refuse a tenant's reasonable request for consent to energy efficiency improvements where finance is available (e.g. under the Green Deal or the Energy Company Obligation).

National Planning Policy Framework (NPPF)

The NPPF supports a 'presumption in favour of sustainable development'. This has proved a controversial document, with environmental groups calling for a single detailed definition of sustainable development, produced by the government, to guide planners in drawing together the sometimes competing demands of environmental, social and economic issues, and more detail on issues such as energy efficiency, recycling and low-carbon energy targets.

Although the NPPF sets out the Brundtland definition of sustainable development it is difficult to come up with a more technical and detailed definition that would be appropriate in all local areas and stand the test of time. It is in the nature of localism that local authorities should be able to apply the definition of sustainable development in a way that meets their local circumstances, while ensuring all relevant themes are considered and evaluated.

The RIBA's *Guide to Localism: Opportunities for Architects* (2011) contains further information on localism and the NPPF and is available on the RIBA website.

www.architecture.com/RIBA/Campaigns%20and%20issues/Planning%20 and%20localism/Supportingtheprofession.aspx

The UK Renewable Energy Strategy

The UK Renewable Energy Strategy (2009), designed to comply with the European Renewable Energy Directive 2007, sets a target for the UK to obtain 15% of its energy from renewable sources by 2020.

Feed-in Tariffs (FITs)

FITs for renewable electricity offer financial incentives to those in a position to sell surplus locally generated energy. Through the use of FITs, DECC hopes to encourage the deployment of additional small-scale low-carbon electricity generation, particularly by organisations, businesses, communities and individuals that have not traditionally engaged in the electricity market. This will allow many people to invest in small-scale low-carbon electricity, in return for a guaranteed payment from an electricity supplier of their choice for the electricity they generate and use, as well as a guaranteed payment for unused surplus electricity they export back to the grid. At the time this guide is going to press, the

3

details of the FIT scheme are being clarified. All the latest information is on the DECC website.

www.gov.uk/feed-in-tariffs

Renewable Heat Incentive (RHI)

The RHI offers financial support schemes to those generating heat from renewable or low-carbon sources. These schemes may incentivise building owners to incorporate such measures into their projects.

Low Carbon Construction Action Plan

The UK Government's *Low Carbon Construction Action Plan 2011* was the government response to the Low Carbon Construction, Innovation and Growth Team's final report (2010).

www.gov.uk/government/uploads/system/uploads/attachment_data/file/31779/11-976-low-carbon-construction-action-plan.pdf

www.gov.uk/government/publications/low-carbon-construction-innovation-growth-team-final-report

The Action Plan identifies several key pointers, including:

- the need to align design and construction with operation and asset management;
- the need to close the gap between modelled and actual performance of buildings;
- advocating the use of the 'Soft Landings' project methodology to encourage user and building management input during the briefing and design development process; and
- extending post-contract monitoring and feedback through to occupation.

The objective to 'close the performance gap' was also highlighted in the Zero Carbon Hub's *Carbon Compliance* report (2010), which headlined an objective for an output-based verification of actual performance by 2020.

www.zerocarbonhub.org

References and further reading

Bone, S. and Osborn, P. G., *Osborn's Concise Law Dictionary*, 11th edn (London: Sweet & Maxwell, 2009).

Clamp, H., *Which Contract? Choosing the Appropriate Building Contract* (London: RIBA Publishing, 2012).

Coombes Davies, M., *Good Practice Guide: Arbitration* (London: RIBA Publishing, 2011).

Ostime, N., *RIBA Job Book*, 9th edn (London: RIBA Publishing, 2013).

Phillips, R., *A Guide to Letter Contracts: For Very Small Projects, Surveys and Reports* (London: RIBA Publishing, 2009).

Speight, A. and Stone, G., *Architect's Legal Handbook: The Law for Architects*, 9th edn (Oxford: Architectural Press, 2010).

Uff, J., *Construction Law* (London: Sweet & Maxwell, 2013).

Wevill, J., *Law in Practice: The RIBA Legal Handbook*, 2nd edn (London: RIBA Publishing, 2013).

Williams, G., *Learning the Law* (London: Stevens & Sons, 2010).

See also Section 3.6.

3

Part 2
Practice management

Setting up a practice

> **THIS CHAPTER:**
>
> - examines what's involved in setting up a practice and some of the considerations that need to be taken into account;
> - explains the different forms of practice;
> - describes how to develop a business strategy;
> - lists the various types of business adviser that might be able to help.

4

4.1 Introduction

There has been an increase in the number of new practices starting up in the UK over the past few years, driven in part by circumstances due to the economic climate. Many of the usual considerations for making such a decision remain valid, but there is a greater need for understanding how to make a practice a successful business.

Most architects set out with a view to starting their own practice at some point, and for those that take the plunge it is undoubtedly the most significant decision they will make in their professional careers. The decision brings with it excitement and trepidation in equal measure: you will need to weigh up the benefits of greater freedom of expression and working patterns with the greater risks and responsibilities of managing a business and, potentially, being an employer. It is not for everyone but the rewards can be considerable.

There are many matters covered elsewhere in this book that are pertinent to starting a practice:

- Chapter 2: The profession (in particular Section 2.10.3 on the employment of those seeking practical training)
- Chapter 5: Marketing and business development
- Chapter 6: People management
- Chapter 7: Financial management
- Chapter 8: Office management
- Chapter 12: Computing, CAD, BIM and IT.

4.2   Making the decision

4.2.1   Why, what, who and when

The decision about whether to form a practice must be taken carefully, and with the appropriate information to support it. *The RIBA Good Practice Guide: Starting a Practice* sets this out as 'why', 'what', 'who' and 'when'. Whether triggered by redundancy, or a desire for a change of lifestyle, or even a competition win, it is a decision generally motivated by the architect's desire to have greater control over their projects and working life, and the potential to build a reputation in the industry and the community.

There is clearly a balance between starting as early as possible and waiting until an appropriate level of experience has been gained and a network of potential clients and collaborators developed. The time will probably never feel perfect, and a point may come where you need to take a leap of faith. However, you must be clear exactly what you are going to do in order to develop a business plan and a marketing plan (see Chapter 5). Although there is some overlap, these are two distinct activities; both are critical to success and a sustainable business. A business plan is a critical tool in this respect – this is covered in Section 4.4.

One of the key decisions is whether you are prepared to spend as much or possibly more of your time in business management and business development as you do in designing and managing building projects. You will also need to determine how you will manage increases (and decreases) in work flow and how you will resource them. It is critical that you manage cash flow (see Chapter 7) so, from a financial point of view alone, taking on personnel and paying monthly salaries is a major step.

Although some way off, it is important to consider how the practice might continue after the founders leave the business. Although not strictly necessary upon start-up, it is worth thinking about this carefully at an early stage in the life of the practice.

4.2.2   Collaboration

Another way of managing work flow, especially in the early stages of the business, is to form collaborations with other practices or individuals. This has to be carefully managed and it is important to choose partners you know well and feel you can trust and who are reliable. They will have other projects and you need to be certain they will be willing and able to maintain their input on your projects when they have new work coming in. It is a fine balance, but collaboration can bring other benefits, such as having someone to bounce ideas off and – assuming you have a number of people to call on – broadening your own practice's experience and capabilities by proxy. The RIBA Plan of Work 2013 is built on collaboration and this is a core matter for architectural practice today. BIM is an enabler for collaboration in the design team – this is covered in Chapter 12. See also Section 4.3.8 below.

4.2.3　Choosing a name

There are varying formats for practice names:

- the surnames of the founding partners or directors;
- parts of the principals' names used to form another name;
- an arrangement of the principals' initials;
- a word or words that evoke the nature of the practice; or
- something that just stands out from the crowd and is memorable.

Whatever name is chosen it should, either in its entirety or as an abbreviation, be capable of becoming a web and email address. It should also be something that rises to the top of a web search.

If some arrangement of the names of the principals is chosen, consideration must be given to what would happen if one person leaves the business. It is, however, the traditional way of naming a practice and demonstrates a willingness to 'stand up and be counted'. It will also stand the test of time, whereas something that feels contemporary now or is related to the sort of work the practice is currently involved with might become outdated or irrelevant in the future.

4.2.4　Website

Websites (which are covered in Chapter 5) are an important business development tool to have right from the start. Clients will invariably look at them initially to see whether they think your practice is right for them. It need not be expensive to develop, but as a designer it is critical that it demonstrates your design aesthetic as well as communicating previous work, the sectors you cover and the way you work. Try to convey something of what clients will experience if they commission you to design their buildings.

4.2.5　Getting clients

Obviously without clients the business will not exist, but they won't just fall into your lap; you must seek them out or generate PR that will bring them to you. This is as important when the practice is starting up as at any time and you should make the best use of your existing network of contacts to generate leads. Set up a programme for regularly communicating with your contacts – either by phone, email or through social media – so that they

4

know what you are up to and remember you next time they commission a project or make a recommendation to someone that does. Not everyone is comfortable making cold calls or attending networking events, but these are important skills to develop; you never know where the next lead might come from. See Chapter 5 for advice on this critical matter.

4.3   Forms of practice

There are no legal restrictions on the form of practice architects might decide to adopt in order to operate their businesses – you will need to determine which of the following best suits your needs and situation. Data from the RIBA on its Chartered Practices show that more than two-thirds of practices now trade as limited liability entities, with the proportions being:

- sole trader/principal/practitioner 20%
- partnership 9%
- limited liability company 60%
- limited liability partnership (LLP) 10%
- others (unlimited companies, co-ops, etc.) 1%.

It is interesting to note the changes since the previous edition of this book; the main one being that partnerships have more than halved in number, with limited companies increasing from 52% to 60% of practices. Sole traders have increased by 2% and LLPs by 3%.

4.3.1   Sole trader

Architects can practise as sole traders (also referred to as sole principals or sole practitioners) either entirely alone, or with employed staff. Many architects choose this form of practice, attracted by the freedom of carrying on a business on their own account, in tune with their own talents, over which they have absolute control. Although the portfolio of work of sole traders can be limited to small projects, this is not necessarily the case, and sole traders often handle a limited number of medium-range projects, particularly if they have efficient IT systems in place and employ or sub-contract some assistance. However, this is generally considered one of the hardest forms of practice in that sole traders can feel isolated from their fellow professionals. While they are entitled to all the profits from the business, they also have to manage it single-handedly and face the risks alone. Sole traders are responsible for debts and any damages awarded against them for breach of contract or tort, and are liable to the full extent of their personal and business assets. They can be made bankrupt. Many sole traders may work with a non-architect co-director and trade as a limited company to limit these liabilities.

4.3.2 Partnership

The Partnership Act 1890 defines partnership as 'the relationship which exists between two or more persons carrying on business in common with a view to profit'. Although there is no legal requirement for a written agreement, it is strongly recommended that a partnership be established by a formal deed of partnership setting out the rights and responsibilities of the partners. These should be discussed and agreed before they are written into the deed, which should ultimately be drawn up by a solicitor. Compatibility of objectives, skills and personalities is of crucial importance, and the executive responsibilities of each partner must be clearly identified. Matters such as the name of the practice, the apportioning of profits and losses, payment of interest on capital, and banking arrangements and authority should be agreed and recorded in the partnership deed. Other matters it should clarify are pension provision, retirement, and the admission of new partners. It is usual to include some form of provision for dispute resolution, such as mediation, adjudication or arbitration.

In a partnership the equity is owned by the partners; they share both the profits and the risks, and have the right to participate in the daily management of the business. Partnership offers many advantages, and it remains a popular form of practice. It is generally more efficient for several principals to combine staff, facilities, accommodation, etc., although this could be done without forming a partnership (see below). The key advantages lie in the profit sharing, the greater potential for new work through the pooling of client contacts, the security a partnership offers to a client and, of course, the benefits of sharing and developing design ideas. However, partnership carries with it a high level of individual responsibility and risk, and there are other forms of collective practice that can offer many of the benefits of a traditional partnership while limiting individual liabilities.

Each partner is liable jointly with the others for all debts and obligations incurred while a partner, and should he or she die, this liability falls upon the estate. The partnership is liable for all negligent acts committed by any one of its partners, even though the others might have taken no part in such negligent action. The same applies to people who were partners at the time, but who have subsequently retired from the practice. A partner's liability extends to all his or her business and personal assets. Someone bringing action for damages against a partnership may bring it against one or several partners, or against the partnership as a whole, or any combination of these. If brought against one person, that partner may recover the damages from the others but initially may have to bear the loss alone.

4

To join an existing partnership, a new partner will in some cases have to 'buy into' it. This will involve contributing a capital sum calculated on the basis of the share of the annual profits the partners will receive. As it is often difficult for a young partner to raise this sum, it is usually paid in stages over several years. It is increasingly common to offer a share in the partnership without any capital sum requirement, but in return the partner agrees to leave a proportion of earnings in the partnership as working capital. In some cases, the partnership agreement provides for a salary to be paid to one or more of the partners in addition to a share in the profits. Such partners are referred to as 'salaried partners'. This is often a difficult position to be in, as the share of the profits is often very small, yet the liability is no less than that of the other partners.

New partners are sometimes drawn from outside the practice, but as a great deal of mutual knowledge and understanding is needed to make a partnership work successfully, they are frequently appointed internally. In many practices promising staff and potential partners are offered 'associateships'. An associate does not normally share in the profits or risk, although they are often placed on a bonus scheme, and may be offered other additional benefits such as a health care package.

When a partner retires or leaves the partnership this does not remove liability, and similarly liability is not removed if the partnership dissolves. It is usual for partnerships to retain professional indemnity cover for any retired members.

4.3.3   Private limited liability company (Ltd)

The private limited liability company is a legal entity separate from its members (i.e. shareholders), where the liability of each shareholder is limited to the nominal value of his or her shareholding. It is governed by the various Companies Acts, and must register with the Registrar of Companies. There is no limit to the number of members. Companies must have at least one director and may also have a company secretary. Annual accounts must be filed with the Registrar where they are available for public inspection. These may or may not need to be audited.

A company has a clearly identified management structure administered by a board of directors, who may be paid a salary. The senior level of management might include equity and non-equity directors (i.e. directors who are not shareholders). Under this structure, young architects of calibre are not deterred from reaching the top of a firm by the prospect of having to buy themselves in, as they might have to with a partnership, as they can be appointed directors on a salary. Non-architectural staff of calibre such as finance, computer or office managers, are also able to enhance their status and progress their careers as well-rewarded directors. In both cases remuneration could be increased if share options are available.

Under English law, directors and other employees, as agents of the company they serve, generally enjoy immunity from personal liability for the company's debts and its obligations towards third parties. However, all employees of a company owe a duty of care to the company itself, and directors owe more rigorous duties to act in the company's interest.

VAT registered?

Strictly speaking it is only necessary to register for VAT if the practice's annual earnings are over £81,000, although practitioners may choose to register regardless of anticipated income to project the image of a larger business. If the intention is to take on larger commercial projects, clients will generally expect to pay VAT and so not charging it may not necessarily be a benefit to them. This approach would not suit a practice intending to work on house extensions and other similar-sized projects however, where the increase in cost might make them uncompetitive against other small practices. For a sole practitioner the set-up can be changed relatively easily, but this should be part of the initial business-planning process (see Section 4.4). If the business is VAT registered it can be set up on a flat rate. For architects this means only paying 14.5% of the gross amount (13.5% in the first year of trading). This reduces the administration required, but expenses cannot then be offset separately as they are considered to be subsumed within the lower rate.

4

There are a number of operational advantages over a partnership:

- The directors are not normally personally liable for the debts of the company.
- It is easier for a company than a partnership to raise outside finance, as security can more readily be created over the assets of a company.
- The taxation position is relatively simple, and overall taxation can be lower than for a partnership.
- All employees, including directors, are subject to PAYE, which they may prefer as it avoids sudden large tax demands later.
- All salaries, including those of directors, are deductible before calculation of profit for corporation tax purposes.
- An interest in a company may be given more readily than in a partnership, by making architects and non-architects with useful expertise directors on a salary or shareholders.

- It is easier to remove an unsatisfactory director than an unsatisfactory partner.
- The company does not dissolve when a director leaves or shares change hands, and there are no complex legal procedures involved.
- Companies are internationally recognised: therefore it may be easier in many cases to develop business relations overseas than it would be with a partnership.

Issues to consider when forming a limited liability company:

Management

An apparent advantage of incorporation is that the separation of ownership from the management should lead to improvements in operational efficiency and cost-effectiveness.

However, in the company situation there is always a danger that ownership may pass outside the original architectural proprietor, whose professional control and influence may thereby be diminished.

Companies have to comply with the formalities laid down by the Companies Act, which relate to all aspects of the company's formation and operation. Management is therefore less flexible than with a partnership, and there can be a considerable additional administrative and financial burden. Companies whose turnover exceeds a certain limit are required to have their audited accounts published, and in any event their abbreviated accounts, whereas a partnership is able to keep its financial affairs confidential. Companies also have a duty to provide their shareholders with prescribed information, and this can be a significant extra cost.

Liability

The personal assets of a director of a company are not entirely safeguarded if the directors conduct their business without regard to the detailed legislation governing the management of companies. Trading through an incorporated business does, in theory, limit the liability of shareholders to the extent of the funds that they contribute as share capital, but this advantage can be eroded if shareholders and directors are required to give personal guarantees to the company's bankers or a landlord. However, there remains some protection for shareholders and directors where trade creditors are concerned.

Pension provision

The pension benefits that can be provided for directors and employees of a limited company tend to be more beneficial than those that can be

---

provided via retirement annuity and personal pension schemes entered into by an individual.

The benefits that a company pension scheme can provide are, in the main, flexible and generous, depending on the type of scheme adopted. The company's contributions into the pension scheme are generally deductible in calculating the company's taxable profits. This should be compared with the fairly rigid limits that apply to the tax relief available on contributions into retirement annuity and personal pension schemes.

Professional indemnity insurance

In terms of exposure to indemnity claims, a change from partnership to limited company does not materially change the risk from the insurer's point of view. However, the insured will now be the company, a separate legal identity from its directors. The policy must therefore be extended to indemnify the individual directors and employees as well as the company. It is vital that any change, whether to a new partnership or to a company, does not leave the practice unprotected vis-à-vis its continuing liability for claims. It may be best to incorporate this cover in the new policy, but legal advice should be taken (see Chapter 11).

Tax and National Insurance

The implications of incorporation for tax and National Insurance can be significant because, at the time of writing, there are different rules for employees/directors of a company and self-employed persons/partners. However, a potential tax advantage for companies is the ability to defer tax liabilities by retaining profits within the company rather than paying them out as remuneration or dividends.

Succession

The proprietors of the business need to consider their future plans in terms of disposing of or passing on a family business. Trading through a limited company has the advantage that shares in the company can be gifted to other members of the family as potentially exempt transfers for inheritance tax purposes. Such gifts can therefore be made without there necessarily being any effect on the running of the business.

A fundamental disadvantage of trading via the medium of a company is the potential double tax charge that can arise on winding up the firm. The company pays corporation tax on retained profits and also on any gains that it makes, and individual shareholders will also pay capital gains tax on the disposal of their shares. This only becomes a problem where assets or the business of the company are sold. If the business

4

is expected to run for many years and pass to future generations, this point may not be of concern to the proprietors.

Considering incorporation

The practicalities of incorporating a business do tend to be underestimated, and it is important to consider all taxes and their impact on the parties involved. Also bear in mind that it is difficult to disincorporate a business once it has been incorporated, so it is not a decision to be taken lightly.

Clients should be advised of any change in the composition or form of a practice, and the firm's advisers should be asked about the legal implications and how best to notify clients. Some clients prefer to trade with partnerships because they consider the formation of a company to be unprofessional. They may see it as an attempt to avoid personal responsibility for work undertaken, as in extreme circumstances a company can be wound up, whereas partners remain liable even after the partnership dissolves. This notion of 'unprofessionalism' is often a key factor in practices deciding to remain as a partnership.

4.3.4   Public limited liability company (plc)

The difference between the private limited liability company and the plc is that members of the public may buy and sell shares of the latter. The plc also requires a higher level of share capital, and has to operate under stricter rules. A company that intends to offer its shares for sale to the public must register as a public company, include the letters 'plc' after its name, and have a subscribed share capital of not less than £50,000. It cannot obtain a certificate from the Registrar of Companies to allow it to start trading until the stipulated sum has been subscribed.

4.3.5   Limited partnership

A limited partnership must be registered under the Limited Partnership Act 1907. In this form of practice one or more of the partners must agree to be responsible for all the liabilities of the practice. Other partners can contribute capital to the partnership, but their liability is limited to the proportion of capital they contribute. It is very little used, its only advantage being to enable the taking on of partners who would otherwise be unwilling to contribute owing to the liability position.

4.3.6   Limited liability partnership (LLP)

This form of practice, governed by the Limited Liability Partnerships Act 2000, combines some of the characteristics of both partnerships and limited liability companies. It is a separate legal entity distinct from its members. It is treated as a partnership for the purpose of UK income tax and capital gains tax. It must register with the Registrar of Companies and submit annual audited accounts. The members are not jointly and severally liable in the normal course of their business, and their liability is limited to their stake in the partnership. There is no requirement to appoint directors.

Internally the LLP may be run very much like a partnership, in that it has complete freedom of internal organisation, except that two people must be designated to perform duties similar to those of a company secretary and director. Externally, however, they are accountable in a similar way to companies.

4.3.7   The unlimited liability company

Very few practices are in the form of unlimited liability companies. The main advantage is that, unlike a partnership, a director's liability ceases 12 months after he or she leaves the company. There is also no requirement for filing reports with the Registrar of Companies. However, members of an unlimited liability company can be required to contribute personally if the company's assets are not sufficient to pay its debts.

4.3.8   Cooperative and collaborative arrangements

The terms 'cooperative' and 'collaborative' are used to describe various forms of practice. There are a number of registered architects' cooperatives; these are in effect workers' cooperatives. Those who work in the enterprise both own and control it. A cooperative may be owned collectively, in which case nobody has an individual shareholding beyond a nominal £1 – this is a common ownership cooperative, and is the type most frequently found in architecture, often for ideological reasons.

There is also a co-ownership cooperative in which dividend-earning shares are held by the members. In some schemes the shares remain at a fixed value; in others they increase or decrease according to the value of the business. Control is dependent on votes (one per person) and is independent of shares. Where an established partnership is converting to a cooperative, this model might be more appropriate, as long-standing partners can hold personal shares commensurate with the value of the assets they have built up.

Both types of cooperative can be legally established by registering either as a cooperative with the Register of Friendly Societies under the Industrial and Provident Societies Acts 1965–87, or with the Registrar of Companies as a

4

company limited by guarantee of £1 per member. Both kinds of organisation carry limited liability.

Two or more firms may arrange to help each other with varying degrees of commitment on individual projects, or a range of specialisations, or other market activities. This is likely to be a short-term cooperation, and might take the form of a simple sub-consultant arrangement. Other firms might wish to engage in a continuing association, either for mutual help or the sharing of facilities, but stopping short of carrying out projects jointly. On a more formal basis, firms may wish to join in partnership for a particular project, exercising a joint venture method of working. This would need to be a legally constituted arrangement with joint and several liability.

Firms of different disciplines may elect to collaborate by establishing a consortium arrangement which could offer the benefits of an integrated approach. Such an arrangement could simply be a continuing informal association, or one which carried out projects jointly. The identity of each firm in the consortium could still be retained for other concurrent projects handled separately.

Whenever formal collaborative arrangements are contemplated, appropriate legal advice should be sought, and professional indemnity insurance arranged to cover the particular situation.

The opportunities for practice in the European Union are increasing as British architects explore the potential of the wider market. The forging of links between British and overseas practices provides informal means of promoting joint architectural opportunities. More formal associations and collaborative working can be expected to develop as business relationships are actively encouraged by Chambers of Commerce in the respective countries. In some cases British-based firms have opened branches or subsidiaries abroad, while others have elected to collaborate with local practices in carrying out projects. Legal systems and insurance obligations in particular differ throughout Europe, and any arrangements for collaborative working should be subject to appropriate legal advice.

4.4 Developing a business strategy

4.4.1 Strategic planning

At any point in its life, a practice should be operating in the context of a described strategy: it should know where it is going and how it is going to get there. It is important to set goals and work to them, both as a means of quantifying achievement and as an expression of purposeful leadership that unites the efforts of all those who work for the practice, and focuses them on worthwhile objectives.

Just having a plan will put you ahead of most of the competition: the RIBA Business Benchmarking Survey 2012/13 showed that 62% of architectural practices do not have a formal business plan and that only 13% of the profession is planning beyond the current year. Participation in the RIBA Business Benchmarking survey is obligatory for all RIBA Chartered Practices and provides invaluable data to inform proactive business planning. Go to www.architecture.com.

Every new practice should formulate a business strategy. Its existence allows the principals to evaluate their decision-making against a described position, and the plan itself will constitute the basis of the practice's business plan when it needs to seek funds or financial backing. It should cover a period of between three and five years – the fluctuating nature of architectural work makes it almost impossible to make more distant assumptions and predictions. Short-term targets will be set in the firm's annual budget. Formulating the strategy will take much time and thought, and requires an honest and objective attitude (see Sections 5.2 and 5.3).

An existing practice will need, first, to evaluate the current position of the business; second, to decide where the principals would like the business to be in, say, five years' time; and third, to devise an operational plan for moving the business from its current position towards achieving its defined objectives. These should be set out as goals and targets, and a SWOT analysis (strengths, weaknesses, opportunities, threats) may help with this (see Section 5.3 for more detail on SWOT analysis).

As with planning for expansion or change to an existing business, the starting point for a new practice is to assess where you are now (however limited this may be) and determine where you want to take the business to. This can be aspirational but, even if you don't achieve the goals set, it will give you a direction of travel. The plan will very likely change over time but, so long as this change is accompanied by proper analysis and introspection, that is fine. Too much change will, however, impede progress, so try not to do it on a whim but only as a result of internal or external forces.

4.4.2   The business plan

The business plan should comprise a full version and an edited summary. The edited summary – which must be as brief as possible, no more than two sides of A4 – should comprise:

- Ambition, brand and USP (unique selling point)
- Objectives

- Strategy (to achieve the objectives)
- Key actions (with costs and marketing requirements)
- Key client targets and sectors
- The team (who will deliver the business plan).

The full version should be as succinct as possible but should in addition include:

- Practice particulars:

  - name, address, etc.
  - company and VAT numbers
  - main activities/sectors
  - existing clients/client types
  - current project locations and size
  - suppliers and sub-consultants

- Financial matters:

  - income to date and forecast income (say for the next 12 months)
  - budget detailing all overheads (e.g. salaries, premises, rates, suppliers)
  - calculations of income per architectural staff member, plus income per member of all staff and percentage of non-fee earning time
  - resources, including IT, etc.

- SWOT analysis (see Chapter 5).

The business plan is a living document, not something to be written and never referred to. It will change to adapt to the changing business environment and aspirations of the management of the business. It should therefore be accessible and straightforward, not overly academic or wordy. It should, however (as noted above), include a section that expresses the ambition and brand of the practice, which can be written in whatever way best expresses those facets.

4.5   Business advisers

The support of good advisers is essential for successful business management – and an accountant is the principal one to get on board initially. It is wise to look for a firm or individual who has other architect clients and will know the kind of special needs that architectural work generates. A fellow practitioner may be able to recommend someone suitable, but otherwise the practice must either make its own enquiries or approach the relevant professional institute. It is important to consider a firm's reputation and prosperity, whether the range of services offered will meet the practice's current and future needs, and whether its offices are conveniently placed.

It is also wise to consider whether the attitude and philosophy of the firm is in tune with that of the practice – whether, that is, the professional chemistry is right.

For some practices it might be worthwhile to consider bringing in one or more non-executive directors or board-level advisers. Non-executive directors focus on board matters rather than executive matters and can provide an independent view of the company, distinct from its day-to-day operations. Non-executive directors are appointed to the board to bring independence, impartiality, experience, specialist knowledge and personal qualities. For example, a company wanting to expand its international presence may look for someone with particular experience of foreign markets and working practices. As an 'outsider', the non-executive director may have a more objective view of external factors affecting the company in its business environment than the executives. The normal role of the non-executive director in strategy formation is therefore to provide a creative and informed contribution and to act as a constructive critic in looking at the objectives and plans devised by the management team.

The accountant will be able to help you determine the most appropriate form for the business (see Section 4.3). They will also be able to keep you appraised of changes in tax legislation, etc. When you are starting out it is advisable to undertake as much of the administration yourself as you can. This will not only reduce the cost (the more you can do, the less the accountant will need to charge) but will also give you a firm understanding of business accounting processes.

Other advice on setting up a practice will come from the bank (although in the current economic climate you are unlikely to be given a loan), and from insurance brokers to arrange professional indemnity and, if appropriate, premises insurance.

4.5.1 Accountants

An accountant is a professional keeper and inspector of accounts. Accountancy firms vary in size from the small office that offers mainly auditing and tax advice, to the large prestigious firm with an international network of offices offering a wide range of financial and management services.

The standard services that an architectural practice might engage an accountant to provide are:

- preparation of the firm's annual audit;
- advice on tax matters;

4

- advice on book-keeping procedures;
- advice about the practice's financial state of affairs.

Many accountancy firms also provide management consultancy services, and some offer services connected with corporate recovery and insolvency, and corporate finance and investigations.

Under the Companies Act every company above a certain size is required to submit audited accounts to Companies House, where they can be inspected by interested parties. Accounts also have to be submitted to the Inland Revenue. The auditors' duty is to review the accounts and the systems from which they are derived and give a professional opinion as to whether they give 'a true and fair view' of the company's results.

The question of fees should be clarified at the outset of the consultancy, and it is important, particularly when any extensive piece of work is commissioned, to set a budget for it and to stipulate that this is not to be exceeded without express permission. It's a good idea to build up a good working relationship with the accountant; they can not only save the practice money in the short term, but also may be able to warn it of troubles ahead.

The Institute of Chartered Accountants in England and Wales (ICAEW) provides an online search facility for chartered accountants. Go to www. find.icaew.com/.

Year-end tax return for small practices

At the financial year end, small practice principals will need to collate the following information for their accountant to enable them to prepare a tax return:

Income from employment

- Income and expenses from the business.
- For those who, having started their practice that year, were in full- or part-time employment earlier in the tax year:
  - Form P60 (gross pay, tax deducted) and/or P45 where applicable.
  - Form P11D (return of benefits) if any.
  - PAYE Coding Notice (for the current and next years) if available.

UK property rental income – if any

- Details of rental income.
- Details of property expenses.
- Loan interest certificate or copy of statement.

Income from investments

Any income from investments:

- interest received from banks and/or building societies
- certificates or vouchers for income received
- dividends received
- whether any accounts held jointly with your spouse/partner.

Other income

Any income received from abroad.

Other outgoings/reliefs

Any pension payments or charitable covenants or Gift Aid payments.

Capital gains

Details of any shares or other assets sold during the tax year.

Other matters

Any other sources of income or outgoings which may be relevant to your tax return.

If child benefit is relevant and if your income has been over £50,000, advise if you or your partner received any child benefit after 7 January 2013. If you did, advise if your income was higher than your partner's.

4.5.2 Legal advisers

Legal services are provided by solicitors and barristers. Lawyers qualified in other jurisdictions are available if such special advice is needed, and lawyers employed by banks and accountants will often offer an advisory service to third parties. Since 1990 architects have been able to instruct barristers directly without having to use a solicitor as an intermediary. This direct access to barristers for architects and their clients is available through the provisions of the Bar Standard Board's Licensed Access Recognition Regulations.

An architectural practice might need various legal services. Its first needs might relate to the form of practice to be adopted and the conveyancing of practice premises, followed by a continuing general consultancy as the practice finds its feet. It may need specialist advice about appointment agreements, building contract conditions and claims, professional indemnity, construction litigation, planning legislation, copyright of drawings, and so on.

Fees are likely to be on a retainer basis to cover routine and day-to-day advice, and time charged for major consultancies. As with architects' work

4

there are various hourly rates, and the procedures for charging expenses and disbursements and for billing will need to be agreed.

Solicitors have to be meticulous in their work, and it may come as a surprise to the architect client to be charged for amounts as small as the price of a first-class postage stamp or to receive an invoice with time charges based on six-minute units of time. There are lessons to be learned from the way the legal profession renders its accounts.

The Law Society, which represents solicitors in England and Wales, provides an online search facility to help in finding a solicitor, advice on what to expect, guides to common legal problems, and advice on what to do if things go wrong.

solicitors.lawsociety.org.uk/

4.5.3   The bank

It is in the interest of banks to support local business initiatives, but clearly their approach to lending has altered over the past 5 years. They may be prepared to lend money if they consider that a firm's approach is businesslike and its prospects are good. Banks make money from the interest they charge on loans, and may allow a running overdraft provided they are confident that the architect will be in a position to pay the interest. Similarly, they will consider sensible intentions for business expansion – which may mean an increased need for borrowing.

Although banking has become an intensively competitive business, banks are aware that the best way to keep their customers is to give them support and advice, and this can be invaluable, particularly to a new architectural practice.

A wide range of banking services is available, some of which may help a practice to streamline its financial administration. For example, payment of creditors' accounts can be made through BACS (Bank Automated Clearing Service). Arrangements can also be made whereby surplus funds in current accounts are automatically transferred into an interest-earning account as soon as they reach an agreed level. New electronic services are coming on stream all the time, and it is always worth seeking the bank's advice about ways of making the most of the practice's finances.

4.5.4   Insurance brokers

A broker is an intermediary between two parties – in the case of insurance, between an insurer and the person buying the insurance. Only registered brokers can call themselves an insurance broker, although anyone can operate as a broker under any other name or description.

The insurance broker's remuneration is the commission he or she receives from the insurer. It is important to remember that insurance brokers are therefore not obliged to place the interests of the client first: they are commission-driven, and the service they offer should not be compared with that provided by, say, the accounting or legal profession. Insurance claims are evaluated and met (or not, as the case may be) by the insurer, not the insurance broker.

Insurance brokers are well placed to give advice about the best deals going among the insurance companies, their promptness or otherwise in meeting claims, and which companies specialise in the particular insurance cover required. Firms of insurance brokers tend to specialise in certain types of insurance cover, and as soon as the first job comes in an architect will need to look for one who specialises in professional indemnity insurance. Risk management, including trade credit risks, is another specialism of interest, and so is claims handling.

The RIBA Insurance Agency offers PI insurance on terms agreed with the RIBA. It is the only broker whose clients can refer disputes with their insurer to the President of the RIBA, where an arbitration system is in place to help resolve such issues. The terms of the RIBA Insurance Agency's main PI policy include an innocent non-disclosure clause to protect the architect in the event of accidental non-disclosure of claims. Refer to Chapter 11: Risk management and insurance for more detail on this subject.

4.5.5   IT consultant

Unless you have a very solid understanding of computing and IT it is advisable to have an arrangement with an IT consultant in the event of computer hardware or software problems. Most will be able to provide an as-needed service and will limit the expensive down-time that can result.

Be careful about software licences; it is illegal not to have a valid licence for all the software you are using. Of the Software Alliance's successful cases in 2010–2013, 7% were against architects.

Regardless of what arrangements you have with external consultants, back up all your work regularly. You should also consider insurance for accidental data loss and other business disruption. Refer to Chapter 11 regarding risk management and Chapter 12 for advice on setting up an IT system.

References and further reading

Foxell, S., *Good Practice Guide: Starting a Practice* (London: RIBA Publishing, 2006).

Ostime, N., *Small Projects Handbook* (London: RIBA Publishing, 2014).

Marketing and business development

THIS CHAPTER:

- briefly defines what marketing is;
- looks at how to structure a comprehensive marketing plan;
- details the steps involved in putting together such a plan, from SWOT analysis to gaining press coverage;
- details a series of new business development techniques.

5.1 Introduction

Marketing is the link between a business and the outside world: customers, competitors, potential employees and other stakeholders. It is both the ears to listen to the needs of existing and potential clients and the mouth with which to promote and sell a business. Often people only associate marketing with the promotional element of advertising, brochures and websites, but without the essential connection to what is happening around a practice it will operate in a vacuum and will struggle to be responsive. Marketing is about understanding the requirements and characteristics of potential and existing clients, and matching or developing skills and services to meet those demands. It is an essential activity for a healthy business and not just a bolt-on to sell its wares.

Questions that need to be asked from the outset include:

- What kind of work do we want/are we able to do?
- What markets are buoyant and who are the clients within them?
- How big do we want to be?
- Where are the key growth markets?
- How do we want to be perceived?

The nature of the construction industry means that relationships between client and provider are close and long term. Understanding clients and their aspirations is key to a successful project and potential future commissions.

5.2 Drawing up a marketing plan

This chapter will focus on how to structure a comprehensive plan to focus a business's marketing activity, broken down into four distinct phases:

5

1. **Where are we?** What is happening in the industry and how does it affect us? What issues are we facing internally that will affect our performance?
2. **Where do we want to be?** What are our goals? Where do we want to be this time next year, or in five years?
3. **How do we get there?** What are the activities that we need to undertake to reach our goals?
4. **Did we achieve our goals?** If not, why not? What have we learned and what do we need to do differently?

Such a plan will help maximise long-term growth, highlight short-term opportunities and prepare for change if it occurs, no matter how large or small the practice is.

5.3   Where are we?

It is important to first set out a brief overview of where the business is in relation to its key markets. This sets the context of the marketing plan and is often most simply presented in a SWOT analysis, such as the one shown in Table 5.1:

- **Strengths** – These are internally focused. This lists the positive elements about the business, so they can be expanded upon and brought out in any promotional material.
- **Weaknesses** – These are also internally focused. This lists the areas in need of attention within the business. Addressing these is key to ensuring overall success of the marketing plan and ultimately the business.
- **Opportunities** – These are externally focused. This lists where prospects for growth and development occur in the chosen markets/industry and should be the main targets of new business development activity (see Section 5.5.1).
- **Threats** – These are also externally focused. This lists elements outside the business's control that may have an external focus. Although they cannot be altered directly, if the plan is flexible and adaptable enough, it can respond to them.

The key points above can be highlighted in a brief executive summary for anyone glancing through the plan.

5.3.1   PESTLE analysis

A second valuable exercise can also shed light on the position of the business in relation to external factors that may affect trading in the long term (see also Section 7.3.1). This is known as a PESTLE analysis. A short statement should be written on the possible impacts on the business direction of the following six high-level factors. For example:

Table 5.1 *Examples of SWOT analyses*

For a *new* practice:

Strengths	Weaknesses
Respected founders with good contacts Talented staff with good mix of skills Good internal culture and mutual respect Good location and offices	New practice leading to: • High start-up costs • Low profit level • Lack of significant built projects • Limited sector spread • Unrecognised name/brand
Opportunities	**Threats**
New government pledge to invest in cultural project development RIBA competitions playing to our strengths Openness to UK architects working abroad	Strong competition from established firms High business tax rates

For an *established* practice:

Strengths	Weaknesses
Respected design capability Talented staff with good mix of skills Recognised name/profile National spread of offices Strong client relationships High turnover and cash flow	Top-heavy management = high costs Low profit level 'Corporate' portfolio Wide sector spread with no perceived specialisms Brand lacks personality
Opportunities	**Threats**
New government pledge to increase public spending Good labour market Increased inward investment to UK construction Openness to UK architects working abroad	Revised planning laws Collapse of housing sector Increased competition Rise of multi-disciplinary firms Downward market pressure on fee levels

5

- **Political** – A change of government and the likely effect on the construction sector.
- **Environmental** – The impact of a government target to cut UK emissions.
- **Social** – An ageing population and increase in requirements for single-person homes.
- **Technological** – Advances in broadband technology, changing the way we work.
- **Legal** – Planning gain legislation and its effect on our sectors.
- **Economic** – Government spending being cut to stem public debt.

5.3.2   Research

The data required to complete both analyses can be gleaned in a number of ways. Desktop studies and the internet are the easiest forms of research to undertake and can provide a reliable basis on which to build. Most trade publications have online versions with in-depth sector reports available to download.

The RIBA Plan of Work 2013 Stage 7 *In Use* (see Figure 10.1) can provide a foundation for collecting project feedback, including feedback on a practice's service from the client's point of view. Interviews and surveys are an excellent way of gaining feedback on a business and its performance and gaining a more holistic view of a practice. This can be done in person, by post or telephone, or increasingly online, using free specialist web tools (such as www.surveymonkey.com) that allow the user to structure internal and external satisfaction or perception surveys and track the results. However, if there is time to speak directly to key clients in person, information can be gleaned from those with the greatest impact on the business's future; it also demonstrates that their views are of interest and that the business wants to improve.

External market data and research can also be purchased from research companies or commissioned especially for a business's requirements, although this can be costly and needs good planning.

Information on international markets is freely available from the government via the UK Trade & Investment website (www.gov.uk/government/organisations/uk-trade-investment).

For competitor activity and performance, the weekly journals carry regular stories of interest, but for more detailed data on performance, Colander undertake an annual benchmarking survey for architects on behalf of the RIBA.

Participation in the RIBA Business Benchmarking Survey is the best way to accurately compare practice performance with a practice peer group.

The scheme, which is mandatory for RIBA Chartered Practices, provides valuable information that can help to develop the business, including tailored reports showing:

- key business development and staff training issues;
- objective assessments of business strengths and weaknesses;
- identification of best practice in a particular architectural service sector(s);
- ways to develop a business based on hard facts;
- how the business performance of a practice measures up.

The use of business benchmarking is now well established as a key business planning tool in many professions.

5.4   Where do we want to be?

Once you have established the current position of your business, whether it is established or new, you need then to consider where it is you want to get to. This stage is all about setting clear, concise goals or objectives.

Objectives need to be market led: a business cannot be built on false pretences if the work isn't out there to get.

The objectives need to be agreed at Partner or Board level before progressing with the development stages (below), to ensure the marketing plan is targeting the right goals and everyone is in agreement over where the business is heading.

It is essential that every member of staff is aware of these objectives as they should fundamentally drive every action undertaken. They also allow

---

Objectives should follow the 'SMART' rule by being:

- **Specific** – Avoid woolly statements, such as 'get bigger' or 'increase income'. You need to know in 12 months' time whether you have succeeded, so be clear about what you want to achieve.
- **Measurable** – How can you decide whether you met your goal? Was it based on financial value or some other numeric, i.e. 'Increase income in our retail work by 20%', or 'Get two new clients this year'?
- **Achievable** – Can goals be met with the available resources?
- **Realistic** – Don't set goals that cannot be achieved, such as doubling income while reducing costs/resource by 15%. Not only will you become disheartened, but you will also expend a lot of energy and cash that could be put to better use elsewhere.
- **Timed** – As well as being specific, put a timeframe on the objective, so that it doesn't slip.

5

every member of staff both to promote the practice at every opportunity and to assist the practice in reaching its objectives in whichever way possible. A marketing plan is a powerful document that can clearly translate what the practice is trying to achieve in a business sense. If it is circulated to all employees at the start of a new trading or financial year, they will feel engaged and armed with the necessary tools to sell the practice.

5.5   How do we get there?

Once you have established where you want to be in the next 12–24 months, you need to decide what activities will get you there. For this you need a strategy, setting out exactly what activities you will undertake to meet your objectives.

It is here that a marketing plan can succeed or fail. Most fail because the activities necessary to reach the objectives are not set at this stage. Another common mistake is to set too many ambitious activities which will take up too much time. A few key activities, well implemented, will generate greater success.

Strategic activities can be simply broken down into various categories:

- New business development
- Client relationship management
- Advertising
- Branding and marketing collateral
- PR.

5.5.1   New business development

Promote the business when things are really busy – if you wait until you have no work it will be too late to make any material impact upon the business. A commonly heard maxim within the industry is that most work is derived from repeat commissions, which is generally referred to as a sign of good-quality service and client retention. Data from the RIBA Business Benchmarking Survey 2012/13 shows that 46% of business for architects comes from repeat clients. However, while this may be true to an extent, it can often be the result of failing to engage new clients or enter new markets, sectors and services, which are vital to a thriving practice and exciting work.

Developing new business opportunities, whether through new clients or as repeat commissions through existing ones, can be achieved in a number of ways. Having identified the areas where there is existing demand for the specific skills identified in the SWOT analysis and research (see Section 5.3), those markets can be approached in a number of ways.

Competitions

Many practices seek new work and also publicity through entering competitions. Open or invited design competitions can provide an opportunity to present the practice's strengths and thinking clearly without size or other preconceptions getting in the way. They are also an excellent way for new or smaller practices to gain commissions over larger, more powerful competitors. If the practice is small, the project may be beyond its physical capabilities, but partnering with a larger practice should be considered. Smaller practices can often bring a freshness and clarity that larger practices seek. Larger practices can bring the support of more resources, adequate PI cover, material resources and experience. The RIBA hosts speed dating services between large and small practices (contact Member Services for further details or visit www.architecture.com).

All competition announcements should clearly state:

- the scope of the competition and a design brief;
- the terms and conditions of the competition;
- the conditions upon which the fee (if any) is based;
- the number of practices invited to take part, or if the competition is open;
- the time available for a stated (and reasonable) amount of design.

They should be regarded as unacceptable if any of the above information is missing.

Under the RIBA Code of Professional Conduct, members undertake to withdraw (or attempt to rectify) any competition process that is not known to be 'reasonable, transparent and impartial' (Principle 3.4). Current information on competitions, both in the UK and internationally, is held by the RIBA Competitions Office (www.ribacompetitions.com). The web page contains information about the briefing documents, submission requirements and assessors for each approved competition.

Tendering

There are also many online sales leads products that can filter design competitions and other opportunities to specific requirements and send regular email alerts. For example, www.ted.europa.org is the Official Journal of the European Union and publishes daily architectural opportunities for the public sector in the UK and Europe. (This service is free but note that it will be necessary to register.) The site www.worldarchitecturenews.com also publishes a subscription-based architectural leads service that can be

5

sorted by international region or sector type. There is a subscription fee for using this service.

It is worth noting that clients are increasingly seeking the competitive pricing brought about by open tendering, which means more project opportunities are being advertised on sales leads services. Not all are free and most duplicate the TED notices, and there is a charge for the filtering mechanisms to return hits against personal criteria. The Official Journal is a European Union initiative aimed at reducing competitive advantages and allowing European suppliers to bid for services anywhere across the region. This means not only that competition can be intense, but that it also can be complicated and procedural. Responding to OJEUs should be avoided unless there is time to respond well. Be realistic about the chances of succeeding, by asking a few simple questions such as:

- Do I know the client (do they know me/us?)
- Have I been involved in the project to date?
- Do I have the skills/resources to complete the project if I pre-qualify?
- Do I have an adequate track record to demonstrate my experience?
- Do I need to form a consultant team? If so, can I get the right/best people and what structure does our group need – formal joint venture or loose arrangement?

Networking

A more long-term method of developing new business opportunities is through networking. The construction industry is built upon relationships and having a good personal network is essential for long-term success. There are many different events, clubs and associations set up to bring construction professionals together, so it is important to be clear about what is intended to be achieved. It is worthwhile checking out various events to assess whether they meet requirements in terms of attendees, format, location, etc. Networking clubs and associations transpose different sectors, disciplines and regions, so spend time researching what options are available. It is also worth joining the membership associations of the practice's main sectors, such as the British Council for Offices, which has a main and regional Boards and events, as well as a new 'NextGen' club for younger professionals under 35; the British Council for Shopping Centres in the retail sector; or the British Airports Group. The Movers & Shakers Breakfast Club is a London-based, cross-sector networking event aimed predominantly at commercial sectors such as offices, retail and residential, but attracts a large diverse crowd of high-profile property professionals.

The key to successful networking is not to see what opportunities can be elicited from a particular event, but to meet as many people as possible and strengthen relationships that may, in the future, bear fruit or provide opportunities. There are several consultancies offering training in networking, which can be found online.

Another way to meet a broad spectrum of new people is by attending conferences and exhibitions within the practice's target sectors. Again there are many events held around each subject and so it is important to research the options well before committing. Enrolment fees for most conferences can be high, added to which there is the time lost out of the office earning fees. So although they can be an excellent way of meeting relevant new people and gleaning the latest thinking on a particular subject, they must also return the value of investment.

5.5.2 Client relationship management

The most successful businesses are often based on a few long-term key accounts. The effort put into serving these key clients generally includes a high level of liaison, continued service and above all a good depth of understanding about a client's business and plans. A strong personal relationship can help enormously and it is wise to ensure there are a number of personal links throughout the businesses.

Creating a key client list requires careful research to identify likely clients, preferably by building up a database of information, including relevant people, their current and future projects, and contact details. There have been many changes to the Data Protection Act in recent years which restrict the use of unsolicited marketing for selling purposes (see https://ico.org.uk/). Lists can either be purchased, or built from individuals and organisations met at networking events, by referral, etc.

When approaching clients it is important to use their language, or at least a universal one, and to work out their approach to value. CABE has identified six 'value types' and any client or any project will lean more towards some than others. These are:

- exchange value
- use value
- image value
- social value
- environmental value
- cultural value.

5

Approach can be by telephone, fax, email or letter. Mailshots and e-shots are ideally targeted at a particular individual or group of individuals, and it should be clear to the client that the practice is aware of their background and that they have been approached for specific reasons. Such a move might spring from a casual introduction or social conversation, or be generated by reliable intelligence reports, or simply be a routine follow-up to earlier commissions. A practice brochure, regularly updated and capable of being assembled with a particular interest in mind, is an indispensable marketing tool in such situations (see Section 5.5.4).

An alternative method is to identify a potential project, for example to prepare proposals for developing derelict or under-used land, or finding new uses for redundant buildings, etc. and then to target specific clients on the strength of the proposed scheme. This could be a speculative move, which would create interest from firms known to have sympathy with such initiatives (e.g. contractors, developers, conservation bodies). It might be a loss leader and would need to be kept under tight control, but it could generate some welcome publicity and spin-off benefits.

If the practice has invested in the development of specific expertise in areas of topical concern, this will be a great help in directing the approach. This could be in an operational respect (e.g. as sustainability/energy consultants, principal designers, specialists in upgrading premises to health and safety requirements, specialists in adapting buildings for disabled access). It could also be in respect of building types (e.g. health centres, housing association work, building conservation, community architecture), particularly where these respond to current political strategy or seem likely to feature in funding programmes.

The architect may no longer be the first point of contact for a client considering investing in a building project. Bearing this in mind, it may well be wise to broaden the catchment from commissioners of building projects to include other members of the procurement team.

The architect could approach a contracting organisation, perhaps offering a package approach – preferably design-led. Such a partnering could broaden the client base, but needs close control. It could also extend to working with construction management contractors. Many contractors are the lead organisation in putting together bids for PFI projects, and may consider approaches from practices that can demonstrate special skills or a track record in particular building types. Careful research, particularly on the internet, will identify contractors that are likely candidates.

Another method is to approach other construction professionals, lead consultants or project managers, to secure a sub-consultant's role. This could result in longer-term relationships. Simply working as sub-consultants to another firm of architects might be expedient, but the work is likely to be unpredictable, needed at short notice, and accompanied by considerable pressures.

Alternatively, many consultants group together to put in joint bids for projects. Careful research will pay dividends as it will enable the practice to demonstrate a clear need for the specific contribution the practice can make to the team. Before making any approach it is important for the practice to become familiar with new forms of procurement used for larger projects, and to be clear as to what terms of appointment it is prepared to accept. If in any doubt as to the proposed arrangements the practice should take legal advice.

5.5.3 Advertising

One of the initial promotional tools to consider is to become accredited as an RIBA Chartered Practice. This gold standard accreditation is a mark of quality which assures potential clients of a practice's business effectiveness and service quality. RIBA Client Services maintains the UK Directory of RIBA Chartered Practices as a fully searchable web directory and uses it to match the client enquiries it receives to a suitable practice (www.architecture.com/ FindAnArchitect/FAAHome.aspx). The criteria for RIBA Chartered Practice accreditation are listed in Section 2.9.2.

The *UK Directory of RIBA Chartered Practices* is also published annually in hard copy format and is sent to some 5,000 clients or potential client bodies. It is also the first port of call for potential clients seeking architects' services.

Information on becoming an RIBA Chartered Practice can be found at www. architecture.com/RIBA/JoinTheRIBA/Practices/Practicemembership.aspx or by contacting the RIBA Membership Services Team on 020 7307 3800 or emailing membership.services@inst.riba.org.

In addition, some RIBA regions publish regional directories, and if practices wish to be listed they should contact their regional office. The print and online editions can include expanded entries which, for a fee, can include images and descriptions of a practice's work.

RIBA Client Services helps clients to find an architect by providing a shortlist of practices suitable for the type, size and location of the project under consideration. The practice should be prepared to respond immediately to any enquiries from clients, and should develop a practice policy for dealing with such enquiries as part of their marketing plan.

5

Advertising can also be placed in trade magazines such as *Architects' Journal*, *Architectural Review*, *Building Design* and *Building*, or more sector- or region-specific titles depending upon the nature of the work and what potential clients might read, i.e. for developers in the commercial and private sectors, *Estates Gazette* and *Property Week* are the key publications.

Investment in advertising needs to be carefully considered. It is generally costly and measuring its effectiveness is difficult. Points to consider when assessing an advertising opportunity are:

- If you have been contacted by a publisher to advertise, it is generally in their interest that you advertise, not yours.
- Most publications are now ABC audited, meaning they must state what their circulation is.
- Make sure the audience is appropriate to your objectives.
- Make sure your message/images are appropriate to the publication and your audience.
- Always make sure there is a response opportunity (i.e. your website/ telephone or email address).
- Ensure the image quality is as high as you can get. Print production is of a very high quality and will highlight poor quality photographs. Most publishers will have specific guidelines for image/graphic quality.
- Do you have the skills in-house to design an advert? Print advertising in a popular journal is a different animal from designing buildings, yet many architects attempt home-grown adverts. If you are investing in the space, make the most of it by getting the best imagery, copy and layout available.

Good advertising follows four simple principles:

- Attract attention by standing out from other adverts within the publication through strong imagery. This needs to be instantaneous.
- Interest – maintain that initial attraction through clear copywriting and more detailed content.
- Create desire by how you portray your skills and services.
- Always leave a 'call to action' – contact details that interested parties can use to follow up on what you have promised.

A note on photography: often in the rush to get a project completed and handed over, taking photographs can be overlooked. But good-quality photography is essential to future marketing, as not much can be done to promote the work of a practice without it. Like advertising, photography can be costly, but considering the investment made in a project, one single high-quality image can be used in adverts, brochures, websites and press releases and will more than pay for itself. It is also worth discussing whether a client or other involved consultant will either provide their images or split the cost.

If a photographer is to be appointed, they need to be briefed well on the shots required, and given specific design details. A good architectural photographer will know their way around a building, arrange the shots and remove unwanted clutter. Most also offer a post-production and artworking service that can clean up shots and remove unwanted objects that often occur as photographs are often taken pre-practical completion when landscaping is incomplete or plant and contractors are still on site. Good architectural photographers can be found in the magazines noted above or online. Always review their portfolio before commissioning as it is important to ensure their photographic style meets the needs and expectations of the practice.

5.5.4   Branding and marketing collateral

There is much that can be done to increase the chances of new work via marketing and business development, but one of the hardest yet most important elements to manage is the brand. A business's brand encapsulates everything about it – it is the corporate personality and not just a logo, and should be evident throughout all of the business's marketing collateral.

Think about how the values and key characteristics of major architectural practices are encompassed in their brands. Brands are not created overnight, but are built from reputation. As creative organisations, architectural practices generally have quite strong brands that are closely associated with key individuals within the practice, or a renowned project they have designed.

An easy way to break down what can be a plethora of marketing collateral is to consider how one wants clients or potential clients and audiences to interact with the brand:

- High-level branding – open to anyone, such as websites, generic brochures/books.
- Mid-level branding – advertising, stationery, signage, exhibition stands.
- Targeted material – specific reports, brochures, presentations, etc. produced for a specific audience.

This vital armoury should consist of a few key elements including:

- A practice brochure or book in hard copy, including information about the practice's history and personnel.
- More specific sector- or service-oriented brochures in hard and digital copy.

5

- Customisable capability statements which can be tailored to client requirements.
- Simple stationery including headed paper and business cards.
- Digital presentations for use in pitches and presentations.
- A practice website with easily navigable project case studies and contact details.
- Regular project updates and PR cuttings for use both internally and externally.

Although many architects tend to design their own logos and graphics material, if budget allows it is worthwhile investing in the help of an external branding agency, who can advise on how to create material such as a logo that reflects the company's brand.

An expanded entry in the UK Directory of RIBA Chartered Practices is sensible if the practice is looking for new work. Press releases about significant new commissions or completions may result in some valuable (and free) publicity in the locality. Placing an advertisement can sometimes be stunningly successful as a one-off 'impact' event, but advertising is relatively expensive and can seldom be afforded on a regular basis.

There should be a database for recording details of clients and potential clients, and the production and issue of marketing material. Equipment will also be needed for printing and binding documents, for producing visual materials, and for storing files, photographs and slides, brochures, models and exhibition material.

In a small practice, whoever acts as librarian could be responsible for looking after such material. A large practice with a vigorous marketing department might consider making a special appointment.

5.5.5   Websites

It is essential that every practice, no matter how small, invests in an online presence. The internet is a universal, mass communication platform unique from other promotional materials in that it is constantly available to a potential worldwide audience.

A simple site can be built using off-the-shelf packages such as Adobe Dreamweaver (www.adobe.com/products/dreamweaver) or Serif (www. serif.com). A space to host the site will also be needed and a domain name registered (companies such as www.networksolutions.com offer packages incorporating both). There are various sites on which to check whether a chosen domain name is free, including www.names. co.uk/. If regular updates to the website are required, a more dynamic content management system (CMS) will be needed, of which Drupal

---

The Codes and self-promotion (see also Section 2.5)

The professional codes and standards are now relatively relaxed over what used to be referred to as the 'advertising' of professional services.

'**By abiding by the RIBA Code of Professional Conduct, members undertake:**

- not to allow themselves to be improperly influenced either by their own, or others', self-interest (Principle 1.2);
- not to be party to any statement which they know to be untrue, misleading, unfair to others or contrary to their own professional knowledge (Principle 1.3);
- to avoid conflicts of interest.

If a conflict arises, they should declare it to those parties affected and either remove its cause, or withdraw from that situation (Principle 1.4).'

There are no direct references to advertising and members of the RIBA are expected simply to 'act with impartiality, responsibility and truthfulness' and 'not be a party to any statement which they know to be untrue, misleading, unfair to others or contrary to their professional knowledge'. Presumably this allows architects to feature in advertisements for other products, and perhaps this wider exposure might serve to attract potential clients.

By the ARB Code, Standard 3 requires all advertising of professional services to be conducted in a truthful and responsible manner. It also requires that advertising conforms to the codes and standards of the industry (e.g. British Code of Advertising Practice, ITC and Radio Code of Advertising Standards and Practice) as relevant. Before any approaches to clients are made, architects should take steps to establish that they have the necessary expertise, competence and resources, and that there are unlikely to be conflicts of interest.

5

(www.drupal.org) and Joomla (www.joomla.org) are widely used open source examples. These are database-driven websites that allow the site to be constantly updated with news, stories and images. Be aware that while a CMS can make a site fresh and vibrant, if it is not updated regularly it can give the website an 'abandoned' and neglected feel, so it is important to choose the correct initial design for the needs of the business.

Alternatively, free online tools such as Google Sites (www.google.com/sites/overview.html) or web blogs such as Wordpress (wordpress.org) provide quick and relatively easy methods of creating a web presence.

Without proper web design experience or knowledge of setting up a web space and domain, a website can lack the feel of a professionally designed site, and look amateurish in comparison to competitors. If budget allows, it is best to use a professional website designer to build a bespoke site to a design brief. Good first impressions are essential, and it is likely that a prospective client will be viewing a range of other practices' sites. The design of the site, and the practice's other promotional material, should reflect its design approach and quality as a business.

RIBA Chartered Practices can access a flexible low-cost website development and maintenance service offered through a partner supplier, Acefolio. This allows RIBA Chartered Practices to build and maintain an effective website, and also to exploit their portfolio online in a more proactive way (to find out more, visit www2.acefolio.com/riba_microsite.aspx).

Using specific keywords and additional tools such as Google Analytics (www.google.com/analytics) can also increase visits to a site. Once a website is up and running, depending upon its functionality, this new repository can be used as a tool for embedding e-mailshots and other promotional tools.

Your website is probably the most important means of communicating with your clients and prospective clients, collaborators and so on. Remember the following points when designing it.

Differentiation

The homepage should be memorable and say something about the practice. Some websites have little more than an intriguing image and a link to the site; others choose to present critical information such as contact details and a summary note on what the practice does. You will need to decide what sort of practice you aspire to and select a suitable approach, but whatever you do it should aim to differentiate you from the competition. The homepage must say at a glance what your business is, what sort of work it aims to produce and the way it goes about producing it (e.g. are you design-focused or process-focused, front-end or 'executive' architects – or all of these, and what geographic areas do you cover?). However, don't try to make it cover everything; be selective and pick out what is most important.

If you can afford it, use a web designer – this need not be expensive if you undertake as much of the design as possible. If you have little previous experience of web design they will bring the technical knowledge of how to achieve the look you desire, how to optimise the speed of processing images, etc.

Keep it simple

Make sure visitors to the website can navigate and find what they want easily and quickly. If you are developing a website for a new practice and need to keep costs to a minimum this will also save you much-needed capital and time. Draw a map of all the pages you want and how they are to be connected. Make sure visitors can get back to the homepage from any other page.

Make the page structure simple to understand as well; don't have too many choices, and if your contact details aren't on the homepage make them easy to locate.

Projects

You will of course need to display images (possibly including drawings) of your projects. Only show the ones that reinforce your brand; don't feel the need to show all of them, only the best examples. Categorise them in some way, such as by sector and/or by date. Don't write an essay about them. People don't generally spend more than a minute or two browsing a website, so rely on the images to tell the story – text should be concise. Videos are great, but provide links to hosted sites such as YouTube to improve the load-time of your site. Keep graphic devices to an absolute minimum, which will also keep load-time down, and don't use Flash (an animation tool): users need a plug-in for it to operate, it is hard to update and search engines can't read it, making your site harder to find.

Social networks

Adding share buttons is a simple way of optimising your design for social networks (see Section 5.5.6). Blogging is another way of keeping in touch with your network, but make sure you update your blog pages regularly.

5.5.6   Social media

Another growing area of promotion is social media, and the exploitation of social networking tools such as Facebook (www.facebook.com), Twitter (www.twitter.com) and LinkedIn (www.linkedin.com) to allow people and practices to interact more directly with potential clients and to promote their business.

LinkedIn

LinkedIn is the principal medium for professional networking and a mobile version of the site is now available. Other than giving you the opportunity of connecting with your contacts' contacts ('second-degree' connections) and

5

their contacts ('third-degree' connections) and so on – which can be used to gain an introduction to someone you wish to know through a mutual contact – it also gives people a means to keep in touch with you should your email address change when you change jobs. There are currently more than 225 million users, with 11 million of those in the UK. Users can invite anyone to become a connection, whether they are an existing user or not. It can then be used to find jobs, people and business opportunities recommended by someone in your contact network. Employers can list jobs and search for potential candidates, and jobseekers can review the profile of hiring managers and discover which of their existing contacts can introduce them. Users can post their own photos and view photos of others to aid in identification. The 'gated-access' approach – where contact with any professional requires either an existing relationship or the intervention of a contact of theirs – is intended to build trust among the service's users.

LinkedIn also supports the formation of interest groups and now has over a million, although they can be subject to spam postings. Groups can be private and accessible to members only, or they can be open to anyone to read, with only membership necessary to post messages.

LinkedIn allows users to research companies with which they may be interested in working and to endorse their connections' skills – which can also be a means of catching the attention of someone you haven't contacted for a while.

A premium subscription is available, with a range of benefits according to the fee paid.

You can select who can see your connections, but by default your first-degree connections can see your list of connections. This lets them browse your network and find mutual friends and colleagues. A 'Who's Viewed Your Profile' feature helps you understand who has been looking at your profile in the past 90 days, how many times you have shown up in search results, and other such information.

You can select what others see when you've viewed their profile and there are three different ways to see who's viewed your profile, based on the profile viewer's privacy settings:

- display viewer's name, headline, location and industry;
- display only anonymous profile characteristics, such as job title, company, school and industry; or
- display as an anonymous LinkedIn member. This reflects members who have viewed your profile and chose to remain anonymous.

You can also see trends regarding the people who have viewed your profile. The trends you see depend on whether you have a free or premium account. If one of your goals on LinkedIn is to increase your visibility, this feature can significantly increase the likelihood that your profile will be discovered and viewed by other members. You do also have the option to remove the box from your profile.

Twitter

Twitter is an online social networking and microblogging service that enables its users to send and read messages of up to 140 characters, known as 'tweets'. It has over 500 million registered users, generating over 340 million tweets daily and handling over 1.6 billion search queries a day. Tweets are publicly visible by default, but senders can restrict message delivery to just their followers. Users can subscribe to other users' tweets – known as *following*. As a social network, Twitter revolves around the principle of followers. Users can group posts together by topic or type by using 'hashtags' – words or phrases prefixed with a '#' sign. Similarly, the '@' sign followed by a username is used for mentioning or replying to other users. To repost a message from another Twitter user, and share it with one's own followers, the retweet function is symbolised by 'RT' in the message.

A word, phrase or topic that is tagged at a greater rate than other tags is said to be a *trending topic*. Trending topics become popular either through a concerted effort by users or because of an event that prompts people to talk about one specific topic.

As with any form of social media you must know what you want to achieve by using it. If you want to attract followers and keep them interested, tweets should be entertaining, or at least informative. In this way you can, if you work at it, develop a group of people who are aware of you and what you are interested in. Your tweets should be professional in nature and reflect your business persona, not your private one. If you do use it for business purposes, make sure it is delivering value for the time you spend on it.

Facebook

Facebook is perhaps the least useful of the three for business use but, as with Twitter, it is important that if you do use it you make regular postings. There are a number of websites that offer advice on how to optimise your business Facebook page, which can be found by searching 'Facebook for business'.

Blogging

Many architect's websites have blogging pages, which can be used to provide up-to-date news on what the practice is doing, awards received,

5

corporate social responsibility (CSR) activities and so on. As with all social media, it must be attended to and updated regularly.

5.5.7 Press coverage

Press coverage can be a very useful way of obtaining publicity for the practice. The first step is to obtain the client's agreement to publishing the project. They usually have no objection, and may even contribute if they feel the publicity would benefit their business. The next stage is to identify a possible publication. Architects tend to focus mainly on the architectural journals, as coverage in such journals carries status among their peers. Articles about specific projects or about the practice in general are, of course, a useful marketing tool, as offprints or good-quality copies can be sent to existing or prospective clients. However, it is worth considering other publications, such as local press, technical journals or business journals, as these may reach a larger number of potential clients than the architectural press.

Any approach to the press has to bear in mind the agenda and needs of the publication targeted. It may be that the scheme is of particular interest locally, or that it exploits new technology that would interest a particular trade journal. It helps to have a specific 'angle' to interest the editor, and it is essential to have a clear summary of the key information readily to hand that can be submitted at very short notice. Practices might also wish to access the RIBA membership service 'Media Matters Toolkit' on www.architecture.com/Files/RIBAHoldings/Communications/Press/General/MediaMatters.pdf.

5.5.8 Resources

Layered across the marketing plan are the resources that are required to implement it and run the business efficiently and effectively. Things to be considered are:

- what manpower is needed to deliver the plan;
- who will do it;
- how much money can be spent.

If the strategy has highlighted the key objectives and approach to achieving them, then this will give an idea of the necessary investment required to help obtain it. This is the marketing budget. A marketing budget should take into account the hard costs (material production/advertising costs, etc.) and, if appropriate, the time input of salaries of any full-time staff or the agencies involved. If it is not possible to achieve everything in the plan, it can be adjusted to suit the budget. As a general rule, most practices spend between 1.5% and 3% of turnover on their marketing budget.

5.6   Did we achieve our goals?

The final stage of any marketing plan should be the measurement of activity, reviewing success and failure of the plan as a whole, and building in a response for the future.

Provided that SMART objectives with specific deadlines and time frames have been set, and that the plan had a one-, two- or five-year lifespan, there should come an obvious point by which time actions are completed and objectives either achieved or not. If the practice failed to meet some objectives, it may be that circumstances changed during the life of the plan, or that they were too ambitious initially.

The point of this phase is not to be critical, but to refine future plans and actions and to learn which actions were successful and which were not. However, it is worth noting that a marketing plan is not a piece of paper but a live series of actions and events and whoever is responsible for delivering the plan should be maintaining supervision on its success throughout the year. Consider therefore quarterly updates to tie in with Partner or Board meetings to demonstrate success and also warning signs of areas that are not progressing as planned so that responsive action can be taken there and then.

Questions that need to be asked include:

- Is the overall programme being maintained?
- Are the right staff, in the right numbers, being used?
- Are they performing their tasks effectively?
- Is the budget set at the right level?
- Are the promotional aids sufficient and of the right quality?
- Are presentations well prepared and executed?
- Have the right targets been identified?
- Is action being taken to address future needs?
- How effective are the marketing tools and techniques?
- What are the quantifiable results so far?

The long-term implications of the results will need to be evaluated to allow forecasts of:

- future workload and staffing;
- any change in financial commitment;
- the kind of marketing required in the future.

The results of this control phase can then be re-applied to the subsequent marketing plan, informing actions required and feedback regarding opportunities and market trends.

5

5.7　Pitching to clients

Once your marketing and PR activities have brought you a potential commission you will undoubtedly at some point need to make a presentation, either on your practice and its experience or to communicate your ideas for the project. The following five pointers will help you secure the commission:

1.　**Prepare**

It is critical to prepare thoroughly. Some experienced presenters reckon on one hour of preparation for every minute of presentation time. Also, you need to know as much about the background to the project and the building type as the client does. Other than having the right experience, you must demonstrate to the client that you have the right attitude and care enough to deliver them value and creativity. The project must be as important to you as it is to them. Ask questions and centre the pitch around their needs, keeping it relevant. Don't focus too much on you – other than the project itself, show them you know about their business, competitors, history and goals and what is important to them.

2.　**Preconceptions count**

By the time you stand up to speak you have already missed your greatest opportunities to influence the outcome. These include correspondence before the meeting, the way you walk into the room and introduce yourself and what you say while you set up for the presentation. Take care to remember people's names and use them when you say goodbye at the end. Don't repeat them too often during the pitch as this can appear patronising. Consider what sort of organisation you are pitching to and act (and possibly dress) accordingly. Research shows that perceptions are enormously influenced by tone of voice and appearance, as well as visual imagery. Only a small proportion of the words spoken word are actually remembered in detail.

3.　**Stop selling when you've finished the pitch**

Keep to the allotted time, and don't just keep talking until the interviewer tells you your time has run out. Take care to listen closely to any questions and answer them carefully, but once you've finished the pitch, don't continue trying to sell. Always follow up with a brief email or letter saying how much you enjoyed meeting them and look forward to the opportunity of working with them. You can also reiterate the key messages of the pitch, but don't overdo it.

4.　**Ask for what you want**

Don't pretend that you are doing anything other than pitching for something you want, albeit emphasising the benefits you can bring to the project. Don't be afraid to ask questions directly if there are important matters you need to know about. Make sure they know how keen you are to win the commission and don't be afraid to tell them.

5. **Reinforce your brand**

    You should always take the opportunity to reinforce your core messages so as to give consistency and help potential customers understand where you sit in the industry and what your key offer is.

References and further reading

Elias, H., *Good Practice Guide: Marketing your Practice* (London: RIBA Publishing, 2010).

Haupt, E. and Kubitza, M., *Marketing and Communication for Architects* (Basel: Birkhauser, 2002).

Lindon, H., Clary, L. and Rost, S., *Marketing for Architects and Designers* (New York: Norton, 2005).

Ostime, N., *Small Projects Handbook* (London: RIBA Publishing, 2014).

Sancho Pou, E., *Architectural Strategies: Marketing, Icon, Politics, Masses, Developer, the No. 1* (Madrid: Peninsular, 2012).

Smith, P. R. *Great Answers to Tough Marketing Questions* (London: Kogan Page, 2004).

5

People management

6.1   Introduction

The most important asset of any practice is its people. Keeping them happy and motivated is hugely important, in order to produce work of the highest possible quality. Underlying this, there is a raft of legislation that the employer needs to comply with to ensure the relationship between employer and employee is fair and equitably balanced.

Both aspects are considered in this chapter – the legal and contractual aspects first, followed by the 'softer' issues surrounding selection, appointment, management and motivation of the entire team.

Communication is probably the most important aspect of dealing with people. Keeping staff well briefed and informed about their projects and work as well as about the practice aims, ambitions and developments is key to keeping them motivated and productive. There are no clear rules as to how best to communicate – just the underlying principle that 'more' is better than 'less' or even 'none', in that it demonstrates trust and respect between employer and employee.

The RIBA Code of Professional Conduct (available from www.architecture. com) places various requirements on members in relation to employment of staff. The *RIBA Chartered Practice Manual* also sets out various criteria to be met by Chartered Practices, including the establishment and following of a model *RIBA Employment Policy* that sets out the roles and rights of the RIBA, the Chartered Practice and the employee (for details, go to www. architecture.com and search for 'employment policy').

Although approximately half of architecture students are women, according to the RIBA Business Benchmarking Survey 2012/13 they only represent 25%

6

of fee earners across the profession, and while 40% of Part 1 architectural assistants are female, only 12% of equity partners or shareholder directors are women. A diverse profession – one which reflects the broader society it serves – is not only desirable in terms of fairness but also makes good business sense. It is therefore good practice for firms to have a formal Equality and Diversity Policy. Section 1.3.1 sets out some practical advice on how to ensure your practice meets these criteria.

6.2   Legal and contractual aspects

6.2.1   Legislation

The legislation governing employment of staff is extensive and ever-changing. It originates from both the UK and European governments, and is supported by directives, regulations and rights that are added to and changed on a regular basis.

It is a challenge for practices to keep abreast of all this change. However, there are a number of useful guidance notes/updates that can help principals and others to manage this aspect of their practice in a positive and proactive manner, including:

- the *RIBA Employment Policy* (see above);
- International Workplace (www.internationalworkplace.com/);
- the employment section of the DirectGov website (www.gov.uk/browse/working);
- Labour Relations Agency (www.lra.org.uk/pages/employment-legislation-landingpage).

Various government websites retain complete copies of legislation, including the UK Statute Law Database (www.legislation.gov.uk) and the database of the Office of Public Sector Information (www.opsi.gov.uk/psi/).

The RIBA operates an HR and Employment Law service for RIBA chartered practices in the 'Members only' area of its website (www.architecture.com), run on its behalf by Croner, one of the UK's leading authorities on employment law and practice. This covers a comprehensive range of topics, offers a 'help page' and includes telephone contact details for other queries.

Many of the larger employment agencies and solicitors involved in employment law publish regular updates on employment legislation, most of which are freely available online.

Larger practices might consider employing an HR specialist, either as a direct employee or as a consultant, to ensure that they are complying with all current legislation and following best practice in the organisation and management of their staff. This will give the partners or directors the confidence that employment matters are being dealt with properly and professionally and allow them to get on with the practice of architecture.

Legislation is added to and/or varied regularly and practices should seek detailed advice as to current requirements if there is any doubt.

Comments about some of the specific requirements of employment legislation are included below.

6.2.2   An employee or not?

A practice might engage someone to undertake work and/or provide services to it as one of the following:

- A permanent employee – full time or part time.
- A temporary employee – fixed term or for the duration of a project or task.
- An agency employee.
- A consultant/contractor/self-employed person.

Her Majesty's Revenue and Customs (HMRC) provides various definitions as to whether or not a person is an employee, which have a fundamental effect on the relationship between the practice and the individual and the rights and benefits accorded to the individual. Among these are:

1. Who controls and directs the individual? Does the individual decide how, when and where they fulfil their work-related obligations or does the practice?
2. Is the individual performing services relative to a 'one-off' requirement or is the practice obligated to provide work to the individual?
3. Is the individual required simply to deliver a body of work/services or to undertake the services personally?
4. Does the individual work for more than a single employer or just for one?
5. Does the individual receive any 'benefits' from the practice, such as paid holiday, notice period, pension or other contributions, etc., or are they entitled to these?

In all of the above, if the first option describes the individual's situation, they are likely to be a 'contractor/self-employed'; if the second, they are an 'employee'.

Among other implications, an employer is required to deduct income tax and National Insurance contributions from its employees and pay them to HMRC. If HMRC deems an individual to be an employee, it is entitled to require the practice to pay these sums irrespective of whether or not the practice has actually deducted them from the individual.

6

6.2.3   Permanent employees and the contract of employment

It is likely that most people providing work/services to a practice will be permanent employees. The benefits of this include the establishment of a long-term relationship between employer and employee based on a series of terms and conditions (see below), which engenders mutual trust and respect.

While a simple offer of employment, acceptance of it and 'performance' (turning up for work, doing what is requested and receiving payment) are all that is needed to establish a contractual relationship, it is highly recommended that the basis of this relationship should be set down in a contract of employment signed by both employer and employee. Employers should also be aware that, irrespective of anything specific that is written into a contract of employment, 'custom and practice', for instance leaving early on a Friday or the payment of a bonus on a regular basis, may be deemed a term of employment over time.

There are certain basic requirements that should be set out in a contract of employment (or alternatively in a 'statement of terms', as required by the Employment Rights Act 1996), including:

- Details of the parties – names, addresses, etc.
- Job title/role.
- The date when the employment commenced/will commence.
- The date when the employment will finish, which will be the employee's normal retirement date in most cases, but would be earlier in the case of, for instance, a fixed-term contract. Practices should be aware of current and imminent changes to the law governing retirement ages.
- The date for commencement of continuous employment; this will usually be the date of commencement, but may, at the practice's discretion, include a period of previous employment with the practice or a related/subsidiary practice.
- Details of remuneration – how much the employee will be paid, at what intervals and by what method.
- Hours of work, including lunch breaks, etc. Practices should be aware of the European Working Time Directive, which restricts the number of hours an employee can work, and rest periods during the working day.
- Paid holiday entitlements, including arrangements relative to public and bank holidays and, at the practice's discretion, the period between Christmas and New Year.
- Payment, if any, for time off due to sickness.
- Notice required and conditions surrounding termination of employment, including arrangements for any probationary period following

commencement of employment, and any matters that might lead to summary dismissal.

- Normal place of work, and arrangements should the employer require working away from this location.
- Whether or not there are any collective agreements affecting the employment.
- Whether or not there is a 'contracting out' certificate in force for any pension scheme.
- Disciplinary procedures or details of where these can be found.
- Procedure for dealing with any grievances.

The practice is advised to include, although it is not legally required to do so, terms and conditions relating to:

- Restrictive covenants, which will prevent a former employee from doing various things for a stated period following their departure from the practice – this will usually include approaching clients and 'poaching' of key employees. These clauses will not become operative until an employee leaves, or has served notice to leave, and will continue to have an effect for a period of time after leaving. These clauses apply mainly to senior employees, and legal advice should be taken regarding the extent to which they can be effective (there is legal protection for the employee against a former employer seeking to use restrictive covenants that will restrain the former employee from gaining normal employment).
- Confidentiality. There may be a need to protect the practice against its current and former employees breaching confidentiality agreements signed with clients and to protect the practice's legitimate business interests. Clauses protecting this can remain operative in perpetuity.
- Any arrangements for garden leave in the event of a (usually senior) employee being asked to leave the practice before expiry of their notice period.
- Any arrangements for 'pay in lieu of notice' on leaving the practice and in the event of redundancy. Clauses of this sort are commonly called PILON clauses, and legal advice should be sought before including them, as they can have the effect of negating restrictive covenants.
- Intellectual property. The employee should indemnify the practice against their breaching a third party's copyright in the carrying out of their work and should confirm that the intellectual property in what they produce while working for the practice automatically passes to the practice.
- Any arrangements for overtime payment or confirmation that payment will not normally be made for overtime working.
- Arrangements for the return of company property, such as mobile phones, keys, laptop computers, etc. on termination of employment.

6

The *RIBA Employment Policy*, which must be followed by Chartered Practices, requires staff training and CPD provision to be set out with the employee's contract of employment.

Once a contract has been agreed, it should be signed by both parties, a copy handed to the employee and a copy retained within the employee's personnel file.

The Data Protection Act 1998 is an extensive and complex piece of legislation that seeks to protect individuals from improper storage or use of personal data. Among other things it governs what data can be retained about an individual and how it can be used, and gives an employee the right to access their own personal records and request the correction of inaccuracies. The Data Protection Order 2010 has increased penalties for breach of the Act. A practice is advised to get specialist advice on what data can be stored on individuals, for what lengths of time and data storage methods.

The contract of employment can only be varied by agreement between the two parties, except as provided for within it: for example it would be usual that variations to salary and other benefits could be made upon written notice being given to the employee. Any changes requested by the company should be made the subject of a consultation period with the employee.

When a practice changes ownership, and there is a new employer, it is usual to transfer all contracts of employment. A 'TUPE' (Transfer of Undertakings – Protection of Employment) process must be initiated to either transfer the contracts of existing employees over to the new company in their entirety or to negotiate revised terms. Such a negotiation is usually done on a collective basis and will, in certain circumstances, require the appointment of employee representatives who will interface with the practice management and report back to their colleagues.

6.2.4   Other employees

The definition of an 'employee' is touched on in Section 6.2.2 above, and practices should be aware of this to ensure that tax legislation is not infringed. However, it is possible to employ staff on other bases, including:

- **Part-time employees**. Staff can be employed on a part-time basis, with their working week defined either by numbers of days worked or numbers of hours worked per day. In these instances a standard form of employment contract will normally be used with the various entitlements to pay, holiday, working hours, etc. amended to suit. Practices should be aware that an employer is legally required to consider requests from eligible members of staff for part-time working/job sharing, etc. and to consider these seriously, but is not obliged to agree to them if there are sound business reasons for not doing so.

- **Temporary employees**. It may be that members of staff are required for a set period only, due to work needs, or because they are, for instance, students employed for a limited period only. In these instances a standard form of employment contract will normally be used with the end date of the contract specified. It would be wise to agree, either in the contract or by side letter, the basis on which the employment might be extended. Rarely, it may be that an employee will be engaged to perform a particular task or series of tasks and that the employment will terminate on completion of the task(s). In this instance, suitable specific terms should be drafted into the termination provisions of the employment contract.

- **Agency staff**. The use of agency staff has become increasingly common in recent years. In these instances the member of staff will be employed by the recruitment agency, which will be responsible for all the employee's benefits, etc., and a contract should be entered into between the practice and the agency, setting out the basis of the engagement. The employment of agency staff is usually terminable on relatively short notice, and they can be treated as employees for all other purposes.

- **Consultants/self-employed personnel**. It is usual for a practice to engage consultants/self-employed persons on a specific contract related to a specific body of work.

6.2.5   Statutory entitlements

The UK Government has instituted a number of entitlements over recent years, for instance maternity, paternity and parental leave that confer certain benefits on employees by law irrespective of whether or not they are included within contracts of employment, staff handbooks/policies, etc. It is important for practices to understand these entitlements, which are generally subject to certain criteria including length of service, as they can have cost and time implications for them.

Each practice should establish a policy for dealing with the above scenarios, so that all employees who make requests can be dealt with equally. Once a policy is set it should be applied consistently in all cases until a decision is made to vary the policy.

Nearly all workers, regardless of the number of hours per week they work, have certain legal rights, as set out below. Sometimes an employee only gains a right when they have been employed by their employer for a certain

6

length of time; when this applies the length of time before the employee gains the right is noted. Some workers are not entitled to some statutory rights, i.e. employees who normally work outside the UK or anyone who is not an employee, such as an agency or freelance worker. However, most workers are entitled to certain rights, such as the national minimum wage, limits on working time and other health and safety rights, the right not to be discriminated against and paid holiday. Unless an employee is in the group of workers who are excluded they will have the following statutory rights:

- the right to a written statement of terms of employment within two months of starting work;
- the right to an itemised pay slip. This applies from the day the employee starts work;
- the right to be paid at least the national minimum wage. This applies from the day the employee starts work;
- the right not to have illegal deductions made from pay. This applies from the day the employee starts work;
- the right to paid holiday. Full-time employees are entitled to at least 28 days a year. Part-time employees are entitled to a pro rata amount;
- the right to be accompanied by a colleague to a disciplinary or grievance hearing;
- the right to paid time off to look for work if being made redundant. This applies once the employee has worked for two years for that employer;
- the right to paid time off for antenatal care. This applies from the day the employee starts work;
- the right to paid maternity leave;
- the right to paid paternity leave;
- the right to ask for flexible working to care for children or adult dependants;
- the right to paid adoption leave;
- the right to take unpaid parental leave for both men and women (if the employee has worked for the employer for one year) and the right to reasonable time off to look after dependants in an emergency (applies from the day the employee starts work);
- the right under health and safety law to work a maximum 48-hour working week. This applies from the day the employee starts work;
- the right under health and safety law to weekly and daily rest breaks. This applies from the day the employee starts work;
- the right not to be discriminated against. This applies from the day the employee starts work;
- the right to carry on working until at least the age of 65;
- the right to notice of dismissal, provided the employee has worked for the employer for at least one calendar month;

- the right to written reasons for dismissal from the employer, provided the employee has worked for the employer for one year if they started before 6 April 2012 or two years if they started on or after that date. Women who are pregnant or on maternity leave are entitled to written reasons without having to have worked for any particular length of time;
- the right to claim compensation if unfairly dismissed. In most cases to be able to claim unfair dismissal the employee will have to have worked for the employer for one year if they started before 6 April 2012 or two years if they started on or after that date;
- the right to claim redundancy pay if made redundant. In most cases the employee will have to have worked for two years to be able to claim redundancy pay;
- the right not to suffer detriment or dismissal for 'blowing the whistle' on a matter of public concern (malpractice) at the workplace. This applies from the day the employee starts work;
- the right of a part-time worker to the same contractual rights (pro rata) as a comparable full-time worker;
- the right of a fixed-term employee to the same contractual rights as a comparable permanent employee.

It should be remembered there is an obligation upon RIBA Chartered Practices to remunerate students they employ to at least the level of the national minimum wage. The RIBA does not recognise unpaid internships as a legitimate means of undertaking professional experience as part of architectural education.

6.2.6 Benefits

In addition to those matters that are covered in and controlled by the contract of employment, the practice should consider whether or not it wishes to offer further benefits to its employees. If these are to be contractual obligations they should be written into the contract of employment, but it is more common that such benefits are non-contractual. Irrespective of this, an employee's entitlement to them, and how this may grow over time or because of promotion, should be set down in writing (see Section 6.2.7).

There is a huge variety of benefits that any particular practice may wish to consider offering to its employees, including:

- Increasing holiday entitlements due to length of service and/or seniority within the practice.
- Arrangements for sabbatical leave – a longer period off work, paid or unpaid, after a lengthy period of service.

6

- Bonus payments and method of calculation thereof, which may be linked to overall company performance, but are likely to depend, in whole or in part, on the individual's performance during the period in consideration.
- Share option arrangements. An increasing number of practices are considering employee ownership schemes and any rights that employees will have to obtain equity in the practice should be set out as part of it.
- Employer's contribution to pension schemes. Any contribution may be a simple percentage or lump sum contribution or may be matched to any contribution made by the employee, up to a certain limit.
- Insurance policies. Many different insurance policies can be taken out and offered as a benefit to employees, including:

  ○ death in service insurance (often associated with a company's pension scheme) – insures employees against their death while still employed by the company. Payable in accordance with the employee's written wishes or to their estate;
  ○ dependants insurance (often associated with a company's pension scheme) – pays an employee's nominated beneficiary a certain percentage of their salary should they die while employed by the company;
  ○ employment protection insurance – pays the employee should they become incapable of working full time in their usual job role because of a defined range of injuries or illnesses;
  ○ critical illness insurance – pays the employee a sum following diagnosis of a critical illness.

There are many options and different illnesses covered by different insurance policies:

- payment for sickness over and above Statutory Sick Pay;
- private medical insurance;
- company car or car allowance with or without fuel allowance;
- season ticket or other travel loans;
- payment of professional subscriptions;
- payment for professional examination course and examination fees;
- additional paid study leave;
- payment of 'introductory fees' for the successful introduction of new staff to the practice.

Each practice should have a policy stating the non-contractual benefits it will offer and interpretation in various cases (see Section 6.2.7). Once a policy is set it should be applied consistently in all cases.

Various of these benefits are treated by HMRC as the equivalent of salary, including company cars, some insurance policies and private medical cover, and the employee is liable to pay income tax on them. Such benefits must be declared by the practice annually on a tax form P11D.

The practice should also be aware that increasing entitlements due to length of service need to be carefully considered to ensure they do not breach age discrimination legislation.

6.2.7   Policies/staff handbook

Many of the above benefits will remain outside a contract of employment, but should be written down, collated into a staff handbook or manual and stored in a central place within the practice accessible to all, so that employees are clear about what the practice offers them and the processes by which such things can be claimed, assessed and awarded. These are usefully set down in practice policies, which are generally (unless stated otherwise) not contractual entitlements and can thus be varied to suit changes in legislation or practice circumstances at short notice without the need to consult employees on contractual changes.

Matters of process (how to claim expenses, book holidays, etc.) can also be usefully incorporated into such a handbook/manual.

The staff handbook should be considered as a 'live' document, responding to changes as and when needed.

6.2.8   Other legal/contractual issues

- **Health and safety**. The directors/partners of the practice are legally responsible for the health and safety of their staff both in the workplace and when out on practice business. It is highly recommended that procedures for conduct are established, particularly for such events as fire evacuation and disaster scenarios, and enforced to ensure that these obligations are fulfilled. In particular it is necessary to identify potential health and safety hazards, and undertake (and be seen to undertake) risk assessments and act on the basis of these (see Section 8.2.2). It is possible to buy these services from outside consultants if no one within the practice has appropriate skills, but the appointment of an external consultant does not relieve the partners or directors of their ultimate obligations. It is also worth noting that, if the practice has agreed to a member of staff working all or part of their time at home, they are required to undertake risk assessments of the working environment in the individual's home. It is a requirement of the RIBA Chartered Practice Scheme that a Chartered Practice operates an appropriate health and safety policy.
- **Discrimination**. The practice is legally required to conduct its business in a manner that is not discriminatory against any particular sectors of

6

society by virtue of an employee's sex, age, ethnic origin, religion or disability (which is quite widely defined), pregnancy or varied working arrangements. These requirements also apply to those on part-time or fixed-term contracts. There is a well set out procedure for anyone who thinks they have been discriminated against, whereby they can take their employer to an employment tribunal, which is both costly and time consuming for the practice, and best avoided if at all possible.

- **Disciplinary procedures**. Issues surrounding disciplinary procedures and termination of employment can be very complex and need to be dealt with properly and carefully. Both ACAS and the DBIS provide useful guidance on these issues. It is recommended that the practice has a policy regarding unacceptable behaviour that could lead to summary, instant dismissal – this could include drunkenness in the workplace or being at work under the influence of drugs, unacceptable behaviour in relation to other members of staff, including violence or threatening violence, breach of confidentiality, etc. Procedures for reporting, investigating and dealing with such issues need to be established. Any instances should be recorded in writing for they may lead to a claim of unfair dismissal.

- **Dismissal**. This can happen for a variety of reasons – summary dismissal as set out above; by reason of redundancy, in which case there are established procedures to follow; or by lack of ability to undertake the role the employee has been appointed for. In this latter case, which could involve long-term illness as well as inability to provide work of the required standard, the law requires that a process is introduced to identify the areas of poor performance and give the employee time to rectify them. Fundamentally, the practice has to ensure it has been fair in dealing with the dismissal of an employee. The employee's remedy via an employment tribunal is well established.

- **Insurances**. The practice is required by law to carry various insurances to protect its employees, the general public and its clients. Partners or directors need to discuss and agree the levels of cover required to protect the practice against claims under any of these insurances. It should ensure that its PI insurance (see Section 11.3) protects its employees against claims against them as individuals by the insurance company ('subrogation'); such protection will normally be provided unless the employee has acted dishonestly, fraudulently or vexatiously.

6.3   Appointing, managing and motivating staff

6.3.1   Employing new staff

It is important that a practice, when approached by a client to provide services on a project, assesses its ability to provide the appropriate resources to the project. To help do this, it is a good idea to retain a log of the skills and experience of current employees. Should the appropriate level of skills not be available within the practice, it will be necessary to recruit.

A job description and list of key skills and experience required should be prepared to make sure that the recruitment is as focused as possible and that the candidate appointed has the best chance of succeeding in the role. Factors to consider include:

- skills required (for example, BIM skills, CAD skills, team leading skills, project running skills)
- experience required
- qualifications required
- basis of employment (permanent, temporary), likely salary and other benefits, etc.
- personal qualities desired.

The practice will need to take care to make sure that the role description does not infringe discrimination legislation.

Having done this, there are a variety of ways of going about the recruitment process, including:

- **Personal recommendation** – usually considered the most reliable, and cheapest, way to recruit new staff. Many practices offer incentives to existing members of staff should recommendation lead to appointment of new staff, although care must be taken to ensure staff are not incited to break restrictive covenants from previous employments regarding 'poaching' of staff.
- **Advertisements**. These will usually be placed in the professional press and can also serve to raise the profile of the practice more generally among the profession. It may occasionally be appropriate to advertise in the local or national press. Prices vary according to the publication and size of advert placed; there may be special offers available for repeat placements over a number of weeks.
- **Online recruitment**. A practice's own website may have a 'current vacancies' section inviting applications from interested visitors to the site. Several online journals offer recruitment services including:

  - *RIBA Journal* (www.ribajournal.com).
  - *Architects' Journal* (www.architectsjournal.co.uk).
  - *Building Design* (www.bdonline.co.uk).

- **Agencies**. There are a large number of specialist recruitment agencies, including RIBA Appointments (www.ribaappointments.com), who will

6

obtain CVs and shortlist candidates based on the practice's brief, thus reducing the 'sifting' work needed by the practice. They will also typically have a database of potential candidates, which should ensure a swifter and wider response. They charge a fee for this service, usually a percentage of starting salary, a part of which may be refundable if the candidate turns out to be unsuitable. Practices are advised to approach a limited number of agencies to undertake this service, in order to minimise the number of candidates put forward. If a practice needs to appoint several new members of staff within a short period it may be worth considering establishing preferred supplier agencies, who give a high quality of service and may be prepared to negotiate rates in return for first refusal, for a limited period of time, on all a practice's vacancies.

- **Headhunting**. This operates in a similar manner to recruitment agencies (and many agencies offer a headhunting service), but will generally be more expensive as it involves the agency approaching those already in employment (and many people have views on the morals of doing this). It is usually reserved for relatively high-level or very specific appointments.

- **Unsolicited applications**. Many practices receive unsolicited applications for work, particularly when students are completing their courses and seeking year out or post Part 2 placements. These should be screened regularly by an agreed senior member of the management team to see if any are suitable, and all should be responded to, even if just by email with a simple 'no suitable vacancies at present' message – a courteous response will leave the applicant with a positive impression of the practice.

6.3.2   Employing non-UK, or EU, nationals

There are strict regulations governing the employment of non-UK or EU nationals, and in most cases a work permit will be required. Non-UK and European nationals may not be employed legally unless their right to work in the UK can be verified, and practices are strongly advised to check this right for all employees, and retain evidence confirming this.

The practice is responsible in law for ensuring that all its employees have the legal right to work in the UK before employing them, but is permitted to offer employment conditional on obtaining the appropriate work permit. Guidance for employers is provided by the Home Office on the UK Border Agency website (www.gov.uk/uk-visa-sponsorship-employers).

In general, other than for certain very specialised types of employment, the potential employee will require a sponsor (which will usually be the practice), and the process of applying for the necessary permit should be started as early as possible.

6.3.3   The interview and appointment process

It is often not recognised that appointing the wrong person to a new position is one of the most costly mistakes a practice can make. It takes time and effort to induct a new member of staff into the practice in order that they are producing work of the required quality in the required time frame. The process of making a wrong appointment can be costly, and any re-appointment process is time-consuming. It is therefore important that the practice gives itself the best chance of making the right appointment first time. This means taking the interview and induction processes seriously and allocating an appropriate amount of time – often senior management time – to ensuring it is done well.

Key points to consider in the recruitment/interview process are:

- Decide on the most appropriate method of recruitment – advertising, agency or headhunting.
- Set out a clear role description.
- Establish and record the skill and experience levels appropriate to the role.
- Screen the CVs of candidates for appropriate skills/experience and produce a limited shortlist, ideally around three candidates for each post to be filled.
- Establish an interview process – will it be a single or multiple interview before a job offer is made? Senior appointments should involve more than one of the practice's existing senior management team.
- Establish who will interview the candidates – if there are to be different interviewers for a single post try to ensure a consistent approach that will enable an objective decision to be made.
- Set down a list of criteria (and ideally a set of key questions), to be discussed during the interview.
- Decide on the appropriateness of introducing tests as part of the interview (e.g. for CAD).

Large practices with human resources personnel/departments can devolve the initial selection and interviewing of candidates to them, but the final decision should be taken by senior members of the architectural team, who will understand the needs of the post and the skills/experience offered by the candidate better than their HR department.

The interview is probably the first time that a candidate will meet the practice and it is as important that the practice makes a favourable impression on the candidate as that the candidate impresses the practice. Most potential staff will be looking to ensure that they work in a practice that meets their aims and ambitions and that it is one into which they are likely to integrate well.

6

The interviewer should be courteous and professional and should provide information to the candidate about the practice, its aims and ambitions, as well as the role they are being interviewed for. It is beneficial to show the candidate the working environment, particularly at second interview stage.

In many cases, particularly those where a relatively senior appointment is being made, a second shortlist and interview process is likely to be necessary.

Unsuccessful candidates should be informed as soon as possible and given a brief explanation of why they were not considered suitable if they request one.

Bear in mind that a practice needs a range of different skills and characteristics to best realise its potential, and that a practice of 'clones', however talented, is likely to be less successful than one that has a range of personalities and experiences within it. Successful business derives from good working relationships, and it is not necessary to cultivate personal friendships. For this reason personal prejudices should be kept at bay as far as possible during the recruitment process.

6.3.4   Induction and the probationary period

The way in which a new member of staff is inducted into the practice is vitally important. It will determine how quickly they are able to deliver what the practice wants. A good and thorough briefing about the practice's procedures and, most importantly, the project that the new member of staff will be working on, is fundamental. New employees should not be expected to guess what they are required to do, or how they are expected to do it.

A new employee is likely to be confronted with a whole set of new processes and procedures when they start in the practice, and it is a good idea for induction to happen over their first few days and not all be attempted on the first day. Establishing an induction programme setting out all those aspects of the practice that the new member of staff will need to be familiar with during their initial period with the practice and giving them a copy of this during the initial induction briefing is recommended.

One way to achieve a successful induction is to appoint a 'buddy', a peer rather than someone more senior, who can help the new member of staff become familiar with the practice's processes and procedures.

It is usual to include a probationary period within a new employee's contract, during which a reduced notice period, often one week, is required on either side. While this period will typically be three or six months, it is important to give the new employee feedback about how they are performing throughout the probationary period, rather than springing a surprise on them at the end. These reviews, and the feedback given, can be done on a formal or informal basis, but the new employee will feel more secure in their new position, and more able to adjust their behaviour to be more productive if necessary, if they are given regular feedback on how they are performing.

It may occasionally be necessary to extend an employee's probationary period. In these instances a written explanation of the reason for the extension, together with a schedule of those criteria that are necessary in order to pass the probationary period, should be given together with the date on which the probationary period will again be reviewed.

The conclusion of their probationary period and with it, frequently, entitlement to benefits should be recorded in writing to the employee.

6.3.5   Management and management structures

A clear and simple management structure is important for the smooth working of a practice and essential for the efficient and correct running of the projects that pass through it. Clear roles and responsibilities help ensure job satisfaction for management and employees alike. Good communication is arguably the most important factor in good management, and engenders a sense of belonging and loyalty to a practice. Structures should be established to manage both the work and the business. Understanding who does what is vital.

When a practice is first formed it is common for the owners, who will often be relatively young and fired with enthusiasm and possibly experienced in project organisation but rarely experienced in practice management, to act instinctively. Communication tends to be good, as staff numbers are low, and is usually verbal and direct, with little need to commit things to writing.

While the legal responsibilities of partners in a partnership or limited liability partnership vary slightly from those of directors in a company, the practical day-to-day management needs of the practice and the work flowing through it are similar.

The division of roles between the partners/directors will often happen naturally in the early days of a practice's existence – one may be responsible for the financial organisation of the practice, another for the quality of the work being issued, another for staff, and so on. Of course, in solo practices a single person has to be responsible for all of these, although may well employ accountants and others to undertake various aspects of business management.

6

As a practice develops and grows it may wish to consider employing non-architects to perform some of these roles to allow the architects more time to secure and undertake commissions. It is important to note that the appointment of others does not relieve the partners/directors of their overriding responsibilities for these issues.

There are a range of issues surrounding practice management that need to be considered by the partners/directors of a young practice if it is to grow and eventually move smoothly into a successful second generation once the founders decide to retire. These are commonly known as 'succession issues' and at a minimum the principles of these should be considered early in the life of a practice, preferably at its inception, as they can inform the structure of the practice.

Among these will be:

- What do the founder partners anticipate they will want to do when they no longer wish to be involved with the practice?
- Do they have any idea of when they will wish to effect these changes? This might be by reference to age or to a set of circumstances.
- What do they wish to get out of the practice in return for their investment over time (cash, pension, ongoing consultancy, etc.)?
- Who will they wish to pass the management and ownership of the practice on to? This may be by reference to type of person – all staff, key individuals, someone outside the current business – rather than by individual.

As time passes the founding partners or directors will need to identify and prepare those who will take over responsibility to ensure a smooth transfer.

It is important to understand the difference between the roles of the owners of the practice and those charged with managing it – the directors or partners. Owners have the ultimate sanction of getting rid of its senior management but, until they do, the directors/partners have full authority to manage the practice, including deciding what work they will undertake, who they will employ to do it, including themselves, and how they will reward them. Owners can receive dividends based on their individual shareholding in the case of a company.

There are various legal responsibilities on partners/directors, and it is important that all these are fully understood. Key among them is not to trade insolvently, i.e. be unable to meet their obligations to pay those from whom they have purchased services or goods.

The partners/directors are ultimately responsible for all that happens within the practice, although they may devolve certain responsibilities to others.

Practically, these include:

- Establishing an overall vision/series of objectives (see Section 5.4: Where do we want to be?).
- Setting strategies to achieve these objectives (see Section 5.5: How do we get there?).
- Implementing or appointing others to implement these strategies.
- Managing the financial performance of the practice (see Section 7.3: Establishing a financial system).

As noted above, it is common when a practice is first formed, or in solo or small practices, for the partners/directors to perform all the necessary management functions, and there is no need to establish a structure. However, as the practice grows it will need to organise itself into:

- Directors – those with a practice-wide responsibility for objectives, organisation and management.
- Managers – those with responsibility for organising and managing the work, architectural and other, as it progresses through the practice.
- Others – those who will actually do the work.

Management structures can be as simple or as complex as the needs of the practice demand, though with a general recommendation to keep them as simple and as clear as possible. The management tier is commonly accorded titles such as 'Divisional Director', 'Project Director' or 'Associate Director'. The roles and responsibilities that sit with these titles should be clear to the entire staff, as should the reporting structure through the practice.

6.3.6 Motivation and staff development

Having recruited the best staff available, it is of the utmost importance to keep them motivated and loyal to the practice, working to maximum effect to deliver great work that contributes to moving the practice forward to achieve its long-term ambitions.

Factors that have a positive motivational effect on architects and architectural staff include:

- Working on worthwhile/high-quality/high-profile/interesting work.
- Recognition, both internally and among their peers, for involvement with well-designed and well-delivered projects.
- Role and responsibility given and opportunities for advancement.
- Social aspects.
- Training/personal development.
- Financial reward and benefits offered.

6

Significant among these is making the member of staff feel part of the long-term future of the practice and facilitating their development in it.

All staff should have regular personal reviews with a member of the senior management team, which should cover not only their performance but also their aims and ambitions and the training/reallocation of work needed to realise these. Outcomes of the review must be actioned, and be seen to be actioned, or the member of staff will rapidly lose faith in the practice management. Reviews should be held regularly, preferably twice a year – one major review and one to verify that things are on track.

For key members of staff, those who have been identified as having the potential to rise to the most senior level within the practice, establishing a personal development plan is a good way to identify key skills they need to acquire in order to achieve their longer-term ambitions (and those of the practice).

A system of mentoring high performers, by pairing them with a senior member of staff who is charged with helping them develop and advance within the practice, can also be beneficial.

Finally, many practices believe that regular staff surveys are a good way to keep in touch with their staff and their concerns. They can be, but the objectives of the survey need to be clearly set out and used to frame the questions within the survey. Surveys should be anonymous, and criticism of the practice not discouraged. It is important that the results are made public and that some action is seen to flow.

Staff surveys, personal development plans and regular personal reviews are all features that will help the practice, should it so wish, to become an accredited 'Investor in People' (www.investorsinpeople.co.uk). This is an organisation dedicated to improving business performance through increased staff motivation, and IIP accreditation is increasingly seen as beneficial in securing new business, particularly from government or quasi-governmental organisations.

6.3.7   A few thoughts

The start of this chapter asserted that a practice's staff are its most important asset, so one or two pieces of homespun philosophy might be of assistance in relation to people management:

- Brilliant staff will not perform well without leadership. People respond to being given information about the practice and to being given clear guidance and a good understanding of how their efforts will help achieve the project goals and the practice's strategic objectives.

- Any idea is potentially a good idea. It does not matter who promotes an idea – this is not the exclusive domain of senior management – what is important is that the practice continually seeks to improve itself, its product and its methods of producing its product.
- Credit where credit is due. A 'pat on the back' for a job well done or a positive contribution from a senior manager will frequently do more to promote morale within the practice than any amount of more tangible reward. A good manager will never be afraid to make public the good work of his or her team.
- Never hide a problem. If a problem is known about it can (usually) be solved – if it is hidden it cannot be resolved. Staff should be encouraged to discuss their concerns and not be pilloried for raising them.

References and further reading

Clayton, M., *Brilliant Time Management: What the Most Productive People Know Do and Say* (Harlow: Pearson Education, 2011).

Gegg, B. and Sharp, D., *Good Practice Guide: Employment* (London: RIBA Publications, 2006).

McGee, P., *How to Succeed with People: Remarkably Easy Ways to Engage, Influence and Motivate Almost Anyone* (Chichester: Capstone Publishing, 2013).

Naoum, S., *People and Organizational Management in Construction* 2nd edn (London: ICE Publishing, 2011).

Peppitt, E., *Retaining Staff* (London: Hodder & Stoughton, 2004).

6

Financial management

- looks at the financial considerations that need to be taken into account when setting up a practice;
- explains how to establish a suitable financial system, including business planning, monthly forecasting and invoicing;
- discusses the key financial performance indicators and how best to use them to monitor the business.

7.1 Introduction

Most architects go into practice to create great buildings, but it is vital to recognise that it is a business and there are certain financial imperatives if it is to survive. The establishment and management of a practice incurs cost, and so it is essential to make money both to survive and to invest in the practice's future.

There are certain legal requirements on the practice, including the filing of annual audited accounts, the deduction of tax and National Insurance from its employees' salaries, the collection and payment of VAT and the submission of various returns relating to taxes. There are also strict legal duties on partners/directors as individuals not to trade insolvently (where they continue to practise in the knowledge that they cannot pay their bills).

Architects are frequently accused of being their own worst enemies – they have, with some justification, acquired a reputation for undercutting one another on fees and doing large amounts of work for free. What architects have is a valuable skill set that is used to add value to a client's buildings and/or land, particularly at the front end of a project. Architects should recognise this value-creating skill and ensure that their clients pay for it appropriately.

Architects need to understand the financial risks associated with working free of charge or at significantly reduced rates and make sure the financial management of their practice is sufficiently robust to accommodate this before agreeing to it. Without sound financial management, a practice is likely to struggle.

'Cash is king' in all businesses, and architectural practices are no exception – no matter how much profit you make on paper, the practice will struggle for survival if the cash doesn't get to the bank. Analysis of business failures suggests that most fail, not because they are bad or unprofitable businesses, but because they simply run out of cash. The establishment and maintenance of a sound financial system that projects, monitors and regulates the financial success of the practice is therefore essential.

This chapter endeavours to set out basic methods to ensure the financial health of the practice in such a way as to leave the partners/directors free to focus on securing and undertaking commissions.

7.2   Establishing the practice

Chapter 4 sets out a range of considerations in relation to setting up a practice. A number of these are financially related. It is a good idea for the practice to appoint its own financial advisers to help with its establishment and the creation of the financial management processes. It is also useful to have an external, expert overview of the financial health of the practice on a regular basis. That said, one of the partners/directors should take responsibility for finance at board level. They don't necessarily need to have a day-to-day involvement in financial management because they will usually have better things to do with their time, and their level of expertise is likely to be less than that of someone trained for the role. Sole practitioners will inevitably have to assume these responsibilities personally.

A new practice is almost certain to need cash for its establishment costs, including premises, equipment, etc., and ongoing costs, including salaries, lease and other running costs, as income is unlikely to flow for some months. This cash can come from a variety of sources:

- the partners'/directors' own money;
- borrowings, usually from a bank, but potentially from other sources;
- a bank overdraft.

It is common for the initial costs of establishing the practice to be secured from a combination of these. In most circumstances a bank will need to be involved and, of course, the practice will need an account to manage its cash in and out, so one of the first visits prospective partners/directors will need to make is to their bank. A well-founded and well-developed business plan will be necessary to convince the bank to help with funding. This will include projections showing the likely income into the practice over its initial period, supported by the likely sources of that income; and projections of the likely costs for establishment and running of the practice and consequently the likely profit to be made. It is important that the projections are as realistic as possible, as the lending institution will gain progressively more confidence in the practice if it is regularly meeting its projections.

7

'Working capital' requirements will need to be assessed in order to establish the quantum of loan and/or overdraft required by the practice.

The bank will be principally interested in three things:

- when it is likely to get its money back;
- the degree of certainty that it will get it back;
- what return it will get on the money it is lending.

The business plan will enable a bank/funding institution to take a view on the first two of these. They will require the partners/directors to give them as much security as they can, and will frequently look for personal guarantees of this in the form of charges over their homes, etc. Partners/ directors need to be very aware of the terms of personal guarantees and to think carefully before entering into them.

The degree of security will have a direct effect on the rate that an institution will charge for lending money – the better the degree of security provided, the lower the fee likely to be charged for the loan.

The partners/directors should not be afraid to approach more than one bank to seek alternative terms and select the one that suits their needs best.

Once a loan/overdraft facility has been agreed the new practice will need to open bank account(s), usually with the lending bank. It will also be a requirement to register with HMRC for tax and VAT purposes. Anyone in business offering a service that requires the addition of VAT can register with HMRC for VAT purposes, but those that turn over in excess of a certain sum (currently £79,000 per annum) must register. The practice's financial advisers should be asked to help in these matters.

7.3   Establishing a financial system

A practice's financial management system needs a number of components:

- A long-term plan setting out ambitions and targets.
- An annual business plan budget setting out anticipated income, expenditure and profit. Once set, this should not be altered, but should be used as a benchmark to monitor against during the year ahead.
- Shorter term, usually monthly but more frequently if circumstances demand, forecasts of income, expenditure and profit.
- A project-based system for forecasting and monitoring resource needs and other project costs.
- Monthly management accounts reporting performance against the budget and forecasts.
- A system of ledgers and timesheets to record invoices issued, cash collected, time spent, supplier invoices received, and other expenditure.

All of these are ideally managed by a single package of accounting software, of which there are a number on the market. It is important that the practice selects a system appropriate to the likely scale of the practice and the likely uses for the accounting system. The partners/directors should prepare a brief detailing what they require their accounting system to do, which might be simple accounting functions only or projecting/forecasting/ monitoring on a project-by-project basis or including/interfacing with databases, etc. Having established this brief, the practice should approach potential providers for quotations and specifications. They should be aware that most systems carry annual maintenance/support charges as well as initial purchase/set-up costs.

7.3.1   Long-term plan

The practice should set a long-term (up to five-year) plan to establish the direction in which it would like to develop. It is not imperative that this contains financial targets; indeed there is a strong argument that financial return is just one product of a great practice rather than a driver to success, but many practices find it useful to set headline targets for financial growth in both income and profit terms.

If the practice does set such a plan, it should be regularly reviewed and updated to reflect changing circumstances and ambitions.

7.3.2   Annual business plan

It is important, before the beginning of each financial year, to set an annual budget of income, expenditure and profit. This should be carefully put together and each component fully considered and used to control/monitor expenditure.

Planned expenditure should ideally be built 'bottom up', by assessing the needs of the various component parts of the practice and then testing them for affordability against the income and profit figures, rather than driving purely financial budgets 'from the top down'. If the sum of the individual elements cannot be afforded, a discussion regarding priorities should be held and the annual business plan adjusted accordingly.

The projected income will be derived in part from the anticipated returns from the practice's marketing initiatives (see Chapter 5).

When setting budgets, it is important to engage with those who will be responsible for controlling them to ensure, first, that they fully understand what is expected to be delivered for what cost and, second, that the agreed budgets have their support.

7

However, the practice should be light on its feet and review its forecasts periodically, particularly if circumstances and/or ambitions change significantly. The annual budget exists as a benchmark to be monitored against and should not be changed too frequently.

The annual budget should also be used to assess and update the practice's hourly/daily cost and charge-out rates for its services.

7.3.3   Monthly forecasting and monitoring

The practice should review its predicted invoicing and costs on a monthly basis by way of a monthly forecast. This is of particular value to spot trends and to predict hiatuses or shortfalls in workload, and hence resource and other needs-planning, in advance of them occurring. It is easier to identify trends if a limited amount of historic performance is reported as well as future projections.

When preparing the monthly forecast it is important to distinguish between those invoices that are 100% secure and have a signed appointment and an agreed programme and those that retain elements of risk, and to project accordingly. Perceived wisdom would suggest that somewhere between 10% and 30% of a practice's annual income will arise from commissions that come into it during the course of that year, and some acknowledgement of this should be made in the later months of the projection period.

The number of months of forward projection is a matter for the practice to decide, but it is often appropriate to project for a rolling period of time rather than, for instance, to the end of a financial year, in terms of the management of the practice, although the practice's accountant will need this projection to year end.

7.3.4   Monthly management account

The practice, or its financial advisers, should produce a monthly management account to show how it has actually performed against the annual budget and the previous month's forecast in terms of income, cost and profit. This does not have to be complex (indeed, the simpler it is, the better), and should be used to spot trends and as an aid to plan additional/reduced spending as well as simply monitoring and recording performance.

The monthly management account needs to be based on reliable data (salaries, expenses, suppliers, etc.), so requires the regular inputting of income, expenditure and time records.

7.3.5 Cash collection

Cash collection is the other vital piece of the financial jigsaw and should be reported regularly. Understanding what the practice is owed, particularly those invoices that have not been settled within the practice's normal terms of business, is critical. A full report should be prepared every month setting out details of each invoice rendered and when it is/was due for payment. This will enable the partners/directors to agree how to address outstanding debts and can give an early warning of potential problems on a project (see Section 7.4.6 below). It is sensible to agree a level of debtor days over which more severe action will be taken to recover money due.

7.3.6 Bank reconciliation

A monthly bank reconciliation setting 'money in' against 'money out' and the balance accruing is needed in order to confirm the practice's actual cash position. This reconciliation should be checked against bank statements received.

7.3.7 Weekly monitoring

The weekly submission and aggregation of timesheets is important in order that projects can be monitored for performance against plan in both cost and time terms.

Petty cash should be reconciled on a weekly basis.

7.3.8 Daily monitoring

The practice administrator/finance team should keep daily records of:

- fee invoices paid;
- suppliers' invoices settled;
- fee invoices raised;
- invoices received from suppliers;
- petty cash utilised.

All of these should be compiled and reported on once a month, or more frequently if necessary.

7.3.9 Other reports

In addition to the financial controls/reports needed by the partners/ directors for the smooth running of the practice there are other reports needed from time to time, including:

- **Annual audited accounts** – prepared by the practice's accountants and audited by an accredited external agency for accuracy and compliance with statutory requirements. These have to be submitted to Companies House within a set period following the end of the practice's financial year, and there are fines for failure to comply.

- **VAT returns** – HMRC requires all businesses turning over in excess of a certain threshold to be registered for VAT. This threshold, which is varied from time to time, is currently £79,000 per annum. Registered businesses must submit a quarterly return setting out VAT charged and paid and a balance owing to HMRC. There are strict time requirements for submitting this information and paying sums due.
- **Bank reports** – assuming the practice has taken out a bank loan to establish itself, or to raise funds for a certain purpose, there will be one-off requirements for reporting performance to the bank/funding institution.

7.4   Day-to-day financial management

7.4.1   Appointments

Before accepting a commission the practice should decide whether it is happy to work for the client. One of the key considerations in reaching this decision will be whether the client is likely to settle the practice's invoices. Reference to previous payment records will confirm this in the case of repeat clients but the practice should not hesitate to ask for financial references on a new client. There may be situations where the practice wishes to request an initial payment before starting work – this is frequently the case on international projects.

The appointment documentation for a project should record the agreed fees to be paid for the services to be provided and other relevant arrangements relating to the financial management of the project. It is important that these are clearly established with the client at the outset of the project and, once agreed in the appointment contract, adhered to throughout its life, unless varied by agreement between the parties. Chapter 9 sets out more detailed recommendations to be considered when negotiating appointment terms.

Set out below is a list of the principal issues to be covered within the appointment relative to financial matters:

- The fee and the basis for calculating it – lump sum, percentage, hourly charge, etc.
- Cash flow for payment of fees. This might be by way of regular time-related or milestone payments. Monthly instalments are recommended to help the practice's cash flow and provide an 'early warning' of a client who may be having financial difficulties.

- Arrangements for VAT (refer to the 'rate prevailing at the time an account is issued' as opposed to a set percentage – it does change occasionally). The architect needs to ensure that relevant VAT provisions are operated – there are a number of instances, for example foreign commissions, which do not attract VAT.
- Time for settling accounts (RIBA Appointment documents specify 14 days for both consumer and commercial clients).
- Arrangements for payment of interest in the event of late payment of accounts.
- Arrangements for payment of additional fees for additional services.
- Arrangements for payment of expenses/disbursements. It is important to state very clearly what has been included within, or excluded from, the agreed fee. The practice should consider whether it wishes to charge an additional management/handling charge in respect of expenses/disbursements.

7.4.2   Invoices

It is exceptionally rare for a client to pay a fee before receiving an invoice, and so it is important for the practice to develop a well-managed system for the issue of invoices. It helps cash flow if invoices are raised as they are due, rather than waiting for a set time each month. It is useful to understand the client's procedures for approval and payment of invoices. Many, particularly contractor, clients will have set times during a month when they raise cheques/settle invoices and the practice will receive prompter payment if they gear submission of their invoices to fit in with the client's payment dates.

It is particularly important to ensure that the client is expecting to receive the invoice being sent, so it should be issued in accordance with a previously agreed schedule or discussed with the client before submission.

It is possible to submit a pro forma invoice to the client, in effect an advice note that is supplanted by a VAT invoice following payment. This delays the payment of VAT by the practice, but is not commonly agreed to by clients and can delay payment to the architect.

The invoice should clearly set out what it relates to, how much has been paid previously and what is being invoiced at this time, and the VAT payment. Invoices must show the practice's VAT number, assuming it is registered for VAT. Either the invoice itself or the covering letter should confirm any preferred payment methods and the timetable for settlement.

The key issues relating to the submission of invoices are to:

- issue promptly when they are due;

7

- ensure they are expected;
- understand the client's approval/payment process;
- ensure clarity/avoid queries.

> It is critical to agree a cash flow to an agreed programme at the outset of the project and submit invoices punctiliously. You should then send reminders for accounts that have not been settled on time.

7.4.3 Key financial performance indicators

It is recommended that practices maintain records of financial performance and use these to measure improvement/variation over time. Included in these might be:

- Income by fee earner, partner/director and/or others, but be aware of differing roles and agree targets to monitor against that correspond to roles.
- Turnover by group – client, location, sector, project/procurement type, etc. This information can be of great help in preparing future fee proposals.
- Profit as percentage of turnover.
- Profit by fee earner.
- Profit by group – client, location, sector, project/procurement type, etc.
- Average creditor and debtor days.

In order to effectively monitor many of the above, it is necessary to have implemented a project-based costing system.

All of the above will help with long-term business planning (see Chapter 5) – what type of work is most financially beneficial to the practice, which clients does it want to do work for, where is the best location in financial terms, etc. Having said this, it is important to stress that decisions about what projects to seek should not be driven solely by these principally financial considerations – but they should be given an appropriate amount of weight when making plans/decisions.

RIBA Chartered Practices participate free of charge in the RIBA Business Benchmarking Service. This annual survey is the definitive benchmarking database for the UK architects' profession. It provides an opportunity to assess business performance against recommended benchmarks devised by Colander. The analysis covers business development, management systems and HR issues, as well as key financial performance indicators. In addition to comparing data with recommended Colander benchmarks, practices are able to make comparisons with average data for practices of similar size and in the same region. The financial analysis includes a practice efficiency measure, based on a target fee income calculated from the number of fee earners, targeted chargeable hours and practice charge-out rates. For further details of the RIBA Business Benchmarking Service email benchmarking@inst.riba.org.

7.4.4   Financial budgeting/reporting by project

Budgeting and monitoring/reviewing budgets is at the core of running a financially effective practice. The setting of a resource profile for the various stages of a project as early as possible following appointment and the development of a financial model utilising this are fundamental. Such a projection can then be used as the basis of a fee proposal, by applying the practice's standard cost/charge-out hourly/daily rates. Testing against previous experience and percentage of construction costs is highly recommended before settling on a proposal.

Individual profit percentages can be applied to standard cost rates on different projects, enabling a fine level of control by the practice.

It is important to involve the project team in this process and achieve their 'buy-in' to the projected resource profile and fee quotation.

A simple process for preparing a project resourcing/financial projection might be:

- The practice allocates all staff to different grades – partner/director, associate director, senior architect/technician, architect/technician, etc. – and ascertains the ratio of average salaries of each grade to the others.
- The practice sets hourly cost rates, either by individual or by 'grade' of staff (see Section 9.2.3 for an illustration of a method of calculating hourly rates).
- The team leader projects the numbers of staff needed at each stage of the project by grade and the number of hours/weeks they need to spend at each stage, and makes an allowance for necessary expenses and sub-consultants' fees (see Section 9.2.3 for an illustration of a method of calculating resource requirements at different work stages on a project).
- The partner/director uses this as the basis of fee proposal by taking the cost rate calculation and applying a profit percentage to the cost.
- The fee proposal should set out expenses and/or external sub-consultants included and ensure appropriate fee allowances are included. If the architect is appointing sub-consultants he or she will need to agree compatible cash flow arrangements with them via their appointment documentation.
- Once agreed this becomes the project budget in terms of both time and money and should be monitored against actual performance over time.

It is important to assess that the progress made on the project matches that which was budgeted.

7.4.5 Resource allocation and budgeting

Predicted project resource needs can be accumulated into a practice-wide resource needs forecast, which will help the practice plan future workload and resource requirements.

It needs to be borne in mind that all staff will engage in 'non-productive' time – administration, marketing, training, holiday, etc. – and an appropriate allowance should be made for this.

The practice also needs to be aware of those who are resourced (for example) only 50% of their time against a project. They need to be allocated something productive to do for the remaining 50% of their time.

7.4.6 Cash collection

Cash collection is fundamental to the success of all businesses. A business can appear hugely profitable on paper but if it cannot collect the cash it is owed it can rapidly head towards receivership. Late payment, particularly where it has not previously been a feature of a particular client's behaviour, can indicate that the client is experiencing financial difficulties.

Practices should agree standard payment terms with their clients during the appointment negotiation process. These terms, while agreed to by the client, are sometimes not adhered to in reality, and the practice needs to consider what to do when this situation occurs. The partners/directors should institute a rigorous process to ensure prompt collection of what it is owed, which might run along the lines of:

- Issue the invoice.
- An agreed number of days later check that it has been received and whether there are any further requirements before it is paid (signing off by project managers, etc.). Also check likely payment date and payment method – automatic bank transfer (BACS) is the quickest and most reliable.
- Issue a statement of outstanding account(s) a number of days before the invoice is due. The practice should decide the appropriate timing for this.
- If the invoice is not paid by the due date an agreed member of the practice telephones the client's organisation to get an update on why it has not been paid and when it is likely to be. It is generally recommended that, in larger practices, the partner/director leaves the initial chasing to his financial team in order to maintain a good personal relationship with the client for as long as possible.

- Agree a series of contacts to be made at certain intervals and who will make them. If the financial team is having no success, the partner/director will need to become involved in the chasing process personally.
- Send a letter stating that legal proceedings will be instituted if payment is not made within seven days.
- Institute legal proceedings. Architects should note that their professional indemnity insurers sometimes require prior notice of the intention to commence legal proceedings for fee recovery, as it can produce a counter-claim by the client for non-performance. Some professional indemnity policies may cover the practice for costs associated with fees recovery.

Practices need to be aware that most forms of appointment give them the right to charge interest on late payments, and should seek to apply this in appropriate circumstances. Practices may consider employing debt collection agencies to chase outstanding debts.

It is important that the partners/directors receive an 'aged debtor report' from their accounts team on a regular basis, so they can discuss and agree how to chase overdue accounts. This information will also help in agreeing which clients to accept future commissions from.

7.5   Conclusion

It is worth repeating the observation that, while making money is frequently not the reason that architects go into practice, poor financial control is often the reason they go out of business. Profit is essential as it ensures the practice will continue to exist and grow in the future, and sound financial management, particularly in respect to collection of cash due, is of fundamental importance.

It is also extremely important to take care about who the practice works for – a client who is difficult to work with, who wants to pay low (or no) fees and who is difficult to part from their cash for work properly undertaken may well be a client not worth having, no matter how good the design opportunity is.

References and further reading

Phillips, R., *Good Practice Guide: Fee Management* (London: RIBA Publishing, 2012).

Pinder-Ayres, B., *Good Practice Guide: Painless Financial Management* (London: RIBA Publishing, 2008).

RIBA, *A Client's Guide to Engaging an Architect* (May 2013 revision) (London: RIBA Publishing, 2013).

Office management

> **THIS CHAPTER:**
>
> - examines various aspects of running an office, from choice of premises to health and safety regulations;
> - discusses how to manage premises efficiently and sustainably;
> - gives information about the various types of insurance available.

8.1 Introduction

The premises a business operates from is a visible and tangible representation to clients and employees of what the business is and what it stands for. It can be used as a showcase for the work of the practice and be an example to potential clients of the care and attention to detail given.

Many aspects of running an office are covered by statutory requirements and the major ones are outlined in this chapter. Of course, the smooth running of any office does not simply rely on the operation of the physical facilities, but also on good communication and consistent processes. More information on these latter aspects can be found in Sections 6.3.7 and 10.2.

It is important to run your office in a sustainable way and advice on this is given in Section 8.2.1.

8.2 The office premises

The choice of office is critical to the running of the business, and a number of factors should be considered before signing a lease or buying a property (see Section 8.2.2 for detailed information):

- Location

  - Access for staff and clients
  - Proximity to support services, e.g. printers

- Layout

  - Reception
  - Presentation/exhibition/meeting space
  - Studio space
  - IT

- ◦ Administration, filing and archives
- ◦ Catering facilities
- ◦ Storage
- ◦ Opportunities for business growth

- Running costs
- Maintenance requirements.

For many smaller practices, serviced accommodation can be a good option because facilities such as reception and printing will be provided under the tenancy agreement.

8.2.1   The 'green' office

It is increasingly important to be able to demonstrate that the office a business works from has a minimum impact on the environment and that the business and its operations are ethical. Issues such as travel, water consumption, energy usage and recycling need to be addressed and office policies developed to establish benchmarks of achievement, monitoring of performance and environmental targets.

The following organisations and publications provide information and guidance on environmental performance, such as the measurement of carbon footprints:

- British Standards Institution (www.bsigroup.com). *Guide to PAS 2050:2011 – How to carbon footprint your products, identify hotspots and reduce emissions in your supply chain.*
- Carbon Trust (www.carbontrust.co.uk). *The carbon emissions generated in all that we consume* (CTC603).

BS 8555 and BS EN ISO 14001 can be used to demonstrate a commitment to the reduction of the environmental impact of a practice's own office and operations (see Sections 10.5.1 and 10.5.2). An environmental management policy is a requirement of RIBA Chartered Practice status (see Section 2.9.2).

8

Ten steps to building a sustainable practice

Step 1: Commit to Leadership

The first step is for a practice to support the sustainable development ethos, and commit to leadership from the most senior level downwards to promote a healthy balance between people, planet and profit.

Benefits

Commitment from the top helps generate:

- enthusiasm from all members of a practice, including those at the start of their careers
- confidence to promote a sustainable approach to clients, collaborators, suppliers and the general public through professional advice on sustainability issues
- expertise in showing how sustainability issues can be integrated into the construction process.

Step 2: Benchmark practice impacts

Before starting to measure the impact of a building project at any stage, it is just as important to understand the direct impacts a practice makes on the environment and on people's lives.

A business can benchmark its performance using a carbon footprinting measurement of business impacts. There is more on how to do this on the DECC archive website.

http://webarchive.nationalarchives.gov.uk/20121217150421/http://www.decc.gov.uk/en/content/cms/tackling/saving_energy/individual/calculator/calculator.aspx

In terms of its social and economic impacts, a practice could consider measuring and benchmarking staff satisfaction through, for example, surveys, annual reviews and measurement of staff turnover rates.

The annual RIBA Business Benchmarking Survey provides vital business knowledge about how a practice compares to others across a broad spectrum of criteria, allowing a practice to identify areas of strength, weakness and opportunity.

Some practices may opt for an environmental accreditation such as ISO 14001 – the latter can be linked to ISO 9001 – but even the smallest practices can measure their impacts year on year and aim for improvements using a self-help tool such as the BRE Managing Sustainable Communities (MaSC) benchmarking tool.

http://projects.bre.co.uk/masc/index.html

RIBA Chartered Practices are required to have an Environmental Management Policy that includes ISO 14001.

ISO 9001:

www.iso.org

ISO 14001:

www.iso.org

Benefits

Benchmarking a range of impacts could also provide a useful example of how sustainability:

- is an integral part of the way that day-to-day business is carried out
- can be integrated in forward planning.

Benchmarking environmental, social and economic impacts, such as energy use in buildings and the impact of CO_2 on travel can become a starting point for:

- setting targets for strategy and improvements
- communicating the impacts of staff behaviours in terms of the real consequences.

Step 3: Demonstrate practice performance

In order to be able to communicate and promote the importance of sustainability in projects to clients and to a wider audience, it is important that a practice understands how its projects contribute to the wider knowledge bank.

It is therefore useful to benchmark projects using current methodologies. This can be done in-house even when the projects themselves are not subject to specific scoring systems such as BREEAM, the Code for Sustainable Homes or LEED.

Beyond the design stage, some benchmarking systems consider actual performance in use and the real impacts on people and the environment.

In an architectural practice, knowledge-sharing can become an issue for project competence and succession planning. Regular 'lessons learnt' sessions can be carried out on project completion, and comparable data (including sustainability targets and outcomes) can be stored in an accessible digital location as part of a Knowledge Management system.

Soft Landings procedures

Where possible, Soft Landings procedures should be promoted to clients and adopted through the project process to measure a building's performance in use and to share data.

www.bsria.co.uk/services/design/soft-landings

Benefits

- Even where clients prefer to keep performance data private, it should be possible for the architect to benefit from the knowledge and understanding that real data can provide, e.g. by promoting the provision of anonymised data to a knowledge-sharing site such as Carbon Buzz.
- A post-occupancy evaluation is invaluable for feedback on the successes and failures of a project including social and environmental impacts.
- Actual energy data as used in a Display Energy Certificate (DEC) can be compared with benchmark data to improve the energy efficiency of a building.

Step 4: Build on existing resources

All practices maintain some kind of Knowledge Management system, and store reference material and project-specific data irrespective of whether they are ISO 9001 or ISO 14001 accredited. Existing staff members may have experience of applying sustainability principles to projects or meeting certain benchmarks and standards – it is worth carrying out an audit of skills, experience and enthusiasm in the existing personnel.

Practices may find they have existing staff who already have the expertise or who are willing to upskill for a relatively small capital outlay. The benefit of in-house capability is in terms of the 'ownership' when carrying out options appraisals in design development.

Benefits

It is a worthwhile exercise to introduce sustainability topics into practice discussions and personal reviews. This will:

- raise awareness of sustainability issues; and
- encourage those designers who are interested in specialising or developing their knowledge of sustainability.

Step 5: Upskill with CPD

To deliver truly sustainable building projects it is important for an architect to have a good working knowledge of all the sustainability issues.

Knowledge development is important for all practices and requires CPD about sustainability issues, together with a commitment to share that knowledge with partners where possible. For example:

- through engagement with research and cross-industry programmes such as CarbonBuzz, the Technology Strategy Board, or Zero Carbon Hub
- sharing the lessons learned
- committing, where possible, to publish feedback on performance in use, Soft Landings and post-occupancy evaluation.

Benefits

Collaborating with other team members and specialists is a vital part of:

- synthesising social, economic and environmental demands
- gaining knowledge of specialist areas on a project-by-project basis.

Staff training and CPD can be:

- tailored to specific project needs
- tailored to personal development targets
- regarded as a general upskilling objective when decisions regarding business planning or software acquisition are made.

Step 6: Develop collaborative project methodologies

Practices differ in their project process methodologies. Some have a series of protocols and rules attached to each stage of the work flow and clients can be predisposed to use specific benchmark standards and procurement methods. These will influence the project process, creating different 'ownership' of sustainable tasks and outcomes. In May 2011 the Government Construction Strategy outlined the processes needed 'to ensure the Government consistently gets a good deal and the country gets the social and economic infrastructure it needs for the long-term.'

8

Building Information Modelling (BIM)

The Government's strategy requires fully collaborative 3D Building Information Modelling on public projects by 2016. Most importantly this approach affects the flow of data and resources of a project, particularly at the early stages because of the requirement for the collaboration of project team members around a single integrated design model. There is more information and background about BIM in the NBS National BIM Report 2012 at and the Strategy Paper for the Government Construction Client Group from the BIM Industry Working Group – March 2011.

National BIM Library

The National BIM Library opened in March 2012. It is a free resource offering construction-industry professionals the facility to locate and download a wide selection of generic BIM objects for a comprehensive range of systems.

www.nationalbimlibrary.com

Benefits

The use of BIM can enable:

- collaborative working among project teams to achieve sustainable outcomes
- monitoring of design environmental targets and production of early visualisations for user and planning consultations
- measurements of whole-life costs and Life Cycle Analysis including embodied energy calculations
- facilities management teams to measure actual performance and record future changes and upgrades.

Step 7: Consider the uses of software

It is becoming increasingly possible to integrate CAD and BIM software with environmental design tools. Using open data formats, many software platforms are beginning to talk to each other more effectively. This guide does not go into the various software packages in any detail. It is strongly recommended that practices research for their own specific needs.

Energy modelling and compliance tools

Energy modelling and compliance are becoming increasingly important considerations of design development in new build and refurbishment projects with low-energy targets.

As the Government Construction Strategy develops, so do software opportunities that enable it and many of these software platforms can be integrated around a BIM model. Early specification of building elements can enable construction production information data to be used with software applications for building environmental modelling and simulation.

The Construction Project Information Committee is responsible for providing best practice guidance on the content, form and preparation of construction production information.

www.cpic.org.uk

The Passivhaus Standard

The Passivhaus Standard has been successfully adopted in up to 30,000 buildings across Europe and equates to a 'near zero' heating standard where annual space heating demand does not exceed 15 kWh/m^2 per annum.

Passivhaus certification requires an accreditation of design and build/commissioning quality, and a maximum Primary Energy Demand from all energy uses for new buildings of not more than 120 kWh/m^2 per annum.

Design performance against the Passivhaus Standard is assessed using Passivhaus Planning Package (PHPP) software which is a user-friendly Excel-based calculation of projected energy performance.

www.passivhaus.org.uk

Benefits

Knowledge and understanding of environmental analysis software can be empowering in order to carry out:

- preliminary energy modelling to inform design options and appraisals
- early specification for cost planning
- dialogue with engineers.

Step 8: Adopt a Knowledge Management framework

Knowledge Management systems may already include a practice's existing projects and other case studies. To increase sustainability awareness it might be helpful to cluster construction knowledge around sustainability themes, perhaps based on BREEAM topics or similar, subject to practice needs.

Benefits

Knowledge systems can be extended to include data, when available, on:

- energy and other benchmarks
- performance of projects in use
- project feedback data
- lessons learned workshops.

Step 9: Follow the RIBA Plan of Work 2013

The impact of climate change and broader environmental concerns has started to have a major impact on design and construction practice. Recognising this move towards more sustainable construction, led by innovative clients, designers and construction teams, the RIBA has incorporated sustainability into the RIBA Plan of Work 2013 and the *RIBA Job Book* (2013), based on the earlier 'Green Overlay'.

For all the variations of project methodologies, it is important for the architect to understand who holds the responsibility for the actions required to deliver sustainable outcomes, including the need for design development to be integrated with input from other specialists.

The RIBA Plan of Work 2013, *RIBA Job Book* (2013) and *Small Projects Handbook* (2014) give useful summaries of tasks and checkpoints to better embed sustainability into the appraisal, briefing, design and construction process of an individual project.

They are invaluable tools for architects and construction professionals to engage clients in conversation about truly sustainable design which aspires to go beyond the regulatory compliance of the standard service and product.

www.ribaplanofwork.com

www.ribabookshops.com/sph

Benefits

The RIBA Plan of Work 2013 is the most widely used framework for building design and construction. It provides a simple set of sustainability guidelines for each work stage with which to engage clients in sustainable design.

Step 10: Monitor sustainable projects

Embedding a sustainable design approach into the business process also helps in-house monitoring of integrated design thinking and the delivery of specific sustainability targets throughout the project process.

Using a simple Knowledge Management structure, for example, one that is based on the BRE GreenPrint framework (described in Step 8), a sustainable design process map can be developed in line with any relevant BREEAM, Code for Sustainable Homes or LEED targets, and can easily be used as a prompt at in-house technical and design review sessions.

Topic headings can be developed into detailed criteria as appropriate such as:

- milestones
- performance targets
- contract conditions.

A practice could develop a simple customised knowledge and sustainability mapping process which aligns to specific project targets while remaining unique to each practice's own strengths and aspirations.

Life Cycle Assessment: operational and embodied carbon

Whole Life Carbon Assessment draws together operational energy and embodied carbon calculation in line with CEN (the European Committee for Standardization) TC350 methodology. In this way comparisons can be made between:

- capital costs and costs in use
- embodied and operational energy.

http://www.cen.eu/cen/Sectors/Sectors/Construction/EPB/Pages/CEN_TC350.aspx

As operational energy usage in buildings is reducing, embodied energy is playing an increasingly greater part in a building's energy consumption over its lifetime. Therefore an architect's involvement in specification, detailing and product selection has an even greater significance in the effort to keep energy usage down.

8

Benefits

In a Life Cycle Assessment the implications of key factors can all be measured in CO_2 terms as well as financial ones, including:

- materials specification and manufacturing
- transport delivery to site
- building construction
- in-use operation and maintenance.

Design to reduce embodied as well as operational energy could become an important role for the architect once the CEN TC350 methodology evolves into sustainability standards, testing procedures and regulatory requirements:

- arguably costs very little
- gives structure to regular design and technical review
- can work for small as well as large practice.

Further information

Government bodies

Department of Energy and Climate Change
www.gov.uk/government/organisations/department-of-energy-climate-change

Department for the Environment, Food and Rural Affairs
www.gov.uk/government/organisations/department-for-environment-food-rural-affairs

Also includes the 2005 Sustainability Strategy at:
http://webarchive.nationalarchives.gov.uk/20130402151656/http://archive.defra.gov.uk/sustainable/government/%20

Environment Agency website has a section on SuDS research, techniques and policy at:
http://webarchive.nationalarchives.gov.uk/20140328084622/http:/www.environment-agency.gov.uk/business/sectors/136252.aspx

Department for Communities and Local Government
www.gov.uk/government/organisations/department-for-communities-and-local-government#about-us

Legislation, regulations and policy initiatives

National BIM Library
www.nationalbimlibrary.com

CarbonBuzz
www.carbonbuzz.org

Check your carbon footprint
http://webarchive.nationalarchives.gov.uk/20121217150421/http://
www.decc.gov.uk/en/content/cms/tackling/saving_energy/
individual/calculator/calculator.aspx

Feed-in Tariff (FIT)
www.gov.uk/feed-in-tariffs

Green Deal
www.gov.uk/green-deal-energy-saving-measures

National Planning Policy Framework
www.gov.uk/government/uploads/system/uploads/attachment_
data/file/6077/2116950.pdf

Renewable Heat Incentive
www.gov.uk/government/policies/increasing-the-use-of-low-carbon-
technologies/supporting-pages/renewable-heat-incentive-rhi

Soft Landings
www.bsria.co.uk/services/design/soft-landings

European standards

CEN
www.cen.eu/cen/pages/default.aspx

Energy Performance in Buildings Directive
www.gov.uk/government/publications/improving-the-energy-
efficiency-of-our-buildings

Sustainability benchmarking schemes in UK Code for Sustainable Homes
www.gov.uk/government/publications/2010-to-2015-government-
policy-energy-efficiency-in-buildings/2010-to-2015-government-
policy-energy-efficiency-in-buildings#appendix-7-code-for-
sustainable-homes

BREEAM
www.breeam.org

Other organisations

BRE – Building Research Establishment
www.bre.co.uk

Royal Institution of Chartered Surveyors
www.rics.org

Technology Strategy Board
www.gov.uk/government/organisations/innovate-uk

UK Green Buildings Council
www.ukgbc.org

Source: Sullivan, L., *The RIBA Guide to Sustainability in Practice* (London: RIBA, 2012)

8.2.2 Premises

After salaries, premises are usually the most significant outlay in any organisation. The adequacy and suitability of premises should therefore be a policy matter which is kept under regular review.

Organisations constantly change and develop, and so there may be a need to increase accommodation or use space more efficiently. Furniture and equipment rapidly become obsolete, and the effectiveness of environmental control may need improving. It is recommended that one person in the practice is made responsible for the review and management of all matters relating to premises.

Suitability

A number of inter-related factors need to be considered when evaluating the suitability of premises:

- The size of the practice (e.g. the number of permanent and temporary staff both at present and in the foreseeable future); whether the office is the headquarters or a branch office; whether the office is a self-contained unit, multi-disciplinary or part of a consortium; whether IT-related work arrangements such as outsourcing, hot-desking or telecommuting should be catered for; whether all work stations are planned to be occupied all the time (see Section 12.5.3).

- The form and nature of the practice (e.g. sole principal, partnership, company or collaborative), the range of activities and equipment to be accommodated, and the support spaces likely to be needed.
- The organisation and structure of the practice (e.g. hierarchical, functional or egalitarian). This might influence the space planning and standards to be followed; it might determine the appropriate ratio of open plan to cellular layout.
- 'Fit' and 'feel good' factors. The preferred shape of the premises relative to the optimum space requirements of the practice; the ratio of dead or unusable space to usable area (at least 85% of the available area should be usable); whether a layout will be compromised by the position of structural members, existing services and other elements; and whether there is likely to be flexibility for subdivision of areas with minimal reorganisation.
- The amount of adjustment needed to bring premises into line with modern standards and current legislative requirements, e.g. the Workplace (Health Safety and Welfare) Regulations 1992 and the Disability Discrimination Act 2005. This will particularly apply to circulation routes, minimum room dimensions, planning of workstations, workers' access to windows (for opening and safe cleaning), ventilation of washing and sanitary conveniences, lighting, etc. It may be that an access audit will need to be carried out to establish whether major modifications are needed.

Location

Modern working methods and communications in the electronic age of the wireless-enabled laptop and smart phones make the location of the office less critical in one sense. Working from home might be a satisfactory initial or permanent arrangement given efficient electronic backup and accessibility, but it requires a disciplined attitude and a methodical approach to ensure that all business is conducted in an environment free from domestic interruption. This is more likely where the office can be located in a dedicated area (e.g. converted outbuildings or a purpose-built studio) with a separate entrance for visitors and all necessary support services separate and self-contained.

Otherwise the location of a practice should be a prime consideration, not only in terms of image and identity but also for the sake of accessibility and convenience for staff and visitors. Ideally, there should be good public transport links with shops, restaurants and other amenities close at hand.

Where a suite of offices is located within a building, it is important for access to be direct and obvious, and the entrance well signed with easy access for delivery services and visitors. Any staircase or lift to the practice's floor should enhance the approach and not be perceived as a barrier. The front door – the point where the design philosophy of the practice becomes clear – should open to the main point of contact, i.e. the reception area and desk. First impressions are all-important.

Requirements

Any schedule of office accommodation will typically include requirements for cellular offices, workstation layouts, conference and interview areas, etc. Other matters for consideration might be:

- Library, information and research area. Even with electronic systems and the internet, some hard copy is still needed.
- Archive arrangements, whether completely or partly in-house. These should be conveniently placed to allow for the orderly deposit and retrieval of key material. Access might be needed for up to 20 years, and lawyers prefer original documents (see Section 10.12).
- Appropriate amenity areas for staff, e.g. hot and cold drinks machines, kitchen facilities, rest and first aid area, changing rooms and showers, parking for cars, motorcycles and cycles.
- Adequate storage for equipment, including survey and site visit equipment, materials samples, office supplies and stationery, etc.

Requirements relating to premises which arise from legislation include the following:

Occupiers Liability Act

The title of this Act refers to 'the state of the property or to things done or omitted to be done there', and Section 2 requires that the premises be 'reasonably safe'. This is a provision that could apply to both landlords and their tenants.

The Regulatory Reform (Fire Safety) Order 2005 (England and Wales)

Since this replaced the 1971 Fire Precautions Act, the onus is on individuals to carry out risk assessments on their offices and submit them to their local fire authority. Guidance is available in the form of government-published documents, each pertaining specifically to a particular type of premises. More information on the fire risk assessment is set out below.

The Order lays out the foundation of the risk assessment by saying that the employer must take into account the following for the safety of their employees:

- means of detection and giving warning in case of fire;
- the provision of means of escape;
- means of fighting fire;
- the training of staff in fire safety.

It also tells employers how they must assess these items in order to protect their employees:

- Carry out a fire risk assessment of the workplace by a responsible person.
- Identify the significant findings of the risk assessment and the details of anyone who might be at risk in case of fire. Under the Management of Health and Safety Regulations, these must be recorded if more than five persons are employed.
- Provide and maintain such fire precautions as are necessary to safeguard those who use the workplace.
- Provide information, instruction and training to employees about the fire precautions in the workplace.

In the event of a fire, proof that adequate precautions were taken comes primarily from the risk assessment/file of evidence/log book. Note, however, that the proprietor of the premises is still deemed the overall 'responsible person'.

The fire risk assessment

This is a logical, incremental process of examining and considering the premises. Each area should be analysed progressively using different methods. For example, a physical walkthrough of the area, visually identifying obvious risks, is a good way to start. Then repeat the exercise with the concept in mind that there is an emergency and you want to make your way out. Identify risks as you again walk through with a view to escaping. Finally perhaps, consider walking through again, this time assuming there are additional obstacles to your escape such as inadequate lighting. Is there sufficient emergency lighting in place?

An immediately obvious concern with this assessment approach is the appointment of inexperienced individuals to assess fire safety. With the above example it may not occur to an untrained person that low-level lighting solutions may be required in emergencies. As such it is imperative that appointed persons are competent. Training, literature and guidance are available from a variety of organisations to aid understanding and compliance (for example www.gov.uk/government/collections/fire-safety-guidance).

Another option is to contract a fire safety consultant to perform the risk assessment, who will visit the premises and conduct a risk assessment in accordance with the appropriate guidelines. They should then produce a report outlining the identified risks and give recommendations for improvement.

All advice should be taken under caution – introduction of the Regulatory Reform (Fire Safety) Order has led to a remarkable increase in companies offering risk assessment services, ranging from individuals with no industry experience yet an impressive training history to people with a wealth of industry experience but no formal training (such as retired fire officers). As with training, in the event of an incident where lives are lost any advice or assessments carried out by a third party will be under scrutiny to determine whether they were a reputable service with adequate qualifications. But, ultimately, only the responsible person is culpable for any breaches in compliance with the order, and training and self-training is advisable in all instances.

The Equality Act 2010

This Act seeks to end discrimination, and to promote the civil rights of people in all areas of life, but there are specific sections relating to employment and the workplace.

An employer has a duty to make 'reasonable adjustments' to ensure that disabled employees are not disadvantaged by employment arrangements, or by any physical feature of the workplace.

Examples of the sort of adjustments that might need to be addressed include:

- allocating some of a person's work to someone else;
- transferring a person to another post or another place of work;
- making adjustments to the buildings where a person works;
- being flexible about a person's hours – allowing them to have different core working hours, and to be away from the office for assessment, treatment or rehabilitation;
- providing training or retraining if a person cannot do their job;
- providing modified equipment;
- making instructions and manuals more accessible;
- providing a reader or interpreter.

Employers and employees should engage in a dialogue to ensure that any adjustments are suitable. In certain circumstances professional opinion should be sought from someone with expertise in providing work-related help for disabled people, such as an occupational health adviser.

Access to Work, a programme run by Jobcentre Plus (www.gov.uk/access-to-work/overview) can give employers advice on appropriate adjustments, and possibly some financial help towards the cost of the adjustments.

Health and safety regulations

The relevant legislation on health and safety at work is sometimes referred to as the 'Six Pack':

- Management of Health and Safety at Work Regulations 1999
- Provision and Use of Work Equipment Regulations 1998
- Manual Handling Operations Regulations 1992
- Workplace (Health, Safety and Welfare) Regulations 1992
- Personal Protective Equipment at Work Regulations 1992
- Health and Safety (Display Screen Equipment) Regulations 1992.

The Workplace (Health, Safety and Welfare) Regulations 1992 deal with space allocation, environmental conditions, circulation and sanitary provisions. Note in particular:

- Reg 6. Suitable and effective ventilation, natural or mechanical.
- Reg 7. Reasonable temperature during working hours, normally at least 16°C.
- Reg 8. Suitable and sufficient lighting, natural or artificial. Also refers to fittings, switches, etc.
- Reg 10. Sufficient floor area, height and free space at workstations. Allow
- volume of at least 11 cubic metres per person.
- Reg 15. Position and operation of opening windows and roof lights, so as not to endanger occupants.
- Reg 17. Organisation of traffic routes, both for people on foot and those travelling in vehicles.
- Reg 20. Number of sanitary conveniences, accessibility, lighting and ventilation.
- Reg 21. Number and suitability of washing facilities.
- Reg 22. Provision of 'wholesome' drinking water.
- Reg 25. Suitable rest facilities, including, where relevant, suitable places to eat meals.

Requirements relating to furniture and fittings arise from the Health and Safety (Display Screen Equipment) Regulations 1992. These concern the use and position of VDU screens and minimum requirements (including environmental) for workstations.

8

> **Fixtures and fittings** are usually a major item of office expenditure. Cost can be set against capital tax allowances; refer to the HMRC advice at http://webarchive.nationalarchives.gov.uk/20140109143644/http://www.hmrc.gov.uk/tiin/tiin688.htm and www.gov.uk/capital-gains-tax-businesses. As with all tax or revenue matters, it is essential to check the current situation with the firm's accountants.

If consideration is being given to taking on a lease on existing premises, requirements should include ensuring that accurate records and plans of the area are available and that there is evidence (e.g. copies of inspection reports) that:

- passenger lifts have been properly maintained at regular intervals;
- electrical equipment and installations have been properly maintained, comply with legislation, and have sufficient capacity for intended loads;
- water systems and water heating installations have been properly maintained.

In addition, it would be advisable to check whether a current fire certificate is held (if relevant), and whether a health and safety file is available.

Acquiring premises

The acquisition of premises will have a considerable impact on practice finances. The main considerations are the type of tenure and any associated terms of availability or restrictions on the use of the building; the cost of acquisition; the condition of the building and the extent of liability for its maintenance and repair; and costs in use. The basis for rating buildings used for business purposes varies according to the local authority involved. The amount to be paid may be considerable, and it is wise to discover at the outset what it is likely to be.

Whatever method of acquisition is considered, legal and financial advice should always be sought.

Leasing

The most common method of acquiring premises is to lease them for a short, medium or long term. Normally, leasing payments are met out of income, but some capital outlay may be needed if a premium is required or if fixtures and fittings have to be purchased or provided. These costs can sometimes be recovered upon relinquishing the tenancy. There may also be opportunities to sub-let at a profitable rent or to assign a lease for a lump sum consideration. The negotiation to let may involve agreement on an initial rent-free period.

It is common for landlords to seek confirmation of a practice's financial stability, and of its ability to pay the rent. This can be by submission of audited accounts, or by the provision of a rent deposit, which will be repayable at an agreed point during the lease, or on its termination.

Occupiers of business premises are given some protection in law, but a landlord does have the right under certain circumstances to obtain repossession. Leases should be carefully drafted, and a solicitor's advice should always be sought.

Restrictions on the use of premises are often introduced in a lease. These should be looked at carefully in the light of future development, because even a change of legal persona or a consortium could be prohibited. Such restrictions could make it difficult to dispose of the lease in mid-term.

Practices are from time to time subject to growth or shrinkage at short notice, and need to be aware of the conditions under which a lease may be disposed of before its term, which are likely to be limited by the lease itself. The longer the lease, the more important it is to have the ability to dispose of it with reasonable freedom. The principal ways in which this may be done, some or all of which may be permitted, are as follows:

- **Assignment**, i.e. getting another party to take over the unexpired portion of the lease. It may be possible to take a premium. The right to assign may be subject to certain restrictions and may be prohibited entirely. It is certainly likely to be difficult to find a taker for a leasehold interest with less than five years to run.
- **Sub-letting**, i.e. retaining an interest in the lease but finding a tenant to occupy all or part of the premises and pay a rent. The holder of the lease is still responsible to the landlord. Sub-letting may be specifically prohibited or may be subject to restrictions. In any event, the landlord's consent will usually be required.
- **Break clauses**. Certain leases permit one or both parties to determine the lease at certain fixed points during the term. The effect of this is that the lease, instead of running for its full period, ends at the earlier date. It is important to be aware whether the landlord has this right. If so, it is useful to regard the lease as being for the shorter term with the possibility of extension.

Restrictions on hours of access may be introduced in the lease, particularly where circulation includes common areas where the one building is divided between several lessees.

8

Leases of more than six years usually have a rent review clause, under which rent is to be renegotiated at certain points. New rents are usually adjusted in line with market values, but in some leases the chance of a downward shift is specifically excluded.

Leases should state clearly and precisely the obligations on the lessee concerning repair, maintenance and insurance. Full repairing terms in a lease should be regarded with caution, and never entered into without an agreed schedule of condition. It is common for the tenant to be required to return the property to its original condition on termination of the lease, and the practice should budget a suitable sum of money for rectification of dilapidations.

It is common for leases to require the tenant to undertake repairs and redecoration, known as 'dilapidations', prior to the expiry of the lease. The practice should make sure it is aware of its obligations in this regard, and that it has planned and provided for them.

Buying or building

Instead of renting or leasing, premises can be bought. If capital is available, the property can be purchased outright; alternatively, funds may be borrowed. However, the practice needs to think carefully before tying up capital in such a way, as buildings are not necessarily a good investment and professional advice should always be sought.

Building brings the obvious attraction of accommodation customised to the needs of a practice. It might also be possible to secure income by letting part of the premises, perhaps to another construction professional.

Sale and lease-back

Having purchased or built new accommodation, the asset may then be sold subject to the granting back of a lease. This permits the release of invested capital and may also offer a capital gain. The vendor may try to incorporate terms in the lease favourable to themselves; if so, the sale price may have to be lowered.

Sale and lease-back is sometimes attempted purely for an initial profit, but it may also be a useful method of raising capital.

8.3   Managing the premises

Efficient management of the premises can make an important contribution to the economic as well as the smooth day-to-day operation of a practice, and it should be the responsibility of a nominated person in the practice

– it is essential for someone to have an overview of the operation of the building as a whole.

The operating cost of the premises is the total cost of running and maintaining both fabric and services. The key cost elements are:

- energy and water consumption
- security
- cleaning
- insurance
- maintenance and repair
- waste collection and recycling.

Certain offices may attract heavy service charges, which will add significantly to running costs. With these in mind, attention should be paid to each of the above elements.

8.3.1   Energy and water consumption

These should be monitored. Devices can be introduced to reduce wasteful consumption of energy and water, and staff should be informed of the levels appropriate to particular tasks and circumstances and be encouraged to observe them. Demands on installations change over time, and obsolete or worn fittings can often reduce efficient consumption. It is sensible to establish a policy for regular checking and replacement.

8.3.2   Security

The cost of providing and maintaining a special security system, which might be a priority in some urban areas, will be a significant one-off cost commitment and special financial provision should be made for it. It is advisable to seek advice on security from a specialist firm, or from the local police. Insurers may ask for information about the arrangements made.

Staff must be clear about procedures for locking up at the end of the day, for setting alarms and systems, and for entering the premises outside normal working hours. It is important to make staff security-conscious; many companies have a signing-in book and require all visitors to provide identification and wear a lapel badge.

As well as the building and access to it, various items on the office premises need to be kept secure, including:

- equipment
- personal belongings

- project drawings and documentation, some of which may be commercially sensitive
- accounting and personnel records.

Computer equipment is likely to be particularly at risk, and items should always be security marked. Insurers may impose special security requirements on practices for high-value items.

8.3.3 Cleaning

Responsibility for cleaning arrangements can be a testing task for the person responsible, and reliable operatives are essential. The alternatives are to contract a professional cleaning service, which can be costly, or rely on a more informal service. The essential consideration is the trustworthiness of the personnel involved, because the practice must be sure that people coming into the premises outside normal working hours are not a security risk.

8.3.4 Insurance

Adequate insurance cover against risks is essential, and the advice of an insurance broker should be sought. The practice's policies should be scheduled and reviewed regularly to make sure that they remain relevant and adequate, that the level of cover is sufficient, and that any requirements by insurers for security procedures and fireproof storage are being met.

8.3.5 Programmed maintenance

The cost of ad hoc repairs to the fabric should be distinguished from routine maintenance costs. If the condition of the building is causing excessive expenditure, a major rethink about the viability of the premises may be needed, whereas increasing operational costs within the office are often connected with staff requirements, and might be reduced by better space planning or by replacing obsolete equipment. It is good practice to complete an inventory of all the office equipment, such as printers and photocopiers, to ensure a programme can be established for renewal and replacement in the most efficient and cost-effective way.

8.3.6 Waste and recycling

It is good practice to implement procedures and processes for the reduction of waste, and its disposal in an environmentally friendly manner. Recycling targets should be set and monitored. Note that it is a requirement under ISO1400 that the practice monitor its environmental impact. Refer also to

Section 8.2.1 above and Chapter 10.

These procedures and processes may include management of printing and copying to minimise waste, the use of environmentally sound suppliers and goods from sustainable sources, and the collection and disposal of waste by approved contractors.

8.4   The office manager

Many practices, especially larger businesses, employ a professional office manager to organise and supervise the administrative activities in order to ensure that the office runs efficiently. If the practice cannot support the employment of a full-time office manager then it should allocate areas of work to employees with relevant skills or provide suitable training and set in place a management structure to ensure the tasks are overseen and can be audited.

An office manager will carry out a range of administrative and IT-related tasks, depending on the employing organisation, and the work may vary from running the administrative side of the practice as a sole administrator to overseeing the office work of numerous staff.

The work carried out by an office manager can vary greatly depending on the nature of the practice but could include:

- management of filing systems;
- human resources;
- statutory employment issues, e.g. building insurance;
- management of building and maintenance;
- financial organisation.

8.5   Outsourcing and consultancy

Many functions of the running of a business require specialist knowledge and it can be a drain on time and costs to attempt to manage and direct aspects of work that could be done by external consultants. Delegating and outsourcing to specialists can improve a business's office management but it can also free the business to focus on its talents, thereby improving the quality of its work and subsequently improving economic performance.

Depending on the size of the office, functions that could be considered for consultancy may include:

- finance
- human resources
- information technology

- marketing and specialist graphics
- HIS (QA)
- health and safety
- legal.

8.6　Insurance

Employers are required by law to carry a number of insurance policies to protect their employees, their clients and third parties, including:

- employer's liability insurance;
- public liability insurance.

In addition, architectural practices are required to take out professional indemnity (PI) insurance (see Section 11.3).

The practice may be required by others to take out insurance to protect against losses associated with their property (buildings and contents).

The practice should consider taking out other insurances to offer as benefits to its employees (life and health-type insurances).

Other than where insurance limits are set down in statute or legal documentation, it is at the discretion of the partners or directors to take out such insurance as they deem prudent to cover the risks associated with their practice and decide the levels of cover purchased. The help of a competent and experienced insurance broker is advisable.

Almost all insurance policies are renewable on an annual basis, and the practice will need to declare relevant details at the time of renewal. Failure to do so may invalidate or limit the insurance cover.

Making claims on an insurance policy tends to be time-consuming, particularly for senior management, and the practice should ensure it adopts sound risk management procedures to reduce the likelihood of experiencing or making a claim under its insurance policy.

The RIBA Insurance Agency is able to offer PI insurance on agreed RIBA terms, as well as a range of other office-related insurance products. For further details go to www.architectspi.com.

8.6.1　Buildings and contents insurances

- **Damage to buildings, fixtures and fittings** (from fire, theft, etc.). This is likely to be a requirement of the building's lease, and may be provided by the landlord and charged with the rent.
- **Damage or theft to property/contents**. Contents insurance covers

the practice's contents, petty cash, etc. while on the premises and, with certain limitations, outside the premises. There are likely to be restrictions on value of employees' personal belongings covered, which need to be understood and the employees advised – employees should ensure their personal household policies cover their property when away from their home. Cover can be extended to cover the 'additional cost of working' to get the practice up and running again following a fire, theft, etc.

- **Computers**. This is likely to be a separate insurance distinct from other contents. Insurance can also be provided against loss/replacement of data. There are likely to be requirements within the policy regarding alarm systems, back-up of data and safety of portable computer equipment including laptops, particularly when away from the premises.

All of the above insurances can be extended to include terrorism cover – the practice should evaluate the likelihood of this eventuality and place insurance cover if deemed necessary.

'Business interruption' insurance can also be purchased to cover the practice against loss of fee income, etc. should one of the eventualities covered by other insurances (fire, theft, terrorism, etc.) occur.

8.6.2   Employee-related insurances

- Employer's liability insurance is a legal requirement (to a minimum cover level of £5,000,000), to protect an employer against any claim brought by its employees due to the employer's breach of its duty to protect them against death, injury, disease, etc. arising out of their employment. It is a statutory requirement to prominently display in the workplace a certificate confirming that the employer has this insurance.
- Life insurance (death in service). Although not required by law, many employers provide insurance payable to their employees' estates should they die, due to any cause, while in employment. This insurance is frequently offered as an adjunct to any pension scheme the practice might offer. It is advisable for employees covered by such an insurance to write down an 'expression of wish', which asks the trustees of the insurance policy to consider the employee's wishes when deciding who should receive the proceeds of the insurance.
- Dependant's pension insurance pays a proportion of the employee's salary to their dependant(s) by way of a pension in the event of the employee's death while in service.
- Personal accident insurance covers members of staff usually on a '24 hour' basis in the event that an accident is fatal or causes them to become disabled. There will be varying degrees of cover for different conditions, usually related to a proportion of the employee's salary.

- It is recommended for a practice to restrict its liability to continue to pay employees in the event of their long-term absence from work due to sickness or injury. Permanent health insurance can be offered as a benefit to employees, as it will pay a proportion of the employee's salary after they have been off work for an initial period of time.

A number of the above insurances may be offered as benefits to employees (see also Section 6.2.6), and the practice is advised to consider whether or not it should enroll all employees immediately or after successful completion of their probationary period or some other timescale. They should also consider whether or not an upward sliding scale of benefit should be offered, dependent on time with the practice, seniority, etc. The practice may also consider purchasing 'key person' insurance, whereby it will receive the insured sums to assist it in the replacement of key individuals in the event of their death, or serious injury or illness preventing them from continuing their employment.

8.6.3 Third party insurances

- While not mandatory, public liability insurance is recommended to practices and covers third parties in the event of injury when visiting the architect's offices or for damage to third party property caused by its employees when visiting sites/other premises, among other things. Increasingly, clients are requiring this, and seek confirmation of it prior to approving the practice.

8.6.4 Other insurances

- The practice should consider whether or not to take out travel insurance to cover its property while away from the office as well as covering medical expenses and repatriation costs, curtailment or delay, etc. If employees are seconded overseas for lengthy periods of time, special insurance packages should be considered based on the particular needs of each instance.
- If the practice either gives its employees a company car or operates a system of pool cars, it is a legal requirement to provide motor insurance cover for the usual liabilities associated with driving. Cars insured in this way should be covered specifically for business use.

8.7 Health and safety requirements

The Health and Safety at Work etc. Act 1974, also referred to as HASAW or HSW, is the primary piece of legislation covering occupational health and safety in the UK. The Health and Safety Executive is responsible for enforcing the Act and a number of other Acts and Statutory Instruments relevant to the working environment. The Act sets out that employers have a duty of care to ensure the health, safety and welfare of their employees while they are at work.

A risk assessment must be carried out to identify possible health and safety hazards and a competent person should be appointed to be responsible for health and safety matters. The competent person may require education and training to carry out their duties.

For businesses employing five or more people there is a statutory requirement for:

- an official record of what the assessment finds;
- a formal health and safety policy, including arrangements to protect the health and safety of all staff, which should be made available to all staff;
- provision of appropriate health and safety training (this should also include employees' conduct on site visits and perhaps training for a CSCS card (Construction Skills Certification Scheme), which is increasingly used to illustrate occupational competence in the construction industry (www.cscs.uk.com).

Records should be kept of all health and safety related incidents as they may be required for any future investigations by the HSE or legal proceedings.

RIBA Chartered Practices must set out their health and safety policy in writing and apply it to all employees both in the workplace and on site visits. The policy should set out how the practice manages health and safety and should identify who does what, when and how. Chartered Practices must also operate health and safety risk management in their project work.

The RIBA publishes a generic Health and Safety Policy Template and the Health and Safety Executive publishes information and model risk assessments.

Health and safety law also covers employees when visiting construction sites and the office should prepare a policy that all employees should follow when visiting sites. It should include amongst its central messages that employees should notify the office when visiting a site and when they anticipate returning to the office and that suitable protective clothing must be worn at all times.

8.7.1   First aid and medical services

The Health and Safety (First Aid) Regulations 1981 require employers to have trained first aiders who can give an initial assessment in the event of a medical emergency; they should have access to a medical first aid kit. These requirements apply to all premises, including those with fewer than five employees, and to the self-employed.

8.7.2 Emergency plan

A comprehensive incident management and business continuity plan should be prepared by the office to cover a variety of scenarios from fire to a major services failure outside the control of the office. It should include named individuals responsible for ensuring that the business knows how to cope during any given scenario and what is needed to keep the business running after the initial incident. Protocols should be set up for staff evacuation, work continuity, contact procedures, communications with clients and recommencement plans to start functioning as soon as possible. These protocols should be communicated to all staff.

References and further reading

Gegg, B. and Sharp, D., *Good Practice Guide: Employment* (London: RIBA Publications, 2006).

Health and Safety Executive, *Essentials of Health and Safety at Work*, 4th edn (London: HSE, 2006).

Health and Safety Executive, *Workplace, Health, Safety and Welfare: Workplace (Health, Safety and Welfare) Regulations. 1992 – Approved Code of Practice and Guidance* (London: HSE, 1998).

Mordue, S. and Finch, R., *BIM for Construction Health and Safety* (London: RIBA Publishing, 2014 forthcoming).

8

Part 3
Project management

The architect's appointment

> **THIS CHAPTER:**
>
> - examines the ways in which an architect might secure a commission;
> - explains how to calculate fees and cash flow;
> - sets out the processes involved in confirming an appointment;
> - describes various standard forms of appointment, and gives guidance on responding to bespoke forms.

9

9.1   Introduction

While the essence of any contract (an architect's appointment is of course a contract) is 'offer, acceptance and performance' and the existence of a contract can be proved if these three factors are present, it is essential that any arrangement between the architect and their client is recorded in writing, even at the earliest stages of a commission. Indeed, it is a requirement of both the RIBA and ARB codes of conduct that agreements are recorded in this way.

Many standard forms exist and these are briefly summarised in Section 9.4. These standard forms have been developed by those in the profession for use within the profession, and should be used wherever possible.

However, many clients seek to use their own forms of appointment; these are often drafted by their solicitors who are, for obvious reasons, seeking to protect their clients' interests as best they can, often in such a way as to potentially increase liability on the architect. These 'bespoke' forms need to be carefully examined by the architect, with appropriate advice from their professional indemnity insurers and legal advisers. This advice may involve payment to the advisers, and this should be considered when negotiating the fee. Issues to bear in mind when considering bespoke forms are set out in Section 9.4.2 and also in the *Guide to RIBA Agreements 2010 (2012 revision)* Section 7.

As set out in Chapter 5, there are three main ways in which architects secure commissions:

- direct appointment;
- fee tendering/submissions;
- limited or open competitions.

Irrespective of how the architect has come to be considered, there are usually a series of stages:

- receive enquiry;
- verify that the practice wishes, in principle, to accept the commission;
- verify that the requirements are complete and understood;
- ascertain how the practice will meet these requirements;
- establish the basis for making a fee proposal and prepare necessary fee calculations;
- establish the additional information (if any) to be submitted with the fee bid;
- prepare and submit the proposal.

The *RIBA Job Book* provides a useful reference to the detailed considerations that need to be taken into account, which are noted under Stages 0 and 1.

9.2   Receiving, assessing and responding to potential commissions

Enquiries can be received in a variety of ways at different stages of a project: for instance, many 'design and build' enquiries will only commence at RIBA Stage 3 or (more usually) Stage 4, the previous stages having been undertaken for a different client by a different architect. However, all commissions will start with a client identifying a property- or building-related need that they do not themselves have the ability to satisfy. Many clients are initially unsure as to exactly what it is they need, and the establishment of a brief and scope of services will need to form part of the architect's initial workload.

At the other end of the spectrum certain clients will have a very clear idea of what they want, and draft an enquiry document accordingly. The receipt of competition entry details equates to this initial statement of requirements.

Initial enquiries should be responded to promptly with confirmation of the architect's intention of making a detailed response within a given timescale.

All enquiries, however received, should be recorded in accordance with the practice's procedures, and senior staff appointed to assess and respond to them.

9.2.1   Making an initial assessment

Upon receipt of such an enquiry the practice should verify that they wish, in principle, to undertake it. In making this judgement they should ask themselves a series of questions that might include:

- Does the practice wish to work for this client?

- Is the project likely to proceed?
- Does this project fit with the practice's established ambitions?
- If a competition or an *Official Journal of the European Union* (OJEU) opportunity, is it one the practice stands a reasonable chance of winning?
- Is the commission of a type in which the practice has expertise, or in which it wishes to gain expertise?
- Will the commission help enhance the practice's reputation?
- Can the practice make profit out of the commission?
- Does the practice have the necessary resources to perform the commission, or can it perform them in part and sub-let other parts to those better equipped?

The practice should not be afraid to make proper and discreet enquiries about a client's financial stability. Accepting a commission is a process of mutual selection – the architect should be as happy with the client as the client is with the architect. Contacting other architects that the client has commissioned may be a sensible starting point.

The practice should also beware of spending significant amounts of time chasing unlikely commissions. A swift straightforward assessment at the time of the initial enquiry and a polite 'no' can save much time and cost.

9.2.2   Ensuring complete information

Having decided that the commission is one that the practice wishes to pursue, it is important to ensure that it understands as fully as possible what is required in order to make a full and well-considered proposal for undertaking the work. Important matters to consider include:

- Understanding the client and their interest in the project.
- Are the site and its context clear? What special features may need to be allowed for?
- Are the client's objectives clear in terms of building use, size, build cost, programme, sustainability, other consultants, procurement, other aspirations, etc.?
- Is the scope of services that the practice is being asked to provide clear?
- What expenses does the client expect the practice to allow?
- What are the anticipated terms and conditions of the appointment?

9.2.3   Calculating fees and cash flow

While fee bids need to be competitive if the project is to be secured, it is important the practice adopts an approach to calculating fees that is likely to lead to a successful outcome for it in financial terms should it be successful in winning the work. The offer made by the architect should reflect the value that they will bring to the project, if appointed.

In a competitive situation it is also important to understand what the client is seeking – is it simply the cheapest fee or will other factors weigh equally, or more, heavily? Architects' proposals should be structured to emphasise those aspects they believe will find greatest favour with the client.

Architects should calculate fees taking into account a range of considerations including:

- Personnel likely to be engaged on the project and projected time to be spent.
- Their cost/charge-out rates.
- The services to be provided.
- The proposed procurement method.
- The proposed timescale for the project.
- The required profit margin.
- Added value.

Once estimated, the proposed fee can be expressed in a number of different ways including:

- A percentage of the construction cost.
- A lump sum for the entire project.
- Calculated lump sums for each work stage.
- Charges based on an hourly rate calculation of hours worked against agreed rates.
- A combination of any of the above.

The fee proposal should set out a clear programme for the drawdown of fees throughout the life of the project, which may of course need to be adjusted if the project is subject to delay. A monthly payment schedule establishes a regular invoicing routine for both architect and client, provides early warning of non-payment and reduces the amount of financial risk carried by the architect, as well as the requirement for working capital.

When using a resources-based approach to calculating fees, cross-checks are recommended to ensure that a sensible outcome has been reached. Such checks might include comparing the fee to be proposed against previous similar jobs, and benchmarking the proposed fee against other projects when expressed as a percentage of construction cost.

The resources-based approach to fee calculation involves establishing an hourly rate per member of staff, or grade of staff (director, associate, architect, etc.), and predicting the number of hours to be spent at each stage of the project by relevant people.

There are two commonly used methods for calculating cost rates: with and without overheads. The apportionment of overheads can be difficult and can change regularly, particularly in larger practices. The method described below includes them; the *RIBA Good Practice Guide: Painless Financial Management* sets out the method excluding overheads (the direct cost method).

Figure 9.1 shows a simple spreadsheet for calculating hourly rates for different staff. Such a spreadsheet can be set up using fixed percentages to cover the prevailing rate of employer's National Insurance contribution, overhead allowance and 'productivity factor' (the percentage of the full potential working year that an individual is likely to spend on income-producing work, excluding holiday and an allowance for sickness and working on administration or other non-income-producing work), but the 'other employment costs' (pension contribution, other insurances, car allowances, etc.) and profit percentages (to calculate charge-out rates) need to be established on an individual basis. As noted above, this calculation can be done either by individual or by grade of staff. In this latter case it will be necessary to establish average figures for the grade in question.

The practice will need to calculate its overhead cost allowing for all non-productive costs (including such things as rent, rates, insurances, administrative staff, marketing, business development, etc.), and establish how to apportion these to the individual or grade rates.

The *RIBA Good Practice Guide: Painless Financial Management* provides more detail on how to work out these rates, based on the method excluding overheads. Once this is done, a resource-based fee projection should be established by estimating the number of staff that will be needed to provide the required services on the project and the duration of their time at each stage. This, multiplied by their hourly rates, will produce the estimated cost to the practice of undertaking the project and thus inform the fee sought. A spreadsheet for fee calculation purposes is shown in Figure 9.2, with a typical calculation through the various stages of a project.

What is essential, as set out above, is to record the fee proposal and the method of calculating the fee, if it is not a lump sum, in writing to the client. In addition to this and the services that will be provided for the fee (see Section 9.2.4), the proposal should also confirm a range of other matters (set out in detail in Section 9.3.1 below), including expenses, VAT arrangements, payment schedules, and the basis for charging additional fees.

Cash flow can be expressed either by a simple monthly cash flow or stage payments based on completion of work stages, specific tasks or deliverables.

Figure 9.1 *Establishing hourly rate costs*

Name	Grade	Salary	NI	Other employment costs	Overhead allowance	Total annual cost	Gross hourly cost	Productivity factor	Factored hourly cost	Profit %age	Profit	Charge-out rate
Name			£0			£0						
Name			£0			£0						
Name			£0			£0						
Name			£0			£0						
Name			£0			£0						

Worked example

Name	Grade	Salary	NI	Other employment costs	Overhead allowance	Total annual cost	Gross hourly cost	Productivity factor	Factored hourly cost	Profit %age	Profit	Charge-out rate
Allen Key	Director	£60,000	£7,200	£12,000	£36,000	£115,200	£59.08	60%	£98.46	20%	£19.69	£118.15
Bess Friend	Associate	£47,500	£5,700	£7,500	£28,500	£89,200	£45.74	70%	£65.35	25%	£16.34	£81.68
Chris Packet	Architect	£40,000	£4,800	£6,000	£24,000	£74,800	£38.36	70%	£54.80	25%	£13.70	£68.50
Don Alduck	Techn'n	£35,000	£4,200	£3,000	£21,000	£63,200	£32.41	75%	£43.21	30%	£12.96	£56.18
Ellen Iwater	Assistant	£28,000	£3,360	£2,000	£16,800	£50,160	£25.72	75%	£34.30	30%	£10.29	£44.59

Figure 9.2 *Typical calculation through the various stages of a project. Alternatively, it is possible to vary this to use charge-out rates (see Figure 9.1), inclusive of profit*

Job budget worksheet	
Job name:	**A job, anywhere**
Job no:	**1234**
Date generated	30/04/13
Date revised	****/**/****
Total fee agreed	£0

Fee calculation summary	Budget cost	Fee quote	%age profit
Cost to date	£2,250	£2,250	0%
Stage 0/1	£32,790	£40,988	25%
Stage 2	£67,267	£84,084	25%
Stage 3	£26,949	£32,339	20%
Stage 4	£201,499	£241,799	20%
Stage 5	£187,772	£225,326	20%
Stage 6	£16,056	£20,069	25%
Total	**£534,583**	**£646,855**	**21%**

Fee calculation	

Cost to date (from records)	
Time costs to date	£2,000
Expenses to date	£250
Total cost to date	£2,250
Total fee to date	£0

STAGE 0/1 – STRATEGIC DEFINITION/PREPARATION & BRIEF					
Anticipated dates	01/05/10 – 30/06/10				
Name	Grade	Cost rate	Hrs/wk	No. wks	Cost
Allen Key	A	£98.46	3	8	£2,363
Bess Friend	B	£65.35	15	8	£7,842
Chris Packet	C	£54.80	37.5	8	£16,440
Don Alduck	D	£43.21			£0
Ellen Iwater	E	£34.30	37.5	4	£5,145
Allowance for expenses					£1,000

Total cost stage 0/1	**£32,790**
Profit %age	25%
Fee stage 0/1	**£40,988**

STAGE 2 – CONCEPT DESIGN					
Anticipated dates	01/07/10 – 31/09/10				
Name	Grade	Cost rate	Hrs/wk	No. wks	Cost
Allen Key	A	£98.46	3	6	£1,772
Bess Friend	B	£65.35	20	6	£7,842
Chris Packet	C	£54.80	37.5	6	£12,330
Don Alduck	D	£43.21			£0
Ellen Iwater	E	£34.30	37.5	6	£7,718
Allowance for expenses					£1,500

Total cost stage 2	**£31,162**
Profit %age	25%
Fee stage 2	**£38,953**

Figure 9.2 *Continued*

STAGE 3 – DEVELOPED DESIGN					
Anticipated dates	01/10/10 – 31/10/10				
Name	Grade	Cost rate	Hrs/wk	No. wks	Cost
Allen Key	A	£98.46	3	12	£3,545
Bess Friend	B	£65.35	15	12	£11,763
Chris Packet	C	£54.80	37.5	12	£24,660
Don Alduck	D	£43.21	37.5	12	£19,446
Ellen Iwater	E	£34.30	37.5	12	£15,435
Allowance for expenses					£3,500
		Total cost stage 3			**£78,349**
		Profit %age			20%
		Fee stage 3			**£94,019**

STAGE 4 – TECHNICAL DESIGN					
Anticipated dates	01/11/10 – 31/03/11				
Name	Grade	Cost rate	Hrs/wk	No. wks	Cost
Allen Key	A	£98.46	2	22	£4,332
Bess Friend	B	£65.35	15	22	£21,566
Chris Packet	C	£54.80	37.5	22	£45,210
Don Alduck +1	D	£43.21	75	22	£71,297
Ellen Iwater +1	E	£34.30	75	22	£56,595
Allowance for expenses					£2,500
		Total cost stage 4			**£201,499**
		Profit %age			20%
		Fee stage 4			**£241,799**

Note the need to use additional staff at this stage, budgeted by showing 75 hours rather than 37.5

STAGE 5 – CONSTRUCTION					
Anticipated dates	01/04/11 – 31/03/12				
Name	Grade	Cost rate	Hrs/wk	No. wks	Cost
Allen Key	A	£98.46	1	52	£5,120
Bess Friend	B	£65.35	7.5	52	£25,487
Chris Packet	C	£54.80	37.5	52	£106,860
Don Alduck	D	£43.21	10	52	£22,469
Ellen Iwater	E	£34.30	10	52	£17,836
Allowance for expenses					£10,000
		Total cost stage 5			**£187,772**
		Profit %age			20%
		Fee stage 5			**£225,326**

STAGE 6 – HANDOVER & CLOSE OUT					
Anticipated dates	01/04/12 – 31/03/13				
Name	Grade	Cost rate	Hrs/wk	No. wks	Cost
Allen Key	A	£98.46	0.5	52	£2,560
Bess Friend	B	£65.35	2	52	£6,796
Chris Packet	C	£54.80	2	52	£5,699
Don Alduck	D	£43.21			£0
Ellen Iwater	E	£34.30			£0
Allowance for expenses					£1,000
		Total cost stage 6			**£16,056**
		Profit %age			25%
		Fee stage 6			**£20,069**

Figure 9.3 *Monitoring sheet*

Current situation summary (from records)	
Report date	15/10/13
Stage reached	3
%age of stage completed	50%
Total fee to date	£129,201
Budget cost to date	£105,377
Actual cost to date	£103,694
Fee billing to completion	£534,204
Budget cost to completion	£444,502

Fee budget summary	Budget cost	Fee quote	Planned profit
Cost to date	£2,250	£2,250	0%
Stage 0/1	£32,790	£40,988	25%
Stage 2	£31,162	£38,953	25%
Stage 3	£78,349	£94,019	20%
Stage 4	£201,499	£241,799	20%
Stage 5	£187,772	£225,326	20%
Stage 6	£16,056	£20,069	25%
Total	**£549,878**	**£663,404**	**21%**

Progress summary	Cost to date	%age complete	Fee invoiced	Actual profit
Cost to date	£2,250	100%	£2,250	0%
Stage 0/1	£31,150	100%	£40,988	32%
Stage 2	£33,140	100%	£38,953	18%
Stage 3	£37,154	50%	£47,010	27%
Stage 4	£0	0%	£0	
Stage 5	£0	0%	£0	
Stage 6	£0	0%	£0	
Total	**£103,694**		**£129,201**	

The cost to date is derived from the timesheet records.

Architects should think carefully about cash flow as it can have a significant impact on their business.

In order to inform cash flow proposals it is useful to have benchmark information of costs incurred, both time and expenses, at different stages on previous projects.

It is useful to monitor performance against expectation. Figure 9.3 shows a simple reporting form that could be linked to the calculation sheet.

9.2.4   Services

It is a requirement of both the ARB and RIBA codes of conduct that the architect ensures they have adequate skills and resources to undertake the project that the client seeks. An analysis of the requirements of the project and the development of a resource plan to deliver these, as described above, should be undertaken. This resource plan can be used to calculate the likely cost of carrying out the services (see Section 9.2.3).

This resource plan will be dependent on the method of procurement, and there are an increasing number of projects that require different services to be delivered at different stages of the project. The RIBA publication *Assembling a Collaborative Project Team* sets out a number of alternative procurement methods and the work stage progression applicable to each. See also *Guide to Using the RIBA Plan of Work 2013*.

If the architect does not have sufficient resources to deliver the requirements of the project brief, they may consider sub-letting parts of the work to others with the necessary skills and resource (see Section 9.4.5).

It is vital to state clearly what services have been included in the fee proposal, together with a list of assumptions made and conditions of the offer.

A comprehensive schedule of 'typical architectural duties' and possible additional services is included in the *RIBA Job Book* in Stage 0. The RIBA Standard Agreements 2010 (2012 revision) include schedules of design services and role specifications. A schedule of services is usefully set out, describing typical services that may be performed depending on differing forms of procurement.

Areas of interface between different consultants need to be clearly defined and the architect may wish to consider including a matrix of services to be performed by each of the consultants, plus the client and contractor, with their offer. A typical matrix is shown in Figure 9.4.

If used, this should be completed and added to/adapted on a project-by-project basis. It should be reviewed regularly as the project progresses.

An architect may be asked to provide a wide range of additional services including:

- information manager (for BIM-enabled projects)
- arbitrator/adjudicator
- principal designer
- construction manager
- access consultant
- expert witness
- interior/product/furniture designer
- party wall surveyor
- planning consultant
- project management
- surveyor.

Figure 9.4 *Typical schedule of consultant responsibilities*

Project title: Reference: Date:	Client	Client's rep./PM	Architect	Quantity surveyor	Structural engineer	M&E services engineer	Highways engineer	Principal designer	Fire engineer	Planning consultant	Landscape architect	Interior designer	Party wall surveyor	Main contractor	Others (name)
Appointment of consultants															
Brief information															
Instruct changes to brief															
Design team coordination															
Site ownership and boundaries															
Land and/or building survey															
Soil investigation															
DPMs up to DPC level															
Water retaining structs./tanking															
Foundations/sub-structure															
Building structure elements															
Roads & kerbs setting out/levels															
External works sub-structure															
Underground drainage															
Foul/surface drains above ground															
Int. sanitary installation															
Sanitary fittings															
Rainwater system															
Mains services supplies															
Water storage/distribution															
Structural fire protection															
Fire-fighting installations															
Fire alarm/detection															
Electrical power and lighting															
Communications systems															
Lighting protection															
Heating installation/fuel supply															
Air conditioning systems															
Main gas distribution															
Lifts, conveyors and hoists															
Services BWIC															
Window cleaning cradles, etc.															
Catering equipment/kitchens															
Waste disposal															
Sound control and acoustics															
Planting and cultivation															
Hard landscaping															
Furniture and fittings															
Signs and graphic design															
Cost planning and control															
Building contract preliminaries															
Maintenance manuals															
Site inspection															
Health and safety plan															
Health and safety file															
Party walls, adjoining premises															
Planning application															
Building regs application															
Fire certification															
Disability design															

9

All of the above require specialist knowledge and expertise, and any architect asked to perform any of these must ensure that they, or a sub-consultant appointed by them, have the necessary skills, experience and, where appropriate, qualifications. They should also ensure their PI insurance covers them to perform these services (see Chapter 11).

Historically, architects have been poor at claiming additional fees when the scope of a project or the services to be performed change, even though most appointment forms, including the RIBA Standard Agreements 2010, (2012 revision) make provision for them to do so. In this regard it is important to set out the original scope fully and clearly at the outset.

The Provision of Services Regulations 2009 no. 2999 require service providers (such as architects) to make available to service recipients (clients and potential clients) information about the provider's business and the handling of complaints. The Regulations are available at www.legislation.gov.uk/uksi/2009/2999/contents/made. Separate guidance is available at http://webarchive.nationalarchives.gov.uk/20090609003228/http://www.berr.gov.uk/files/file53100.pdf.

The information required by the Regulations is about the provider's business and is not project-specific. It must be made available in a clear and unambiguous manner in good time before the conclusion of a written contract, or where no written contract is yet in place, before the services are provided. The information should include the legal status of the business and contact details of its PI insurer and its complaints procedure, together with details of websites of relevant regulating bodies relating to codes of conduct and the availability of any non-judicial dispute resolution procedures.

The Regulations apply to any business providing services and its principals. However, the information might include generic data about personnel, particularly those with specialist qualifications relevant to the performance of the business, e.g. the number of accredited conservation architects. Principals who are members of a professional institution should be identified, giving the name of the institution and their registration number.

If the business is an RIBA Chartered Practice, this should also be noted in the information.

9.2.5   Submissions

Architects may be invited to make a submission to be considered for a new project, with or without a formal fee proposal, by a potential client – usually as one of a limited shortlist. Alternatively, they may themselves decide to make a submission for a new project that they become aware of, usually on an 'open' basis, for instance via an *Official Journal of the European Union* (OJEU) process. In these instances it is important to understand what the client is seeking and to gear the submission to this. Particular care should be taken to ensure that appropriate material is submitted and responses given to all aspects set out in the enquiry document. Section 5.5.1 gives some useful guidance on criteria for deciding whether or not the practice should enter these open invitations. It is important to be selective with any such initiatives: the PQQs (pre-qualification questionnaires) take time to complete, and that time may be wasted unless the practice has properly assessed its likely chances of success.

The Construction Industry Board recommends that clients seeking to engage an architect should develop a scoring system to balance their requirements for quality and price. While such a system may be operated formally by only a relatively small number of clients, it is important in all instances for the architect to analyse the skills and experience that will give greatest value to the client and emphasise these in the submission.

Many clients will request that additional information is submitted with a fee bid. In these instances, the architect must ensure they comply with the client's requirements as the offer is unlikely to be considered if it is 'non-compliant', and many hours or days of work may be wasted.

In any event, the practice should consider including some or all of the following with submissions made, in addition to the proposed fees, schedule of services, etc.:

- Previous examples of similar projects.
- The team to undertake the project, including relevant CVs.
- A method statement as to how the work will be undertaken.
- Relevant research projects undertaken.
- Company policies on, for example, health and safety, quality control, sustainability, equal opportunities, etc.
- Qualifications held and awards won.
- Confirmation of PI and public liability insurance.

Some clients will request the architect's audited accounts for previous years; it is prudent to provide these only when specifically requested.

In many instances the architect is invited to submit preliminary design ideas with their submission to secure a project. This is a double-edged sword in that the practice obviously wishes to demonstrate its understanding of the client's brief and its ability to respond creatively to it, but does not wish to give away all its best ideas without charge. There can be no clear guidance on this, but the practice must carefully consider the benefits of submitting even initial design ideas as part of the submission process. Architects should always aim to avoid giving away high-value design work free of charge.

This is obviously not the case when the practice decides to enter a competition. The checklist in Section 9.2.1 should be reviewed when considering whether or not to enter a competition.

It should be noted that the RIBA Code of Professional Conduct prohibits architects who are members from entering those competitions that the RIBA has declared to be unacceptable.

9.3   The appointment

9.3.1   Confirming the appointment

Both the ARB Code and the RIBA Code of Professional Conduct require the architect to record the terms of any appointment before undertaking any work, and to have the necessary competence and resources. A written agreement is therefore essential, and it is in the interests of both client and architect that they fully understand the agreement. The agreement should define and record the services to be provided, state the obligations of each party, identify the associated terms and conditions, and set out the fee basis and method of payment.

Appointment agreements should also include provisions for dealing with:

- assignment
- copyright
- liability
- suspension and termination
- dispute resolution.

The appointment document must also state that individual architects are required to be registered with the ARB, and are subject to its Code and to the disciplinary sanction of the ARB in relation to complaints of unacceptable professional conduct or serious professional incompetence.

The RIBA produces a flexible range of appointment agreements, RIBA Agreements 2010 (2012 revision) (see Section 9.4.1), for use with projects of all sizes and complexity; further information on these RIBA standard agreements is available at www.ribabookshops.com.

For very small projects the appointment agreement may alternatively be set out in a self-contained letter of appointment. The RIBA produces a book entitled *A Guide to Letter Contracts for Very Small Projects, Surveys and Reports*, which gives detailed guidance on such letter contracts, and includes model letters; further information on this publication is available at www.ribabookshops.com.

In exceptional circumstances, for example where the commission is for a limited feasibility study only in the first instance, or the work forms part of a speculative or conditional bid, it may be acceptable to rely upon a client care letter to confirm the initial appointment. This should be sent to the client at the earliest opportunity following receipt of instruction. It should set out the terms and conditions under which the commission will be performed, pending the entering of a formal appointment agreement, and should include:

- The name of the client.
- The name(s) of those within the client body from whom the architect will accept instructions.
- The site address.
- An outline description of the project.
- A description of the services to be provided by the architect.
- Arrangements for any of the services that are to be sub-contracted by the architect.
- The date on which the provision of the services commenced or will commence.
- Services that are to be provided by other consultants (a typical matrix showing project responsibilities for the various consultants is shown above in Figure 9.4).
- Confirmation that the architect will use their 'reasonable skill and care' to perform the services.
- The quantum and basis of calculation of the fee to be paid for the services.
- Any assumptions made in the calculation of the fees.
- Any exclusions to the fees.
- Arrangements for cash flow for payment of the fees.
- Arrangements for payment of expenses and/or disbursements or, if they are to be included in the fee, any limitations on them (e.g. maximum numbers of prints included or maximum travel distance included).
- Arrangements for payment of VAT.
- The time for settlement of accounts correctly rendered and for payment of interest should this not happen.
- Limits of indemnity of PI insurance to be provided by the architect.
- Confirmation that the architect will retain copyright over their designs.
- The terms and conditions that have been assumed to apply to the provision of services and used in the calculation of the fees, and those that will apply to any future services in connection with the project. It is recommended to refer to one of the RIBA standard appointment forms.

9

- Confirmation that the letter confers no rights or obligations on any third parties.
- Reference to the ARB Code and disciplinary sanctions.

The architect should also write to the client advising them of their responsibilities under the Construction (Design and Management) Regulations 2015 (CDM) and in respect of party wall procedures. The RIBA publishes helpful guidance for clients on both of these issues and the RIBA Quality Management Toolkit contains a specimen client care letter.

The architect may also wish to include a reference to additional services they are able to provide (for an additional fee).

The client should be asked to sign and return a copy of the client care letter to signify their agreement to it.

9.4 Appointment documentation

9.4.1 Standard forms of appointment

The agreement of sound and sensible terms of engagement is central to the management of risk. Furthermore, having agreed such an appointment, it is vital that all staff working on the project understand clearly the limits of the services that the practice is contracted to perform on the project. Appointment documents may be entered 'under hand' (in which case the architect will remain responsible for six years), or 'under seal' (in which case they are responsible for 12 years). Building contracts are often entered under seal because it can take more than six years from inception to completion and claims might otherwise be restricted by the Limitation Act 1980, as amended by the Latent Damage Act 1986. Refer to *Law in Practice: The RIBA Legal Handbook* Chapter 2 for further advice in this area.

There are a number of standard forms of appointment agreement, including a suite of documents published by the RIBA that have been drafted especially to respond to these issues, and to protect the interests of the architect while being fair so far as the client is concerned.

The RIBA Agreements 2010 (2012 revision) are endorsed by the Association of Consultant Architects (ACA), the Royal Incorporation of Architects in Scotland (RIAS), the Royal Society of Architects in Wales (RSAW) and the Royal Society of Ulster Architects (RSUA). Information on the RIBA Agreements 2010 (2012 revision) can be found on the RIBA Bookshops website: www.ribabookshops.com.

The core suite of RIBA Agreements 2010 (2012 revision) comprises:

RIBA Standard Agreement 2010 (2012 revision) Architect

This incorporates a flexible schedule of services, which enables its application to a variety of scopes of service and a range of different procurement methods. It has comprehensive conditions making it suitable for use on projects of all types, including larger and more complex buildings. The RIBA Standard Agreement 2010 (2012 revision) Architect comprises:

- the Standard Conditions of Appointment of an Architect 2010 (2012 revision);
- Schedules;
- Fees and Expenses Schedules;
- Memorandum of Agreement and alternative Model Letter, which together form the appointment contract;
- notes on use and completion.

RIBA Concise Agreement 2010 (2012 revision) Architect

This has shorter conditions derived from the fuller provision of the Standard Agreement. It is suitable for smaller and intermediate-sized projects, and the schedule of services assumes a traditional architectural service, but with flexibility to facilitate partial as well as full services. In deciding to use the Concise Agreement the architect needs to consider carefully whether the more concise wording is compatible with the complexity of the proposed project, as the provisions in this shorter form are inevitably less comprehensive. The RIBA Concise Agreement comprises:

- the Concise Conditions of Appointment for an Architect;
- Small Project Services Schedule;
- Fees and Expenses Schedule and Model Letter, which together form the appointment contract;
- notes on use and completion.

RIBA Domestic Project Agreement 2010 (2012 revision) Architect

This is designed for use where the client requires work for their home and is a 'consumer' to whom the Unfair Terms in Consumer Contracts Regulations 1999 apply. The RIBA Domestic Project Agreement 2010 (2012 revision) Architect comprises:

- Conditions of Appointment for an Architect for a Domestic Project;
- Small Project Services Schedule;
- Fees and Expenses Schedule and Model Letter, which together form the appointment contract;
- notes on use and completion.

9

RIBA Standard Agreement 2010 (2012 revision) Consultant

This consultant version can be used when the client wishes to directly appoint another consultant under a separate agreement, but on parallel terms to the architect's appointment.

RIBA Sub-consultant Agreement 2010 (2012 revision)

In certain circumstances, and with the client's consent, the architect may wish to directly appoint a sub-consultant to provide specialist services, but the architect needs to be aware of the associated liability implications and implement any necessary PI arrangements. Use of the RIBA Sub-consultant Agreement ensures that the sub-consultant's obligations to the architect are based on the same terms as those extended by the architect to the client.

The introduction of the lead designer role in the RIBA Plan of Work 2013 is partly in recognition that many clients increasingly expect the person leading and coordinating the design to offer a single point of responsibility. This may mean that in future other designers are more frequently appointed as sub-consultants.

The core suite of RIBA Agreements 2010 is available to purchase in hard copy and electronic versions. The electronic version facilitates easy editing and customisation of the services and fees schedules.

A number of additional specialist services schedules and supplementary agreements are available in electronic format only. These include:

- Access Consultancy Services Schedule
- Contractor's Design Services Schedule
- Contractor's Design Services Schedule Notes
- Historic Building or Conservation Project Services Schedule
- Initial Occupation and Post-Occupation Evaluation Services Schedule
- Master Planning Services Schedule
- Multi-disciplinary Design Services Schedule
- Small Historic Building or Conservation Project Services Schedule.

(N.B. There is no RIBA supplementary switch or novation agreement, but the RIBA recommends the CIC Novation Agreement, which is compatible with the RIBA Agreements 2010 (2012 revision).)

- Draft Third Party Rights Schedule
- Draft Warranty by a Sub-consultant
- Public Authority Supplement.

A number of client guides are also available, on:

- Access consultancy services

- Initial occupation and post-occupation services
- Working with an architect: Repair and alteration to historic buildings
- Working with an architect: Repair and alteration of places of worship.

Other standard forms include:

- ACA SFA 2012 (Association of Consultant Architects Standard Form of Agreement for the Appointment of an Architect)
- BPF Consultancy Agreement, version 2, 2007
- CIC Consultants Contract
- FIDIC Client/Consultant Model Services Agreement, 2006
- GC Works 5, 1998
- NEC 3 Professional Services Contract
- PPC 2000 (Project Partnering Contract)
- JCT Consultancy Agreement (Public Sector)
- JCT Consultancy Agreement for a Home Owner/Occupier who has appointed a consultant to oversee the work.

While these are all presented as standard forms, some are written with the principal interests of other parties paramount. It is therefore strongly recommended that the practice's legal advisers and professional indemnity insurers are consulted to confirm acceptability of the form proposed, particularly if the client is seeking to amend the standard wording.

9.4.2 Guidelines for review of bespoke forms of appointment

Many clients, in both public and private sectors, seek to draft their own bespoke appointment documents. It is important, in addition to one or more of the practice's partners/directors thoroughly reviewing the documents, that advice on the proposed terms and conditions be sought from the practice's legal and PI insurance advisers.

In general terms the architect should seek to enter appointments that leave them in no worse position than they would have been under common law in the absence of an appointment document. There are a number of aspects that regularly appear in bespoke appointments that would extend the architect's responsibility beyond where they would be under common law and these should be resolved wherever possible:

- The standard of care to be used in the performance of the services.
- The provision of guarantees or indemnities.
- The inclusion of services that are not the architect's responsibility or whose performance is not fully within their gift.

In law, it is the duty of an architect, along with other professionals, to undertake their services using 'reasonable skill and care'. This is commonly defined as exercising the skill and care to be expected of an ordinary architect exercising and professing to have that skill. It is important that the architect does not contract to provide a higher standard of service, for instance 'fitness for purpose', as this is likely to fall outside the scope of their PI insurance cover.

Guarantees or indemnities should also be avoided. Again, these are likely to fall outside PI insurance cover.

It is particularly important to review the proposed services carefully and for the architect to verify that they are able to fulfil them all. Any terms that require the architect to ensure that they achieve something should be viewed with particular care.

The architect should also take care to ensure that, unless they agree specifically to it, the copyright in their designs remains with them and is not passed on to others by the terms of appointment.

In order to help RIBA members address the risk management and liability matters associated with the review of appointment agreements, the RIBA, working with the RIBA Insurance Agency, has produced a short guide covering some of the common areas where issues can arise. The points covered apply to the appointment agreement, as well as issues associated with novation agreements, collateral warranties and other associated documents. This guidance can be downloaded free of charge from www.architectspi.com/Pages/RiskManagement.aspx.

Refer also to the RIBA publication *Law in Practice: The RIBA Legal Handbook*.

9.4.3   Collateral warranties

Collateral warranties are a frequent feature of appointment documentation. They create separate contractual relationships between the architect and funders, purchasers and/or tenants, among others. It is important that the parties to whom these will be given and the terms thereof are negotiated at the project inception to control risks in the longer term.

Of particular note in relation to warranties is that it is important to preserve the architect's rights to seek a contribution from all those who may have contributed to a particular failure in any claim brought against them. This is usually possible in any action brought by the client under the appointment as all consultants are likely to have entered similar appointments at a similar time. However, it is less certain that all consultants and contractors with design responsibility will enter warranties at the same time, and therefore it is recommended that a net contribution clause is inserted into warranties whereby the architect is only financially liable to the extent that they have caused the problem.

Certain clients are reluctant to include such clauses, but PI insurers will, by and large, only pay out to the extent that the architect was liable for the problem. This important issue should be resolved early.

The architect's rights to contribution can be protected by including a clause stating that claims made under the warranty will only be valid provided all consultants have entered warranties at the same time in similar terms.

Another strategy to limit risk is to limit the financial liability of the consultant in appointments and relevant collateral warranties, often to the maximum limit of their PI insurance.

A collateral warranty, as described above, creates a new contractual relationship between the architect and the party he or she is granting the warranty to. It is important to clarify that this relationship does not extend further, and thus the inclusion of a sentence confirming that 'nothing in the agreement is intended to confer any benefit or right to any third party pursuant to the Contracts (Rights of Third Parties) Act 1999' is recommended.

There are, from time to time, compelling reasons why a practice may wish to enter an appointment or warranty where a risk of not having full PI insurance protection exists. In these instances the risk to the practice should be evaluated and agreed by the partners/directors.

9.4.4   Novation

In certain situations, particularly under design and build contracts, architects may find themselves appointed by the client and that their appointment is subsequently 'novated' to another, usually the contractor, when the project is moving towards the construction phase.

Novation of the architect's appointment can take place with effect from the date of the novation, or can be 'ab initio', where the architect is deemed to have been working for the new client from the start of the project. While legal and insurance advice should be sought in both of these situations, architects should take particular care when considering whether or not to enter ab initio novation arrangements, as this type of arrangement can bring onerous liability implications.

From the point of novation onwards, the 'old' employer ceases to be the architect's client and the 'new' client assumes all of the responsibilities that were formerly the 'old' employer's. The architect is henceforth responsible for providing the services to the new client, and should take instructions from them alone. The architect should review their appointment in this situation and confirm that its terms do not need to be changed in any way. The new client assumes all responsibilities for payment, etc. and the architect should ensure that arrangements with the 'old' client have been satisfactorily concluded before novation takes place.

The following contain useful guidance on novation:

- Guide to RIBA Agreements 2010 (2012 revision) Section 3.5.3
- Notes to Contractors Design Services
- CIC Liability Briefing Novation of consultants' appointments on design and build.

9.4.5   Sub-consultancy agreements

There will be certain instances where the architect is not able to provide the full range of services required on a project, and will wish to sub-let those. The practice should think carefully about the risks associated with this, most obviously the potential requirement to pay fees to the sub-consultant prior to the client settling the architect's account. If the practice decides that sub-letting a part of its work is appropriate, a sub-consultancy agreement should be entered into, which sets out the terms and conditions that will apply to that portion of the services.

This will mean that the practice is the client's first point of contact should something go wrong with the performance of the sub-consultancy services and thus the practice should seek to ensure that the terms and conditions of the sub-consultancy agreement are 'back to back' with their appointment terms.

Advice on appropriate terms and conditions should be sought from the practice's legal and PI insurance advisers.

The RIBA Agreement suite 2010 (2012 revision) includes a Subconsultancy Agreement, Guidance Notes and a draft warranty by a sub-consultant to the client. It is a requirement of all RIBA Appointment documents that the client has to give permission to the architect to sub-let a part of the work.

9.4.6   Variations to appointment documentation

Appointment documents should be reviewed from time to time and, if necessary, amended or added to as and when there are variations to the services required or to the scope of the project.

This should always happen whenever there is a change of client, for instance following a novation of the appointment to another client (see above). In particular, the services to be provided should be reviewed and amended as necessary to reflect the new relationships.

If additional services or the scope of a project otherwise varies the changes that flow therefrom in terms of fee, timetable, etc., should be agreed in writing with the client.

Any amendments should be set down in writing and signed by both parties in the same way as the original contract, i.e. under hand or as a deed (see Section 9.4.1). See also the Guide to RIBA Agreements 2010 Section 5.2.

References and further reading

Luder, O., *Good Practice Guide: Keeping out of Trouble* (London: RIBA Publishing, 2012).

Murray, M. and Langford, D., *Architect's Handbook of Construction Project Management* (London: RIBA Publications, 2004).

Ostime, N., *RIBA Job Book*, 9th edn (London: RIBA Publishing, 2013).

Ostime, N., *Small Projects Handbook* (London: RIBA Publishing, 2014).

Pinder-Ayres, B., *Good Practice Guide: Painless Financial Management* (London: RIBA Publications, 2008).

Phillips, R., *Good Practice Guide: Fee Management*, 2nd edn (London: RIBA Publishing, 2012).

Phillips, R., *Guide to RIBA Agreements 2010 (2012 revision)* (London: RIBA Publishing, 2012).

RIBA Plan of Work 2013 Overview (London: RIBA Publishing, 2013).

RIBA, *A Client's Guide to Engaging an Architect: Guidance on Hiring an Architect for your Project* (November 2009 revision) (London: RIBA Publishing, 2009).

Sinclair, D., *Assembling a Collaborative Project Team* (London: RIBA Publishing, 2013).

Sinclair, D., *Guide to Using the RIBA Plan of Work 2013* (London: RIBA Publishing, 2013).

Wevill, J., *Law in Practice: The RIBA Legal Handbook*, 2nd edn (London: RIBA Publishing, 2013).

9

Procedures and processes

THIS CHAPTER:

- examines how the standardisation and formalisation of office procedures can help to minimise risk in the business;
- identifies areas of running an architectural business that can benefit from establishing methods and routines for day-to-day processes;
- explains how these methods and routines can, if implemented in a considered and structured way, reduce wastage in time and costs, and ensure quality of output is accepted as the norm.

10.1 Introduction

The RIBA Plan of Work 2013 (Figure 10.1) sets out the industry standard for the way that projects are managed and administered. The publications *Guide to Using the RIBA Plan of Work 2013*, the *RIBA Job Book* and *Assembling a Collaborative Project Team* provide valuable advice on the procedural, technical and legal aspects of running a job, and this chapter outlines some management and administrative tools and techniques that can be used in conjunction with these publications to enable integration with office processes and procedures.

10.2 The office manual

While the *RIBA Job Book* and the RIBA Plan of Work 2013 set the big picture for running a project, there is an equal need for consistency of procedures on the smaller scale, within each individual office. The staff in any office are all trained and should know how to do their jobs, but the reality is that all individuals and groups of people sometimes have idiosyncrasies in the way they carry out their duties. The aim of an office manual is not to suppress individuality, but it will help promote consistency, introducing employees to the specific way a company wants to work, and ensuring employees do not carry out their duties as they did for previous employers. The benefits of a well-written office manual include:

- better knowledge of the company's activities;
- clearer understanding of its duties, methods and results;
- improved clarity of structure and processes to all staff;
- consistency of output from individuals;
- consistency of output from multiple offices;

10

Figure 10.1 *The RIBA Plan of Work 2013*

The RIBA Plan of Work 2013 organises the process of briefing, designing, constructing, maintaining, operating and using building projects into a number of key stages. The content of stages may vary or overlap to suit specific project requirements. The RIBA Plan of Work 2013 should be used solely as guidance for the preparation of detailed professional services contracts and building contracts.

www.ribaplanofwork.com

RIBA Plan of Work 2013

Stages	0 Strategic Definition	1 Preparation and Brief	2 Concept Design	3 Developed Design	4 Technical Design	5 Construction	6 Handover and Close Out	7 In Use
Core Objectives	Identify client's **Business Case** and **Strategic Brief** and other core project requirements.	Develop **Project Objectives**, including **Quality Objectives** and **Project Outcomes**, **Sustainability Aspirations**, **Project Budget**, other parameters or constraints and develop **Initial Project Brief**. Undertake **Feasibility Studies** and review of **Site Information**.	Prepare **Concept Design**, including outline proposals for structural design, building services systems, outline specifications and preliminary **Cost Information** along with relevant **Project Strategies** in accordance with **Design Programme**. Agree alterations to brief and issue **Final Project Brief**.	Prepare **Developed Design**, including coordinated and updated proposals for structural design, building services systems, outline specifications, **Cost Information** and **Project Strategies** in accordance with **Design Programme**.	Prepare **Technical Design** in accordance with **Design Responsibility Matrix** and **Project Strategies** to include all architectural, structural and building services information, specialist subcontractor design and specifications, in accordance with **Design Programme**.	Offsite manufacturing and onsite **Construction** in accordance with **Construction Programme** and resolution of **Design Queries** from site as they arise.	Handover of building and conclusion of **Building Contract**.	Undertake **In Use** services in accordance with **Schedule of Services**.
Procurement *Variable task bar	Initial considerations for assembling the project team.	Prepare **Project Roles Table** and **Contractual Tree** and continue assembling the project team.	*The procurement strategy does not fundamentally alter the progression of the design or the level of detail prepared at a given stage. However, **Information Exchanges** will vary depending on the selected procurement route and **Building Contract**. A bespoke RIBA Plan of Work 2013 will set out the specific tendering and procurement activities that will occur at each stage in relation to the chosen procurement route.			Administration of **Building Contract**, including regular site inspections and review of progress.	Conclude administration of **Building Contract**.	
Programme *Variable task bar	Establish **Project Programme**.	Review **Project Programme**.	Review **Project Programme**.	*The procurement route may dictate the **Project Programme** and may result in certain stages overlapping or being undertaken concurrently. A bespoke RIBA Plan of Work 2013 will clarify the stage overlaps. The **Project Programme** will set out the specific stage dates and detailed programme durations.				
(Town) Planning *Variable task bar	Pre-application discussions.	Pre-application discussions.	*Planning applications are typically made using the Stage 3 output. A bespoke RIBA Plan of Work 2013 will identify when the planning application is to be made.					
Suggested Key Support Tasks	Review **Feedback** from previous projects.	Prepare **Handover Strategy** and **Risk Assessments**. Agree **Schedule of Services**, **Design Responsibility Matrix** and **Information Exchanges** and prepare **Project Execution Plan** including **Technology** and **Communication Strategies** and consideration of **Common Standards** to be used.	Prepare **Sustainability Strategy, Maintenance and Operational Strategy** and review **Handover Strategy** and **Risk Assessments**. Undertake third party consultations as required and any **Research and Development** aspects. Review and update **Project Execution Plan**. Consider **Construction Strategy**, including offsite fabrication, and develop **Health and Safety Strategy**.	Review and update **Sustainability, Maintenance and Operational** and **Handover Strategies and Risk Assessments.** Undertake third party consultations as required and conclude **Research and Development** aspects. Review and update **Project Execution Plan**, including **Change Control Procedures**. Review and update **Construction and Health and Safety Strategies**.	Review and update **Sustainability, Maintenance and Operational** and **Handover Strategies and Risk Assessments.** Prepare and submit **Building Regulations** submission and any other third party submissions requiring consent. Review and update **Project Execution Plan**. Review **Construction Strategy**, including sequencing, and update **Health and Safety Strategy**.	Review and update **Sustainability Strategy** and implement **Handover Strategy**, including agreement of information required for commissioning, training, handover, asset management, future monitoring and maintenance and ongoing compilation of **As-constructed Information**. Update **Construction and Health and Safety Strategies**.	Carry out activities listed in **Handover Strategy** including **Feedback** for use during the future life of the building or on future projects. Updating of **Project Information** as required.	Conclude activities listed in **Handover Strategy** including **Post-occupancy Evaluation**, review of **Project Performance, Project Outcomes** and **Research and Development** aspects. Updating of **Project Information**, as required, in response to ongoing client **Feedback** until the end of the building's life.
Sustainability Checkpoints	Sustainability Checkpoint – 0	Sustainability Checkpoint – 1	Sustainability Checkpoint – 2	Sustainability Checkpoint – 3	Sustainability Checkpoint – 4	Sustainability Checkpoint – 5	Sustainability Checkpoint – 6	Sustainability Checkpoint – 7
Information Exchanges (at stage completion)	Strategic Brief.	Initial Project Brief.	Concept Design including outline structural and building services design, associated **Project Strategies**, preliminary **Cost Information** and **Final Project Brief.**	Developed Design, including the coordinated architectural, structural and building services design and updated **Cost Information**.	Completed **Technical Design** of the project.	'As-constructed' Information.	Updated 'As-constructed' Information.	'As-constructed' Information updated in response to ongoing client **Feedback** and maintenance or operational developments.
UK Government Information Exchanges	Not required.	Required.	Required.	Required.	Not required.	Not required.	Required.	As required.

*Variable task bar – in creating a bespoke project or practice specific RIBA Plan of Work 2013 via www.ribaplanofwork.com a specific bar is selected from a number of options.

© RIBA

- improved productivity;
- more protection in the event of a claim;
- improved communication.

Thus the manual allows the management to communicate to all members of staff the principles behind the running of the practice. A well-prepared manual is the first port of call for new employees, and is a core document in the induction process.

It is more than likely that the manual will be stored as a series of linked handbooks, possibly on an intranet, and examples of the type of information required are outlined below:

- The company

  - Organisation and structure
  - Responsibilities and authorities
  - Stated company policies relating to areas such as health and safety, and environmental issues

- People policies

  - Induction procedure
  - Development, training and performance reviews
  - HR policies such as disciplinary procedures and holidays
  - Equality and diversity
  - Health and safety
  - Email and internet usage

- Office handbook

  - Office security and emergency action plans
  - Administration procedures
  - Office equipment such as printers and telephones
  - Contacts for all office departments
  - Standard forms (these can also be directly linked to quality procedures)

- Instructions

  - Company guidelines on production of external communications such as drawings and brochures
  - Company manuals for specific computer programs and applications
  - Library
  - Quality procedures.

The concept of risk management is essential to a comprehensive office manual as well-written procedures can reduce risk. This starts at the high-level processes such as appointments, and drills down to accurate and well-organised filing systems.

10

Producing a manual is the first step in establishing a quality system. It should be remembered, however, that the QA manual and office manual can be separate entities because the QA manual also has to meet an external standard. The QA manual does not need to detail the minutiae of office operations – an administrative manual may be a better solution. In other words it is a matter of content – careful consideration must be given to those processes that need to be standardised and those that do not.

10.3   Quality systems

For many clients, and for public bodies in particular, the demonstration of the architect's quality through a commitment to a quality system gives assurance that quality is of critical importance to the success of the project.

Processes are used continually in the architect's daily work, from the naming of a drawing and filling in of a drawing register to the review of a design before taking it to the next stage. The aims of QA are the standardisation and auditing of processes to help ensure that products and services meet client expectations, that work is done right the first time, and that a culture of continuous improvement is introduced, all of which give added value to the product and associated benefits to the office in terms of reaping economic gain. A QA system can give structure to and demonstrate compliance with statutory legal requirements, such as CDM and health and safety.

Although a quality system can be implemented without external assessment, for many the strategic aim is to be assessed and ultimately approved under BS EN ISO 9001. This standard promotes implementation of a process approach when developing, implementing and improving the operation of a quality management system. The RIBA also has an online QA toolkit, available for members to download, which can be used as the basis for creating a QA system that relates the requirements of the standard to

---

RIBA Chartered Practice Criteria – Quality Management Systems

- Small practices (up to ten staff in total) are required at least to use the RIBA Project Quality Plan for Small Projects (PQPSP), or equivalent, on each project.
- Medium practices (11 to 50 staff) are required to use the full RIBA Quality Management Toolkit (incorporating the RIBA PQPSP), or equivalent, on all projects, and for office procedures.
- Large practices (51+ staff) are to have an externally certified BS EN ISO 9001: 2008 quality management system in use. This could be based on an externally certified system developed from the RIBA Quality Management Toolkit or another externally certified equivalent system.

architectural practice. It should be noted that in order to become an RIBA Chartered Practice the business must have in place a quality management system appropriate for the size of the practice.

10.4   The quality management system: BS EN ISO 9001

BS EN ISO 9001 sets out in detail the requirements for meeting the standard, but the following are central concepts to its formulation (www.bsigroup.com):

- Identify the processes required for the quality management system, and how they will be applied throughout the business.
- Determine the order and relationship of these processes.
- Determine criteria and methods that both control these processes and ensure that they are effective.
- Ensure availability of resources and information necessary to support the implementation and monitoring of these processes.
- Monitor, measure and analyse these processes.
- Implement actions necessary to achieve planned results and continual improvement of these processes.

10.4.1 Management responsibility

The standard requires a commitment from senior management in creating the system and being involved in its ongoing implementation. This management input can focus attention on strategic business philosophy as it involves establishing the quality policy, ensuring the stated objectives are met by reviewing on a regular basis and ensuring that the resources are available to meet the objectives.

These objectives can be either business focused or philosophical in nature, and may include the following:

- quality
- environmental ambitions
- standards
- growth objectives.

The practice should also consider incorporating a statement as to how these objectives will be met and recorded, which may include:

- application of processes
- development of expertise
- customer satisfaction
- prevention of error
- continuous improvement.

10

10.4.2 Documentation requirements and control of documents

The quality system should document the following:

- Documented statements of a quality policy and quality objectives.
- A quality manual.
- Documented procedures required by the standard.
- Documents needed by the organisation to ensure the effective planning, operation and control of its processes.
- Records required by the standard.

One of the major requirements of the standard is control of the documents produced; this covers keeping records and ensuring that all documents used are current to ensure conformity of standards.

10.4.3 Implementation

In simple terms, implementation means producing a quality manual with procedures put in place to audit its effectiveness. Central to the manual is the production of a quality policy that outlines the ethics, aspirations and conduct of how the business will operate. The manual should cover all aspects of the running of an office to meet the standard including design, contract administration, finance, marketing, HR and administration. A good quality manual and associated processes should fit into the work carried out, and be concise and clear, so it is not seen as a paper-filling exercise and an extra burden on the working day.

BS EN ISO 9001 allows flexibility in how processes and procedures are described, and the various stages do not need to be described in minute detail. The relationship between competence and operational instruction is crucial, and so the level of instruction can be proportional to the level of competence. ISO requires that the person performing the task is suitable and competent, and this can be covered by HR procedures and personal development plans. Examples of procedure headings might be:

- Appointment and project process

    - Enquiries
    - Appointment
    - Documentation
    - Project planning
    - Design control and review

- Drawings and related documents

    - Presentation and production
    - Checking drawings

- ◦ Area calculations
- ◦ Drawing management
- ◦ Receipt of information

- Administration and records management

  - ◦ Administration and project filing
  - ◦ Standard forms and key documents
  - ◦ Archiving

- Quality systems management

  - ◦ Management review
  - ◦ Internal audits
  - ◦ Corrective and preventative action
  - ◦ Feedback
  - ◦ Quality system control

- Personnel management and practice

  - ◦ Interview guidelines
  - ◦ Induction
  - ◦ Professional development and training
  - ◦ CPD requirements

- Health and safety

  - ◦ Health and safety policy
  - ◦ Responsibilities and instructions

- Supplier management and purchasing

  - ◦ Assessment and review of suppliers
  - ◦ Ordering procedures.

These sections can be supplemented and supported with additional process-specific manuals, such as a library manual, and appendices for project-specific work, such as sample letters for appointment documentation and standard forms.

Process maps can be a good starting point to outlining how a practice works. Figure 10.2 is an example of a process map related to the standard RIBA stages that isolates the design stages, and illustrates good practice of when reviews and audits should be carried out for Stages 0 to 4; this could be used to illustrate the 'Appointment and project process' heading above. The same process could be developed for Stages 5 to 7. Figure 10.3 illustrates how this map fits into an example of a management review system that is required by BS EN ISO 9001. Processes and procedures would then have to be written for each element of the process maps.

10

Figure 10.2 *Process map 1: project execution processes. Process owners: project team*

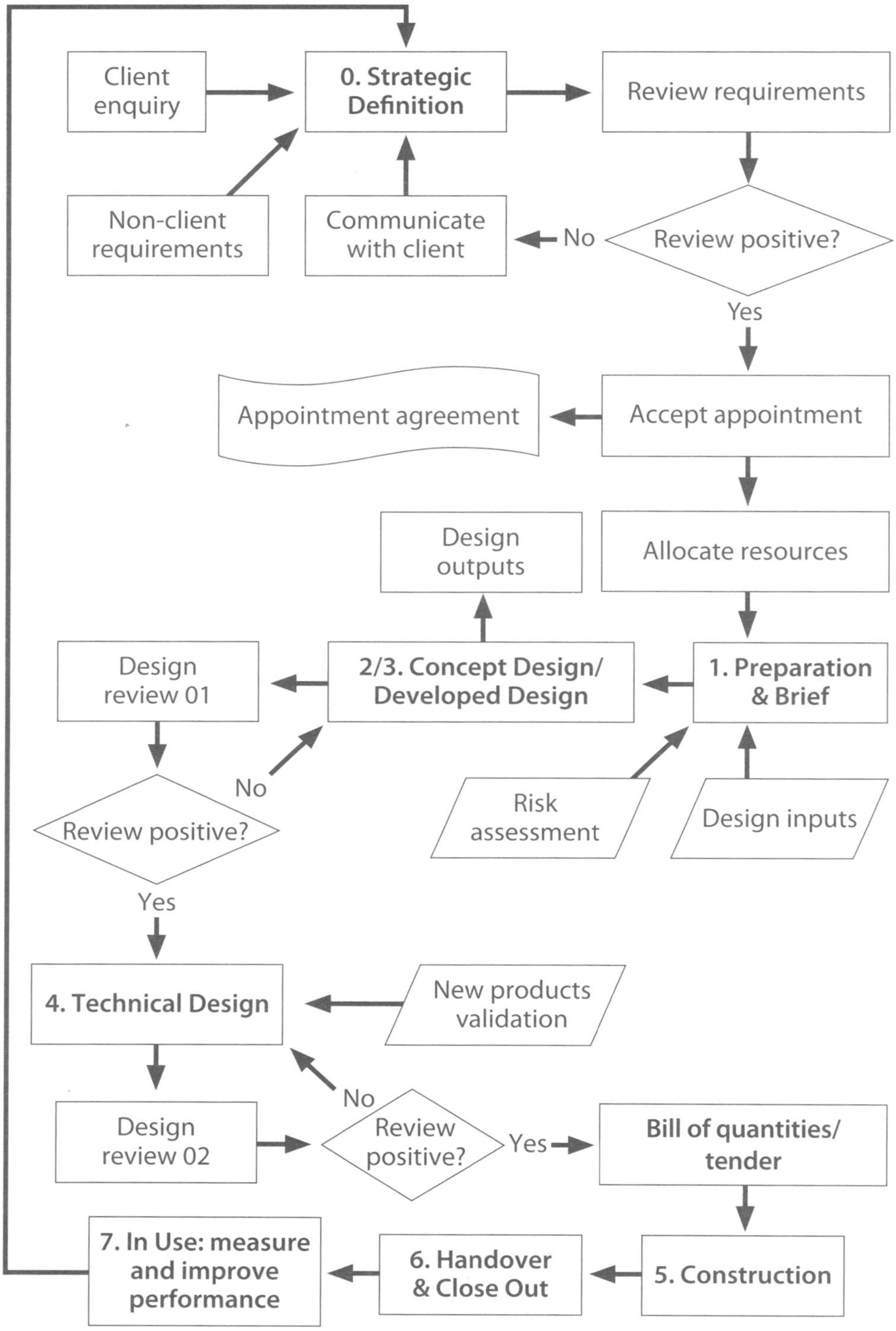

Figure 10.3 *Process map 2: measure and improve performance. Process owners: project team*

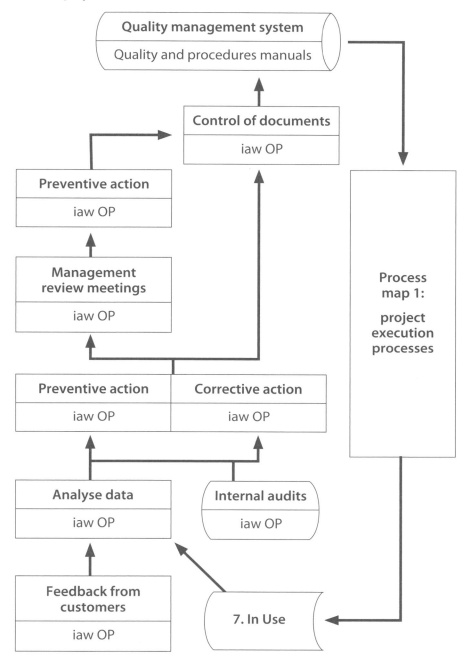

Key: iaw = in accordance with
OP = operating procedure

The production of a good manual or QA system will also allow a practice to demonstrate to PI insurers that it takes risk seriously, and one of the goals of writing these documents should be to satisfy any requirements PI insurers have with regard to their policies.

In practice, the only extra work on a day-to-day basis should be for staff running projects as they will have to record in a project plan that the established processes are being carried out. The project plan is the lynchpin of the entire QA process, and one by which external auditors will judge the success of the system. The project plan can be referenced to the RIBA work stages as outlined in the *RIBA Job Book*.

In order to take the process forward it is necessary to designate a Quality Director and also a Quality Manager. The Quality Manager role will include liaison with external consultants, managing the production of the quality manual, writing specific sections of the manual and reporting progress to the directors.

For larger practices the Quality Manager will need a support network in each office, with a designated QA Manager for each office to ensure the process is being implemented, and given the attention this process will require.

10.4.4 Certification

ISO does not itself certify organisations. Many countries have formed accreditation bodies to authorise certification bodies, which audit organisations applying for ISO 9001 compliance certification. The various accreditation bodies have mutual agreements with each other to ensure that certificates issued by one of the accredited certification bodies are accepted worldwide.

The UK Accreditation Service (UKAS) is a body recognised by the UK Government which accredits certification organisations (these are listed at www.ukas.com). The requirement for RIBA Chartered Practices with 51+ staff to have external ISO 9001 certification does not necessitate the use of a certification body on this particular list. However, many public sector procurement bodies insist that practices are certified for quality management by UKAS-accredited certification bodies.

The applying organisation is assessed based on an extensive sample of its sites, functions, products, services and processes; a list of problems ('action requests' or 'non-compliances') is made known to the management. If there are no major problems on this list, the certification body will issue an ISO 9001 certificate for each geographical site it has visited, once it receives a satisfactory improvement plan from the management showing how any problems will be resolved.

An ISO certificate must be renewed at regular intervals recommended by the certification body, usually around three years. The practice will also be audited between renewal audits by the certifying body to ensure the system is being operated in line with the certification. The frequency of the audits is at the discretion of the certifying body, but as a guide a medium-sized office would be audited externally twice a year.

It should be remembered that QA is not a static process – indeed, one of its principles is continuous improvement – and allowance should be made for positive change at all times which will result in improvements to the way the system works and ultimately the way the practice carries out its work. QA is not just an administration system; it is meant to allow monitoring of production – in architectural practice this is usually the design output, and ultimately leads to a better product.

10.5 Quality and sustainability

Demonstrating and achieving sound environmental performance through sustainable means is now an integral part of the design process. This is being done within the context of increasingly stringent legislation, the development of economic policies and other measures that foster environmental protection, and increased concern expressed by interested parties about environmental matters and sustainable development. Many clients now expect commitment to sound environmental principles as part of the appointment process.

10.5.1 BS 8555

BS 8555 provides guidance on how to implement environmental management systems. The guidance is grouped into four main areas:

- a six-phase incremental approach to implementing an environmental management system using environmental performance evaluation;
- information on environmental management and the use of environmental performance indicators;
- information to satisfy the environmental criteria increasingly being set in contract tenders by clients; and
- information for organisations that wish to self-declare or seek voluntary phased acknowledgement at a specified point throughout the implementation process.

10.5.2 BS EN ISO 14001

BS EN ISO 14001 provides the framework to develop procedures, which can be externally accredited, that take into account the legal requirements of the

10

construction industry and those significant environmental aspects resulting from the architectural business itself and design of buildings. It provides the structure for developing an environmental policy, establishing objectives and processes to achieve the policy commitments, take action to improve performance and demonstrate conformity in supporting environmental protection and prevention of pollution in balance with socioeconomic needs.

It is a requirement of obtaining RIBA Chartered Practice accreditation that a practice operates an environmental management policy. The RIBA Environmental Management Policy template can be used as the basis for developing an appropriate approach. However, for many practices formal accreditation to BS EN ISO 14001 will demonstrate the practice's commitment to this issue.

This standard works in the same way as BS EN ISO 9001, in that a manual should be produced defining the practice's environmental policy and its systems, which will be cross-referenced with a set of office procedures. These procedures could be incorporated into the main office manual or sit as an independent document.

In order to meet the standard it can be convenient to split the procedures into the impact of the business, and the impact that the designs produced by that business have on the environment.

Environmental management systems have identified relevant environmental aspects and include desired environmental objectives and targets. A list of possible topics for consideration in the production of these procedures could include:

Design of buildings	Office operations
Land use and site location	Office location and staff travel
Biodiversity	Biodiversity
Human impacts	Human impacts
Energy: conservation and renewable generation	Energy: conservation and renewable generation
Air quality and pollution	Air quality and pollution
Materials	Materials
Water	Water
Waste	Waste
Project and facility management	Office management

The accreditation process for BS EN ISO 14001 works in a similar way to BS EN ISO 9001.

10.6 Information management and library services

In many ways the term 'library' is a little outdated in terms of architectural practice, and the stored information should be seen as a knowledge bank that can provide inspiration and accurate data to support the design process. However, there is still a need for information to be stored and catalogued in a methodical and organised way, and large practices may need a dedicated librarian with specialist skills. When these are used in conjunction with IT specialists, information will be accessible and catalogued appropriately. For many smaller practices it may be more economical to employ the services of a freelance librarian who can work as and when required, depending on workload. The Construction Industry Information Group (CIIG) is an organisation dedicated to good practice in construction libraries, and can also provide a directory of freelance members (www.ciig.org.uk).

See also Chapter 13: Knowledge management.

10.6.1 The library

With easy access to information online, the contents of the library can be physically reduced compared with a traditional library, and to ensure optimum use of space the office should be specific and ruthless about its needs. An annual audit should be carried out to ensure the library is meeting the needs of the office, and to remove outdated information. There will be a need for core information, which can be grouped as follows:

- Quick reference material

  - RIBA Product Selector
  - ESI Publications (www.esi.info)
  - Barbour Compendium

- Non-trade literature

  - Architectural books and periodicals
  - Official publications
  - British Standards

- Trade literature

  - Trade works that are industry standards

- Maps

  - Historical and purchased OS maps

- Standard forms

  - RIBA contract administration forms
  - In-house standard forms

10

- In-house information

  ◦ Marketing and promotional material
  ◦ Standard specifications and materials
  ◦ Office manual.

10.6.2 Classification

Originally released in 1997, Uniclass allows project information to be structured to a recognised standard. The original version has been heavily revised to make it more suitable for use with modern construction industry practice and to make it compatible with BIM. As a key deliverable of the BIM Toolkit project, NBS have worked with experts from across the industry to develop Uniclass 2015 which contains tables classifying items of all scales and all sectors. It has been restructured and redeveloped to provide a comprehensive system suitable for use by the entire industry, including infrastructure, landscape and engineering services as well as the building sector, and for all stages in a project life cycle. Uniclass 2015 provides a means of structuring project information essential for the adoption of BIM level 2. Information about a project can be generated, used and retrieved throughout the life cycle.

Uniclass 2015 is divided into a set of tables which can be used to categorise information for costing, briefing, CAD layering, etc. as well as when preparing specifications or other production documents. These tables are also suitable for buildings and other assets in use, and maintaining asset management and facilities management information. The suite of tables is broadly hierarchical and allows information about a project to be defined from the broadest view of it to the most detailed.

The tables comprise:

- Complexes
  This describes a project in overall terms. It can be a private house with garden, drive, garage and tool shed, or it can be a university campus with buildings for lecturing, administration, sport, halls of residence, etc. Rail networks and airports are also all examples of complexes.
- Entities
  Entities are discrete things like buildings, bridges, tunnels etc. They provide the areas where different activities occur.
- Activities
  This defines the activities to be carried out in the complex, entity or space. For example a prison complex provides a detention activity at a high level, but can also be broken down into individual activities like exercise,

sleeping, eating, working, etc. The Activities table also includes surveys, operation and maintenance and services.

- Spaces/Locations

  In buildings, spaces are provided for various activities to take place. In some cases a space is only suitable for one activity, for example a kitchen, but a school hall may be used for assemblies, lunches, sports, concerts and dramas. Also classed as spaces are transport corridors that run between two locations.

- Elements

  Elements are the main components of a structure like a bridge (foundations, piers, deck) or a building (floors, walls and roofs).

- Systems

  Systems are the collection of components that go together to make an element or to carry out a function. For a pitched roof, the rafters, lining, tiles, ceiling boards, insulation and ceiling finish comprise a system, or a low temperature hot water heating system is formed from a boiler, pipework, tank, radiators etc. A signal system for a railway has a number of components and products; and the scum removal system is part of a wastewater treatment entity.

- Products

  Finally, the individual products used to construct a system can be specified, e.g. joist hangers, terrazzo tiles, gas fired boilers.

For further information go to www.thenbs.com and search 'Uniclass'.

10.6.3 Online subscriptions

A range of documents traditionally kept in paper form can now be viewed online, and the purchase of an online subscription ensures that all information is currently up to date. There are various levels of service available, and information can therefore be tailored to meet the needs of the office. These services are particularly useful in relation to statutory and legal requirements such as Building Regulations and British Standards. IHS is an industry-wide website providing access to comprehensive information on all aspects of construction:

www.ihs.com/industry/construction.html

National Building Specification (NBS), provided by RIBA Enterprises, can be accessed online by subscription, and is the industry standard for the provision of building specifications:

www.thenbs.com

10

10.7   Project-based communications

The practice of architecture revolves around the communication of ideas and concepts, which in turn become a physical reality. These ideas can be expressed in a variety of forms, but there are core issues to be considered that apply to virtually all types of presentation ranging from a public meeting to the writing of an email:

- Why – Why is the communication needed, and what style is most suitable?
- Who – Who is the intended recipient?
- What – Clarity and accuracy of information.

Communications skills vary, and it is important that channels are managed and that there is a chain of authority visible to all staff.

In terms of architectural practice, aside from drawings, there are essentially two different types of information that need to be presented – reports and technical information, and other material such as marketing and presentation material.

A technical report needs to be objective, concise and above all accurate. Presentation material, although it has some of the qualities of a technical report, has a bias towards style, selectivity and the selling of an idea which can be influenced in a much more personal way.

In support of both these outputs a building information model can be utilised for presentation purposes. A developed model allows both the design and space to be explored in many different ways, either through a planned walkthrough, a fly-through or a series of saved views. Using the developing model in this way allows the idea, the quality of space and the building in context to be better communicated than by 2D and 3D drawings.

In the end these types of presentations require review and reflection to ensure the message reaches the target audience, and careful editing to ensure clarity and consistency which will improve the quality of the communication. The major groups of written project communications and key points regarding their production are listed below.

10.7.1   Audio/visual/verbal presentations

- Who is the target audience?
- Is it part of a larger presentation – tailor the presentation for purpose.
- Visual aids can convey complex messages without the need for verbal explanation.

- Structure and shape – messages will be remembered if the structure has a developed argument with the main points reinforced by evidence.
- Questions and answers – prepare and research possible responses.
- Presentation – think about your body language and voice.

10.7.2 Technical reports

- Before writing be clear about the terms of reference of the report to ensure accuracy and relevance.
- Technical reports usually have a well-organised format to convey a sense of professionalism:

  - Title page
  - Acknowledgements
  - Contents
  - Abstract or summary
  - Introduction
  - Methodology
  - Results or findings
  - Discussion
  - Conclusions and recommendations
  - References
  - Appendices.

10.7.3 Design reports

Design development reports are advised at the end of particular RIBA stages. These are normally presented to the client and the design team, and set out the brief and how it is being responded to, and provide benchmarks for the future development of the design. The reports are normally presented, although not exclusively, at the following stages:

- Stage 2 – Concept Design
- Stage 3 – Developed Design
- Stage 4 – Technical Design.

The client's agreement to the design illustrated in these reports should be confirmed in writing.

As noted above, the building information model can also be utilised as a full summary of the status of the design through a series of agreed saved views and drawings and can form the basis of the stage report supplemented with appropriate information as required. This should be highlighted at the outset of the project so that the model is developed in a way that supports the reporting process.

10

10.7.4 Meetings and minutes

- Record why the meeting was called, what it achieved and actions required (by including an action column or list).
- Minutes record progress and are used as a benchmark to discuss ongoing issues and programme.
- Minutes are issued to external parties to inform progress.

10.7.5 Formal letters and contractual correspondence

- Use a formal style.
- Ensure references are accurate and precise.
- Use concise and clear language to ensure the message is understood.
- If there is potential for a claim, inform legal team and insurers.
- Ensure an early reply is sent to any correspondence, even if only a holding letter.

All these types of communication form part of the business image projected to external parties, and thoughtful arrangement and presentation can enhance the perceived status of the business for producing work of the highest standard.

10.8 Project drawings, specifications and schedules

Drawings are key tools for architects to demonstrate the ideas and solutions to a client's brief, and as such they must be organised in a clear and legible way. Good-quality production information reduces the incidence of site quality problems and leads to smooth-running jobs and significant cost savings. It is important to programme the work required to produce this information, to make sure it is completed on time and to an appropriate standard, because this is a key area where claims can arise for delay and extensions of time from contractors.

As noted above, CPIC is the Construction Project Information Committee, and it encourages the use of a standard system throughout the construction industry. The documents it produces contain useful information on the production information process and its management (www.cpic.org.uk). In general there are three types of production drawing at the construction phase of a project:

- General arrangement drawings:
    - give an overall picture of the shape, layout and form of construction of the building and external works;
    - determine setting out dimensions;

- locate and identify the spaces and parts of the building, e.g. rooms, doors, structural frame members, services terminals;
- identify references to more specific information, particularly to assembly drawings.

- Assembly drawings:

  - illustrate and identify how parts of the building and their junctions are constructed;
  - provide references to more specific information, particularly to the specification and any component drawings.

- Component drawings:

  - give information about components that cannot be given adequately on the assembly drawings.

As with drawings, specifications and schedules should be carefully drafted and reviewed by someone other than the author, and be given a reference number. Any revisions should be recorded and dated on the document, and previous forms marked as superseded.

Drawings and other project information can be produced directly from the building information model and assembly, components and elements used within the design and subject to the level of detail required will remain linked, so subsequent developments, coordination and revisions are reflected directly within the drawings, schedules and specifications.

10

10.9   Presentation and numbering systems

The key to retrieval of drawings is that they should be numbered and presented in a unique way. Apart from presentation material, drawings are now produced on a variety of commercially available programs, but production drawings in general are still presented stylistically in a layout similar to a hand-produced drawing, and should include the following information:

- Name of business
- Contact details
- Project title
- Drawing title
- Drawing number
- Revision date, number and date
- Author and check author
- Scale and north point
- Key to symbols.

Most practices use a unique job identifying number as part of the drawing number followed by a classification number and then a sequential number to give it a unique reference based on the classification.

The following documents set out a standardised approach to document naming and should be identified at the outset of the project so that all information is produced utilising the same system:

- BS 1192: 2007
- PAS 1192-2:2013
- AEC (UK) Model File Naming Handbook v2.4.

Numbering systems have also been developed that are specific to the computer or drawing system in use, and may include references to the storage system of the operating system as this enables ease of traceability. CAD standards are dealt with in Section 12.7.

10.10 Project records

It is important to remember that all project records, such as drawings and instructions, are legal documents, and so filing systems should be developed that are systematic, and logical, and allow for ease of retrieval.

Quality assurance, and more broadly the principle of sound risk management, demands that all such records are stored according to a formal procedure as they will be needed in the event of a complaint or legal proceedings.

There are document management systems that can name and file documents and drawings in an intuitive way, but these should be considered in terms of how the practice works; it may be possible to adjust them to suit a business model that applies specifically to the practice. Uniclass can be used to file project and administration documents, but in general a project number is used as an identifier with an alphanumeric code attached acting as the section and sub-section locators.

Where BIM is used, the workflow process for work-in-progress models and when information is issued for appropriate review should be identified. These models should be appropriately archived as they represent the status of the design at that stage. You should also use appropriate naming protocols, allowing them to be documented accordingly. If a website is being used to manage the design then you should ensure that any issued information is recorded locally as well as being uploaded to the management system. This will ensure that your data always remains retrievable without the need to access a third party storage system.

Records should also be kept of 'informal' communications and decisions, such as telephone calls, as these provide a record of the development of the job, and are as important as official contractual documents; they should be stored and recorded with the same care.

10.11 Email

Email is the standard communication tool in architectural practice, and a transparent and robust filing and retrieval system should be put in place, because management of email can easily become an onerous job in itself. Many practices use electronic filing systems that can be purchased as an add-on to current IT systems. Chapter 12 looks at IT in detail.

It is important to implement an email policy, and use email filtering and anti-virus software. Any email policy should be written in the context of the Data Protection Act 1998, which protects employees against the misuse of personal data, both manual and electronic. An email policy may include the following:

- Security and confidentiality of company information – internet email is not a secure medium of transfer, and password-protected attachments should be used when sending confidential information.
- The limits and obligations of personal use including a clause that prohibits the use of company email for the running or trading of another company.
- Legal obligations – email may be subject to litigation, and should be treated in the same way as traditional correspondence.
- Prohibition of dissemination, storage or viewing of obscene, racist or sexist material.
- Copyright of both internal and external material that is uploaded or sent on the company system.

Email correspondence

Email for business use is distinctly different from personal use, where a more relaxed style of presentation is common, and protocols should be set up and followed for business use to give guidance regarding use, style, presentation and content.

- Email is impersonal, and it may be better to speak to people face to face or make a phone call.
- Use email as the carrier of information, and use attachments where possible.
- Always ensure the subject line is filled in and relevant to the email.
- Think hard before replying to all addressees, as it is good practice to be specific and accurate in who receives and replies to e-mail correspondence.
- Design of headers and footers should be standardised across the business.

10

- Emails are legal documents, and retaining a formal style of business communication in their use is a good discipline; this reduces the chances of sending emails that are hard to understand or irrelevant.

10.12   Archiving

Archiving of material produced by the office needs to be managed and organised to allow easy retrieval, and forward thinking will save much time when a practice is asked to provide information to resolve a query about past work.

An archiving policy should be developed – this can easily be incorporated into the office manual or quality manual. Decisions need to be made as to how archives are to be stored, how long they are to be kept, and who has the authority to destroy records. Although contracts and PI insurances will differ, for many project documents there is a legal obligation to retain information relating to the contract, and it is in the interest of the office to retain drawings permanently as an archive of the work of the practice and a design resource. The RIBA recommends that key project documents are retained for 17–20 years, because of the laws relating to the periods within which claims may be brought. In the event of a claim being made against the firm, or the firm wishing to make a claim, relevant documents will need to be readily accessible. This will be of utmost importance where, for example, a claim is made via the more speedy dispute resolution procedures such as adjudication. Here the adjudicator will expect to see all relevant documentation to enable them to reach a decision within the 28-day period.

As noted above, the BIM protocols should highlight how electronic data will be recorded and stored throughout a project and this data should be archived accordingly with the project documentation and data. Any information shared via a project website should be recorded, stored and archived locally as a record of information shared.

It would be good practice to record and appropriately archive other consultants' information and models issued to form part of a federated model at an agreed review stage. This information represents the level of coordination and completion of the design and contributes to the context of the architectural model.

All current records, information and other live data should be reviewed from time to time, at least annually, by senior staff. Files that are no longer current and regularly referenced should be archived. A register of archived files should be set up in each office to record all hard copy files archived. This should list details of each file (e.g. project number, file reference) and should also state the disposal date. The register of archived files should be reviewed annually by the person responsible for archiving who should, when disposal dates occur, ensure that the expired records are destroyed in a confidential manner. All archives, whether within the office or off-site, should be kept securely with access restricted to the person responsible for archives and persons specifically authorised by a senior member of staff.

If the project has been developed utilising a building information model to a sufficient level of definition then the model could be utilised by the client or building user to manage the facility. The final issue of the model should be recorded and archived accordingly as the facilities management team may alter the model significantly to suit the management software.

Archiving is the final process in the life of a job, and setting up filing and naming conventions correctly at the beginning of a project will ensure the archiving process will be simpler to organise.

The storage of archived electronic data, and its security, should be considered as part of the general requirements of an IT section in the office or quality manual. Any policy for storing, archiving and where appropriate disposing of electronic data should follow that for hard copy documents.

References and further reading

BS 1192:2007. Collaborative production of architectural, engineering and construction information. Code of practice (London: BSI, 2008).

BS 8555:2003. Environmental management systems. Guide to the phased implementation of an environmental management system including the use of environmental performance evaluation (London: BSI, 2003).

BS EN ISO 9001:2008. Quality management systems. Requirements (London: BSI, 2008).

BS EN ISO 14001. Environmental management (London: BSI).

Eynon, J. and Chartered Institute of Building, *The Design Manager's Handbook* (Chichester: Wiley-Blackwell, 2013).

Jeffries, T., *Transition Document for the Quality Management System: To facilitate compliance with BS EN ISO 9001: 2000* (London: RIBA Publishing, 2003).

Langford, D. and Murray, M., *Architect's Handbook of Construction Project Management* (London: RIBA Publications, 2004).

Ostime, N., *RIBA Job Book*, 9th edn (London: RIBA Publications, 2013).

RIBA, *A Client's Guide to Engaging an Architect* (May 2013 revision) (London: RIBA Publishing, 2013).

RIBA Plan of Work 2013 Overview (London: RIBA Publishing, 2013).

10

Sinclair, D., *Assembling a Collaborative Project Team* (London: RIBA Publishing, 2013).

Sinclair, D., *Guide to Using the RIBA Plan of Work 2013* (London: RIBA Publishing, 2013).

Walker, A., *Project Management in Construction* (Oxford: Blackwell Publishing, 2007).

Risk management and insurance

THIS CHAPTER:

- provides advice on identifying and managing risk;
- breaks down the various types of risk a practice may encounter;
- explains the workings of professional indemnity insurance.

11.1 Introduction

Prudent employers will establish policies and procedures to manage risk with the intention of trying to eliminate error. However, even practices that follow the best of systems and procedures will make errors on rare occasions, and they are required by the ARB (by law), and the RIBA (by the Code of Professional Conduct), to take out and maintain professional indemnity (PI) insurance adequate to cover such eventualities.

Dealing with a claim from a client for breach of professional duty is extremely time-consuming for the practice, in particular its senior management, at a time when productive, income-producing work could be pursued. It can also be depressing and sapping on the morale of those involved. The first objective for a practice should be to establish procedures to identify and manage its risks so that claims are, at worst, infrequent, and preferably non-existent (see Chapter 10).

The cost of PI insurance is likely to feature relatively high on the practice's list of annual expenditure; however, the potential consequences of facing a claim without adequate PI insurance could be catastrophic for a practice and/or its partners/directors.

11.2 Risk management

Effective risk management means that the practice is more likely to get it right first time. This leads to less reworking (and therefore more profit), higher morale, and an enhanced reputation for high-quality work, and consequently more commissions from existing and new clients. Conversely, poor risk management increases the possibility of the practice exposing itself to a claim against its PI insurance.

11

The first and most important task is to identify the potential risks that the practice faces. It is only once this is done that measures can be instituted to eliminate or minimise their effect. Certain practices operate on the 'it will never happen to us' principle, but prudent ones will actively plan to minimise the risk that errors will occur.

There are several sources of sound advice on identifying and managing risk, including the *RIBA Good Practice Guide: Keeping out of Trouble*. PI insurers can often provide good risk management advice: for example, the RIBA Insurance Agency undertakes regular risk management audits of member practices to help improve processes and thus minimise the risk of a claim. The RIBA, in association with the RIBA Insurance Agency, has produced a short guide entitled *Understanding Risk Management*, which has been designed to assist architects in understanding and managing risk within their business. (This can be downloaded from www.architectsPI.com/pages/riskmanagement.aspx.)

Included in the risks that a practice should assess and plan to minimise may be:

- The risk that a client may go into liquidation or may not pay fees owing for other reasons, causing liquidity problems for the practice.
- The risk of a key member(s) of staff leaving at a critical time.
- The risk of a key supplier going into liquidation.
- The risk of a deteriorating workload leaving the practice with insufficient income.
- The risk of a disaster, such as a fire or terrorist alert, occurring to the practice or its premises rendering it difficult/impossible to fulfil its obligations.
- The risk of errors occurring on a project leading to a claim against the practice.

The potential risks to the practice should be discussed by the partners/directors and assessed according to the likelihood of them occurring and the severity of the effect should they do so. A simple matrix can be developed to show these two variables, which will show clearly the most significant potential issues:

Description of possible incident:			
		Severity of incident	
		Low	High
Likelihood of incident occurring	High		
	Low		

The practice should prioritise plans to address those incidents that have a high likelihood of occurring and a serious impact should they do so.

Having identified and assessed the potential risks, a strategy should be devised to mitigate the effect of the identified risks should they occur, and communicated to relevant people throughout the practice. Many such strategies, particularly those relating to projects, are covered in more detail in Chapter 10. Risk management plans should be regularly reviewed (at least annually) and updated as necessary.

11.2.1 Client-related risks

Many architects greet the prospect of a new commission with open arms and rush off to start work without having given full consideration to the risks involved or putting measures in place to give them the best chance of avoiding or minimising these risks.

Critical among these is that they won't get paid. It is recommended that a formal process is adopted for verifying as far as possible that the client is financially stable and, at the very least, has a reasonable record for settling accounts.

A long history of working successfully with a client on repeat commissions will render this unnecessary, but architects should consider asking a new client for references from architects or others that they have commissioned previously. For major corporate clients Dun & Bradstreet operate a credit rating system based partially on their payment record.

The chances of an architect being paid for their work reduce if they don't set out the basis of their engagement at the outset. The appointment process, together with recommendations for issues to be covered, is set out in detail in Chapter 9. The need to understand the scope and basis of the appointment cannot be stressed too strongly.

Even the best checks on a client's solvency and the best-drafted terms of appointment may not guarantee payment by the client. The practice should watch out for warning signs that clients may be in financial difficulty, including late payment, excuses for non-payment, and unsigned or undated cheques, and should consider what measures they should take to seek recovery. Chapter 7 sets out the need to initiate a sound invoicing and fee-chasing process. The RIBA Good Practice Guides *Keeping out of Trouble* and *Painless Financial Management* both contain sound practical advice to help the architect get paid.

Architects rarely cease trading because of lack of work – it is lack of cash that brings the majority down, and a reluctance to take money seriously is possibly the largest risk to the long-term survival of a practice.

11

11.2.2   Resource-related risks

Risks that a practice can bring upon itself fall broadly into two categories – those associated with resources, and their adequacy in both quantity and quality, and risks associated with making mistakes during the performance of the services.

Upon being approached to undertake a new commission, the architect should ensure they have the necessary skills and resources available to undertake the services they are contracted to provide. Indeed the RIBA Code of Professional Conduct requires an architect to verify this before accepting the commission.

In order to assess this it is worth maintaining a register of the staff employed, and of their skills, qualifications and experience, recording such things as:

- architectural qualifications;
- other qualifications;
- skill and experience levels in different aspects of design and project management;
- skill and experience levels in different sectors;
- skill levels in different CAD programs and other software;
- specialist skills and experiences;
- training undertaken.

It is important that, having established a suitable set of records, they are maintained and updated to ensure that current information is available when needed. The establishment of such databases needs to be carefully thought through as over-complicating them will make them 'user-unfriendly' and lead to them not being properly completed or regularly updated by staff, or even not used at all.

These databases should be referred to when compiling CVs to be put into submissions for projects, but care should be taken to ensure that any individual whose CV is included in a project bid is available to work on the project should the bid be successful.

The other main staff-related risk is that individuals with a particular skill set or role in the practice can place the practice at risk should they decide to leave. It is any employee's contractual right to leave on completion of the agreed notice period, so it is important that the practice acknowledges this risk, and develops plans to mitigate it.

The risk of departure should, however, never be used as an excuse for failing to train all staff appropriately and adequately to enable them to perform their tasks.

Practices may sometimes sub-let a part of their services – having first obtained the client's agreement. In these instances the architect should check that the person(s) or practice(s) they will sub-contract the work to:

- have the necessary resources to perform the role;
- have the necessary skills and expertise to perform the role;
- have an appropriate level of PI insurance.

A formal sub-contract should be entered with the appropriate party on terms and conditions that are compatible with the architect's appointment with their client. It is particularly important to define fully and clearly the role that the sub-consultant is to perform, the deliverables that are their responsibility, and the timescale for performance of their part of the services.

11.2.3 Project-related risks

No matter how good the practice is, or how well it manages its risks, errors will occasionally occur, and the way in which the practice resolves these may determine the chances of a claim being made against it and its chances of securing future work from the client. As noted above, the practice is required to purchase PI insurance to cover any losses a client suffers due to the architect having failed to perform their services as required under their appointment. These risks can be minimised by the implementation of robust procedures that are applied throughout the practice comprehensively (see Chapter 10).

Particular attention should be paid to establishing a good document storage and retrieval system, which will make documents easy to find should suggestions of breach of duty be made, and that a clear record is maintained showing exactly what was issued to whom, and when.

Another area requiring careful planning and management is control over members of staff, and the checking procedures that are established to make sure that only carefully prepared and thoroughly checked information is issued. It is particularly challenging to keep control of this when the majority of information and correspondence is produced and issued electronically.

Particular attention should be paid to the performance of inspection services. It is critical that the architect's team, including site staff where appointed, understand their role, the scope of their authority, and the requirements that the form of construction contract places on them as architect. It is important that those inspecting the works on behalf of the architect are experienced in this, and have a thorough understanding of the contract documentation, and thus what should be constructed by the

11

contractor. It is recommended that elements of construction to be inspected are planned before the visit. Good records, including photographs, should be taken and circulated as appropriate, and retained for future reference.

Requests to participate in post-completion evaluations should be carefully assessed as these may lead to an extension of the architect's period of liability.

11.2.4 Unusual risks (usually) outside the practice's control

There are a range of potential occurrences that could have a serious impact on the practice which are difficult to avoid through planning, so it is important to develop strategies for dealing with them should they occur. These include:

- failure of energy suppliers;
- computer crashes;
- fire, flood, etc.;
- terrorist attacks.

Any of these may affect the practice's ability to produce the work necessary to earn fees, or may occasion additional unplanned expenditure in order to hire/rent new premises/equipment. Potential situations should be thought about in advance and a plan drawn up setting out how they will be dealt with, and by whom, if and when they occur. Those responsible should be fully briefed, and it is prudent to consider occasional 'dry runs'. Such plans, when prepared, should be reviewed and updated regularly.

National or international economics are also a risk factor for many practices, and contingency plans for dealing with reducing workloads/income streams are best set down before they occur, so they can be actioned rapidly should the need arise.

This is not to say that pre-prepared plans should be followed slavishly, but they should act as good guidelines, setting down a series of actions to be confirmed and implemented should the circumstances occur.

11.3 Professional indemnity insurance

The Architects (Registration) Acts, as administered by the Architects Registration Board (ARB), require all practising qualified architects to be covered by appropriate PI insurance for their professional work, such that a policy exists that will pay out in the event that the architect is found to be in breach of their professional duty and/or has been negligent in the way in which they have carried it out.

The cost of purchasing PI insurance is likely to be one of the practice's largest overhead costs, and it needs to be carefully considered by the practice (see Section 11.3.2).

Although relatively uncommon at present, there are forms of project-based insurance, including decennial (ten-year) insurance, purchased occasionally. In this instance a single insurance policy is taken out, usually by the employer, insuring against error by any of the professional consultants or the contractor. Clients may seek a reduction in the architect's fee should this type of insurance be purchased, and in these instances the practice should verify that the insurer has waived its rights to sue individual practices if it is their error that has led to a claim on the insurance before either offering a discount or omitting cover for the project from their own PI policy.

One advantage is removing the possibility of gaps in cover during any switch of insurers. Although currently mainly in use on very large scale projects, single-project insurance could potentially enable smaller practices to bid for one-off projects that are larger than they would usually undertake and which have a requirement for cover greater than their standard level. There is also a benefit to clients in removing the risk of a consultant ceasing or reducing the level of cover further down the line.

In the USA there is, additionally, a move towards cover on a range of liabilities (PI, public liability, employer's liability) for multiple parties on a single project. Termed 'wrap-up' or 'fully-integrated' insurance, these policies minimise the risk of disputes between the parties involved because one policy covers all of them. Whether this trend moves across to the UK is yet to be seen.

Owner's protective PI insurance (OPPI) is also occasionally purchased by clients in the UK, although it is more common in the USA. In this instance the client will purchase a 'top-up' to the PI insurance of the architect, and possibly the other consultants. It is usually a condition of this type of insurance that the practices being covered are not informed of its existence for fear they may reduce their cover and leave the OPPI insurer more exposed.

11.3.1 Level of cover

The ARB requires architects to carry 'adequate and appropriate' PI insurance, and currently states the following guidance on levels of cover:

- Turnover less than £100,000 per annum – £250,000 minimum cover.
- Turnover between £100,000 and £200,000 per annum – £500,000 minimum cover.
- Turnover above £200,000 per annum – £1,000,000 minimum cover.

Furthermore, the RIBA Code of Professional Conduct requires all members to ensure that their professional work is protected by an appropriate insurance policy at a level commensurate with the type of projects they undertake, and they should inform their clients as to whether or not they carry PI insurance; many clients will ask for confirmation of this, and the level of cover maintained by the practice, in any event. The Provision of Services Regulations 2009 require architects to make available to the client and potential client certain information about their business and the handling of complaints. This includes details of the practice's PI insurer.

The partners/directors of the practice should assess what level of cover is appropriate for them. They must consider whether they purchase in excess of the minimums laid down by the ARB, for any claim that exceeds the sums paid out by their PI insurance will fall to the practice and/or them as individuals to meet. Practices, in assessing their PI insurance cover needs, should remember that in a disappointingly large number of cases the majority of the cost paid out following a PI claim is the legal cost of defending it, which can exceed the pure cost of rectifying the defect.

If the practice offers services over and above those of the 'normal' architect, it is important to check that their PI insurance covers them for these additional services.

While the amount of PI cover, and the terms and conditions of it, are a matter for the partners/directors of the practice, there will be many instances where clients seek to require their architect to purchase a certain minimum level of cover. This is often included within the terms of appointment.

There are some clients who believe that their architects should carry an excessive level of PI insurance. However, it is worth noting that the costs associated with the rectification of faults, and costs flowing therefrom, arising out of a catastrophic failure by the architect in respect of a building are, in most instances, likely to be less than those that may be caused by the structural engineer. History tends to suggest that claims against architects are comparatively common but relatively small in cost as opposed to those against engineers which tend to be fewer but larger.

In these instances, the partners/directors should discuss the PI level being asked for by the client and endeavour to persuade them that, because the risk of inadequate cover rests principally with them, the cover they purchase is adequate for the commission being considered.

11.3.2 Obtaining PI insurance

PI insurance is in most cases annually renewable, and the practice will have to complete a detailed proposal form each year. It has a duty to disclose anything that may affect the premium charged by the insurer – failure to do so may invalidate or limit the insurance cover. Such details are likely to include, among other things:

- Names and qualifications of directors/partners, and number and experience levels of staff (in general terms).
- Turnover for recent years.
- Projected turnover for the current and following year.
- Profile of fees in terms of both services offered and building types constructed (usually split into public and private sector fee income). It is also usually a requirement to advise the quantum of fees from non-UK projects.
- Services offered by the practice to be covered by the policy.
- Details of claims made against the practice during the past ten years, and of any events that may give rise to a claim against the practice. It is usually a requirement of the proposal form for the practice to enquire of its employees whether or not any of them are aware of any such event, and this should be done and recorded.
- Largest projects completed and about to commence.

PI insurance is available from a number of commercial providers. Practices should choose their PI insurance broker and provider with care. Policies offered by the RIBA Insurance Agency are specifically tailored to the needs of architects, and include the benefit of a discounted legal advice service to comment on proposed forms of appointment. The RIBA Insurance Agency provides PI insurance on agreed RIBA terms, including an innocent non-disclosure clause, and, exclusively among PI policies, the right to refer a dispute to the President of the RIBA.

It is recommended that, once a practice has placed its PI insurance with an underwriter, it should seek to remain with that underwriter. Over time, the insurer will get to know the practice and vice versa, ensuring an efficient line of communication between the two, as much certainty as is available in the market of consistency of terms and cover, and the highest likelihood that the underwriter will provide full cover for a claim on a project whose appointment was agreed a number of years before. Changing underwriters every year for the sake of saving a small amount of money is not recommended – the costs to the partners/directors of the practice of not having proper PI cover when a claim is made are likely to be much more significant.

11.3.3   Basis of cover

PI insurance is offered on a 'claims made' basis, where a claim is set against the insurance policy for the year in which the event that leads to a claim is

11

notified, rather than the year when the project was undertaken or when the damage first occurred.

The basis of cover does change from time to time, as does the overall availability and cost of PI insurance, depending on market circumstances. Furthermore, the wording of different PI policies varies, and it is therefore important for the partners/directors to ensure that their particular policy covers risks relevant to their practice.

Most architectural PI policies in the UK are offered on an 'each and every' claim basis, whereby an amount up to the maximum of the consultant's insurance cover will be paid for all claims against the architect, enabling a client to make a number of claims on a single contract, if the architect has caused a series of different failures. However, it is still relatively common for other, particularly foreign, consultants to have 'aggregate' insurance policies where the payments made by the insurer are limited in total in any single policy year rather than in respect of each claim.

The premium for PI insurance will depend on a number of factors, but chiefly the turnover of the business. Recognising the 'claims made nature' for the payment of claims, PI insurance is relatively cheap to purchase for a new practice, which has no history of potential claims as it has done little work, and increases over time as the practice builds up a portfolio of completed buildings, and therefore potential claims.

Most insurers will consider the practice's claims record before offering terms, although one of the benefits of remaining with one underwriter is that they can see a good claims experience over a number of years, and are less likely to penalise the practice for one poor year of claims.

All policies are subject to an excess, which is a matter for agreement between the insurer and the practice. In broad terms, the greater the excess that the practice is prepared to bear against each claim, the lower the premium will be.

The partners/directors need to consider who should be covered by their PI insurance policy. Clearly current staff, including agency or contract staff, should be covered, and the policy should be checked to ensure it includes no rights of subrogation against employees (where the insurance company can seek to recover any monies they have paid out from the employee who made the mistake). It is usual for policies to include this provision; however, employees will not be protected if they have acted fraudulently, maliciously or illegally.

Cover for retired partners/directors should be considered, as should cover for parent or subsidiary companies, joint ventures or sub-consultancy and other working arrangements with other practices.

11.3.4　Claims

It is essential that a practice notifies their PI insurer as soon as they become aware of an event that may lead to a claim against the practice. Failure to do so may lead to a claim being rejected. Insurance companies, by and large, do not penalise practices for the number of notifications they make. Indeed, it is sometimes held that they respond more favourably to the practice that notifies events that do not ultimately lead to a claim.

It is important that the practice, and its employees, do not say or do anything in relation to a particular problem that may prejudice their defence should the problem escalate into a claim. For this reason, it is recommended that the practice maintains a good level of dialogue with its insurer relating to any difficult situation, and takes guidance and advice from them before responding to allegations of defects, etc.

It is common for many weeks or months, or sometimes even years, to pass between the notification of an event likely to lead to a claim and the practice actually receiving a claim. Upon receiving notification of an intended claim, usually from the client's solicitors, or a formal claim, the practice should immediately inform their PI insurers, and seek their advice on action to be taken.

Should the claim be pursued, the insurance company will usually appoint a firm of solicitors to act on their behalf, and a process of 'discovery', 'statements of claim', 'disclosure of relevant documentation', 'preparation' and 'exchange' of witness statements will begin. If it looks likely that the claim will proceed to trial, the defence team is likely to be increased by the addition of barristers and/or expert witnesses. It is at this time that the costs associated with a claim can escalate dramatically, as can the time needed by senior members of the practice to research events and prepare its defence.

Many insurers believe that an architect seeking to instigate legal action against their client for non-payment of fees may encourage a counter-claim alleging mistakes on the part of the architect, and therefore may require the architect to notify them of their intent before instigating such proceedings.

There are a number of alternative dispute resolution procedures, which may be referred to in the appointment documentation. Where specified, these should be followed, as they set out to provide a swifter and less expensive form of dispute resolution. Included in these forms are mediation, adjudication and arbitration. Any practice faced with the need to initiate or respond to these types of situations should consult its PI insurance and legal advisers for guidance on how best to proceed.

11

Proper risk assessments and top-quality management processes cannot be recommended highly enough as a way of avoiding, or at least minimising, the number of claims incidents experienced by a practice. See Section 11.2 and Chapter 10.

References and further reading

Bateman, M., *Tolley's Practical Risk Assessment Handbook* (London: Butterworth-Heinemann, 2006).

Burkitt, J., *Disputes without Tears: Alternative Methods of Dispute Resolution* (London: RIBA Publishing, 2000).

Luder, O., *Good Practice Guide: Keeping out of Trouble* (London: RIBA Publishing, 2012).

Pinder-Ayres, B., *Good Practice Guide: Painless Financial Management* (London: RIBA Publishing, 2008).

RIBA, *A Client's Guide to Engaging an Architect* (May 2013 revision) (London: RIBA Publishing, 2013).

Walker, P., Greenwood, D. and Chappell, D., *Construction Companion to Risk and Value Management* (London: RIBA Publishing, 2002).

Computing, CAD, BIM and IT

12.1 Introduction

The way we produce, manage and communicate information is constantly changing, and with the increasing use and expansion of the internet, architectural practices are frequently being asked to produce faster, better and more economical information.

Determining and developing the right systems and tools to meet these needs, and the future requirements of any practice, is critical, and should always be based on an understanding of exactly what information will be produced, both now and in the future. Knowing this will ensure that any decision regarding the right hardware and software will be made significantly easier, as well as defining the best fit for any supporting systems that may be required.

This chapter will review the basic principles of the internet, and the opportunities presented through its varying forms of interface and networks. In addition, in line with these expanding connections, it will provide an overview of the potential of these associations and the development of building information modelling (BIM).

With both the internet and BIM in mind, the following is a brief overview of the hardware, software and peripheral systems available, highlighting the options and opportunities for using and managing them to best effect within any size of practice. The review of software will not be product specific, but will take a more generalised view of the kind of information that can be produced, and in what way.

12

12.2   Choosing a set-up that suits the business

It is essential for a practice to understand how best to build and develop its systems to produce information suited to its aims, objectives and business model.

Whether a small, medium or large practice, this understanding of what information represents the majority of the workload will help define the types of terminals/workstations, their platform, the software and systems needed, and any required peripheral systems. Not only is knowing the shape and form of the 'end product' key to determining a computing and information technology (IT) strategy, but it should also be a key consideration within the overall business strategy (see Section 4.4).

Creating and communicating this information can then be managed through the use of different types of system and application, with varying levels of sophistication tailored to suit both aspirations and budget.

12.3   Building information modelling (BIM)

Before reviewing the components that constitute the set-up options, it is worth highlighting the principles that define BIM, and how they might influence the design of a system.

The three-letter acronym 'BIM' has been taken variously to stand for either 'building information management' or 'building information modelling'. The use of the two definitions has almost been interchangeable, although consensus is beginning to settle on the latter. However, BIM is much more than a digital representation of the design; it is a multi-faceted technological approach for the whole building process and should be considered as a methodology, an approach and a process for delivering a coordinated architecture, engineering and construction (AEC) project.

Design, manufacture, assembly and management are encompassed in a single philosophy, which is in part about the team, the approach and the technology, and all about the overall collaboration.

BIM is not just the software that facilitates the team's delivering a single project model, or the way that model is stored and accessed; it is the process through which the whole team collaborates and coordinates the design towards a common output. This can, if managed appropriately, be delivered through a more straightforward and simplified route than a sophisticated architectural computer model reflecting the finished functioning design. The principles of collaborative working and workflow protocols are outlined within PAS 1192-2:2013 as well as within the AEC (UK) Drawing Management Handbook v2.4, which will define how the models are produced and allow models to be hosted and reviewed online via a number of extranet sites, such as www.asite.com, www.conject.com, www.en-gb.viewpoint.com/ and www.cpic.org.uk.

Following the idea of BIM being an approach rather than just a system, it is more commonly defined as a 3D, object-oriented approach to computer-aided architectural design, which allows the complete management of the design-specific information throughout the lifespan of the project.

It is a system that enables information and data from specific or generic manufacturers' details to be imported into the design, and it locates these 3D products 'as constructed' within the building model.

It allows these elements to be reviewed and tested against the other building systems, and it also allows the reverse of this process to occur, with design elements being imported directly into manufacturing technology to produce full-scale products from the modelled elements. A suitably developed model can also allow the environment and building systems to be tested to determine the most sustainable approach for the site and related systems.

The model itself comprises building geometry, spatial relationships, geographic information, quantities and properties of building components, specifications, costs, schedules and maintenance requirements, and represents a significant shift from the more traditional computer-aided drafting methods of drawing with vector file based lines that combine to represent objects. BIM objects are 'intelligent' in that they assess the objects around them and react to any change in the parameters they have been assigned.

These parametric objects highlight clashes and coordination issues with other systems when they can't adjust to the information adjacent to them, e.g. a duct object passing unplanned through a wall object or another duct.

BIM also represents a shift both in working methods and in the transfer of information, as all the design team consultants, contractors and end users share and utilise the single-project model. This decreases the potential for coordination errors, as each discipline's objects combine to form the model, and with the use of additional clash detection software issues are easily identified and resolved.

The data stored in the model can be named and coded appropriately and then serve the client/user in helping to manage each element of the actual building, defining attributes and maintenance requirements as well as replacement suppliers. The benefits of BIM services include:

12

- full collaboration within the project team;
- detailed project information documenting the design life and lifecycle of the project;
- complete coordination of the components of the building, facilitating the review, analysis and elimination of discrepancies and clashes;
- pre-fabrication and design for manufacture opportunities;
- support for construction process and project management techniques;
- automatic scheduling and costing of elements and components;
- elimination of waste within the design, construction and maintenance processes;
- an internet-based model providing 24/7 access.

Ultimately the aim of a collaborative workflow is to produce and utilise a single project model that is hosted in a web-based location (Level 3 BIM), allowing the design to be accessed and viewed by the client, users, stakeholders and building team and permitting the design to be interrogated, reviewed and perceived in real time. However, current best practice employs a federated model workflow (Level 2 BIM).

A federated model allows each consultant to produce a specific model relative to their discipline; the models are coordinated at a relevant and pre-planned stage following their progress through a number of work-in-progress developments, creating a single federated model. The review of the federated model can be completed within the native BIM software, or it can be done using additional software that allows models generated in different formats to be combined for numerous forms of analysis, such as spatial and component coordination, clash detection, costing and programming purposes.

When Level 3 BIM is finally achieved, access to all the integrated project information will be typically through an internet-based website that hosts the single project model, ensuring that teams can collaborate from anywhere and at any time.

12.4   The internet

If BIM or an alternative collaborative approach to the design process is the way forward for the AEC industry, then this transition is made a little easier through its accessibility via the internet. Single-project models – whether in a 2D or a 3D format, or simply a set of project drawings and data – can be accessed, stored, communicated and reviewed via the web, either directly or via intra- or extranets (see Section 12.5).

The internet affects everything we do, and is increasingly simplifying all forms of communication and information management. It has and will continue to have a significant impact on the way we design and construct, both now and in the future.

However, the internet, like BIM, is a process and a methodology – a philosophy and an approach. Neither is actually tangible; they simply exist and are accessed and utilised through a series of applications and tools.

How a practice chooses to utilise the internet within its business, and its IT and computing strategies, will greatly affect the information it produces and the way it will be communicated, as well as influencing the way the practice procures, sets up and progresses its systems.

Internet security

When considering access to the internet, the primary concern should be security, and ensuring that the business is not at risk of data loss or lengthy system downtime from an intrusion by an unknown user.

Very basic measures will involve password protection and a backup of computer data (see Section 12.6); however, systems should have some form of anti-virus, anti-spyware and email security run automatically, with regular updates, to be certain that they are always protected. Viruses, along with the dangers involved, are constantly evolving.

For larger systems with increased internet usage through a significant number of terminals it may be more beneficial to include, in addition to the anti-virus and spyware software on the individual terminals, a hardware firewall through which all data has to pass in order to be reviewed.

In addition to the firewall, a content filter could be applied to stop users accessing sites that are known or are likely to harbour data or information that could be harmful to the system.

The same type of filter can be applied to all incoming emails via a hosted filter site that scans all emails addressed to the company before passing them through its own security measures. These measures are very simple to apply, but the implications of ignoring them can be catastrophic, with the possibility of losing projects, databases or even the entire network.

12.5   Networking

In order to allow files and information to be shared easily within the office or other locations it is necessary to connect all or some of the practice's workstations together to form a network. Networks essentially allow a computer's operating system to access the resources of a remote computer to support the same functions as it could if those resources were connected directly to the local computer.

12

Simple networks can be formed using a physical ethernet type of connection between terminals, or via a connection using wireless technology.

Once created, a network can be expanded to include all the computers in an office, in local offices, or even globally through the internet, which represents the simplest and the largest system of interconnected networks, facilitating the global transfer and use of all forms of information and data.

12.5.1 Types of network

The most common network is a local area network (LAN), which can interface anything from two computers to hundreds in one physical area. Wide area networks (WANs) link computers or a group of computers (LANs) that are far apart and connect via the internet, phone or satellite.

The levels of use, accessibility and security rights differ between different types of network; LANs tend to suit internal use through internal systems and workstations in individual physical locations, such as a building, whereas WANs may physically connect separate parts of an organisation to each other, and may include additional connections to third parties.

Types of network interfaces can be classified typically as:

- an intranet
- an extranet
- the internet.

Intranets

An intranet, in contrast to the internet, is a network or a group of networks within an organisation. It tends to be interfaced using web browsers that control access to all forms of information and data, and is managed in a single location with control over security and accessibility. It can be used to allow the flow of information between locations, internal communications and marketing, management of projects and management of work streams. The advantage of an intranet is that all users will access the same data through an identical interface, no matter what type of hardware and software they are using.

Extranets

An extranet, on the other hand, is a private network or internetwork that allows access, typically across the internet, to a selected group of users or workstations, to share and utilise information. Commonly, whole projects can be hosted on an extranet, allowing all members of the design team from multiple organisations to upload and publish their drawings to the project. This allows everyone to share and comment on information as it progresses, but it also manages and tracks the progress of the project throughout its development.

When using a project-hosting extranet it is important to make and/or receive a copy of all the information relating to the practice at the end of the job, because projects are often archived, and a fee will be charged to access them in the future.

The cost of a project extranet also tends to be shared within the project, and following completion these costs are no longer met, which can result in deletion of the data. It is therefore vitally important to research and understand what happens to all the information after the works are complete.

Many design-based extranets are appearing on the internet, with newer and better ways to share and develop live information between project teams. With the transfer of data becoming as important as the data itself, it is worth spending time reviewing what will, if required, best suit the practice's methods of working.

12.5.2 The fundamental components of a network

The simplest network is commonly two PCs connected together to share files or a printer. It is created and managed using:

- two terminals
- security software
- an interface (LAN, WAN, etc.)
- cabling or wireless connectivity
- servers (for larger networks).

Obviously, once a network has been created it can accommodate remote connections over the internet, allowing any roaming laptops to connect back to the office and the data held within it. However, as a network increases in size, so will it need to be managed, and the appointment of an IT specialist should be considered to service the system on a full- or part-time basis.

12.5.3 The workstation

Workstations represent the coalface of the business – where the key information is created, managed and controlled. These can either be laptops or desktops, but whatever the size of a practice, it is likely that a mixture of both will be preferable.

12

Laptops allow flexibility and remote working, but have smaller screens and often less processing power, whereas desktops are limited only by the spatial constraints of the office and the number needed. Laptops:

- are constrained by their screen size;
- have battery limitations;
- do provide a 'work anywhere' ethic;
- can create and demonstrate work out of the office;
- can connect to the internet almost anywhere;
- can utilise a number of wireless peripherals.

It is worth noting that laptops are easily stolen: not only do you lose the computer, you also lose all your data. Types of insurance, and how data is backed up, may also therefore influence the decision about which type of workstation to invest in.

Desktops:

- are larger, non-portable machines;
- also require a keyboard, monitor/s and a mouse;
- have more computing power for a little less cost;
- can handle more powerful technologies;
- can be upgraded easily to meet changing needs.

Obviously, an administration terminal will not need to work as hard as a CAD terminal, and the latter will not require the processing power of a 3D rendering terminal, so workstations will need to be set up and tailored to the nature and type of work to be produced. This may also mean that some terminals have dual uses, so that file storage locations will become important, to allow access to data from anywhere within the network.

When deciding on a monitor, budget tends to be the deciding factor; however, a workstation for predominantly CAD users may benefit from having two screens rather than one, especially when using BIM and 3D design, so that a number of views can be developed simultaneously.

There are a number of ergonomic issues involved in the layout of computer workplaces, all of which can have serious implications for the health and safety of the user if a workstation is set out incorrectly. Some of the key issues are:

- the right desk
- monitor location
- sitting correctly
- the right working chair
- good lighting for productive work

- optimum climate
- acoustics.

It is important to be familiar with all these issues, and those highlighted on the HSE website (www.hse.gov.uk/msd/dse/index.htm), as well as ensuring that workstation users are aware of the implications of amending any workstation set-up. See the HSE's guidance leaflet *Working with Display Screen Equipment (DSE)* (www.hse.gov.uk/pubns/indg36.pdf).

The operating system is the interface between the hardware and the user. It is responsible for the management and coordination of resource sharing on the computer. When deciding which operating system to use it is vital to understand what information is to be produced and how, both now and in the future, to ensure that the OS used will always offer compatibility, durability, flexibility and adaptability to the business.

It may be that the business requires the use of more than one type of operating system to enable the efficient use of some programs, and it is possible to network computers running dissimilar operating systems for sharing resources such as files and applications, as well as printing and scanning peripherals, using either wired or wireless connections.

It should be noted that currently some 2D and 3D drawing applications, as well as some BIM applications such as Revit, cannot be run natively on operating systems other than Windows; however, a secondary piece of software such as Boot Camp or Parallels (for the Mac platform) can allow additional operating systems to run either virtually or in native mode, allowing applications such as Revit 2010 to run. However, a copy of the Windows OS will be needed as well.

When considering an operating system, it is essential to understand what needs to be done and research the system fully to ensure it will support any requirements, both now and in the future.

The hard drive is generally where all files and programs are stored in a basic network, and should be chosen based on its speed, size and the type of interface. The faster a drive spins, the faster data can be accessed and transferred, and the faster it runs, the more expensive it is, but if a network is supported by a server the storage capability of the hard drive is not as relevant as the speed.

Networking workstations allows data and information to flow freely within an office, as well as allowing both software and hardware to be shared. They also mean that data can be stored in a single location on a server and backed up automatically and remotely from a single location, ensuring that all information has a basic level of protection.

12

The server is critical to the success of a large network, and choosing what to buy should be relatively easy with the advice of an IT specialist, but an awareness of what the server needs to do is paramount. Key considerations include:

- How many people will be accessing the server?
- Will multiple users affect the processing speed?
- Will frequency of access to the information affect speed?
- Will different types of data be stored on different servers?
- Will servers be in different geographic locations?
- Which servers will require a shared internet connection?

A good server should meet as many of these needs as the budget allows, but it should also make provision for the expected rate of growth.

Virtualisation technology should also be considered, for desktops and servers, as advances in desktop technology mean that even some of the more resource-hungry applications can be virtualised.

A virtual desktop environment allows a company to manage its desktops better, as all the data is stored centrally, and a new desktop, application, patches or service packs can be deployed for all users at once, rather than having to carry out the process at each workstation, one by one.

This type of technology can also save on the cost of PCs and workstations, as all that is required on the desk is a 'thin client', i.e. a smaller machine allowing access to the network.

Again, it is important to understand the budget, and what is needed, and to seek advice from an IT specialist to help design the basis of the system: this can save both cost and time when expanding and developing a system in the future.

12.6   Backing up

Backing up data is vital for any business; lost information can cause a major crisis or, worse, lead to business failure. Individuals who don't regularly back up computer data run this risk. Backups are needed in case a file or a group of files are lost because of a hardware failure, accidental deletion, a software corruption, or a stolen drive. Whatever the reason, it may just be good to have access to older versions of files.

Business impact analysis

In order to determine the effects of a loss of systems or data, or of denial of access, a business impact analysis (BIA) should be carried out – this can be done internally or outsourced to a professional organisation.

The purpose of the BIA is to help a company identify which information, operations and processes are essential to the survival of the business. The ultimate aim of a BIA is to understand what is required to protect systems, data – and staff.

The BIA will identify how quickly essential business information and/or processes have to return to full operation following a disaster situation. It will delineate the impact of disaster scenarios on the ability to deliver product, or to support mission-critical services. In addition, the BIA will facilitate identification of the resources required to resume business operations to an appropriate level.

Impacts are identified based on a worst-case scenario that assumes that the physical infrastructure supporting the essential systems has been destroyed, and all records, equipment, etc. are not accessible within a 30-day period.

A completed BIA should also allow a company to identify two key objectives:

- **Recovery point objective** (RPO) – defining the amount of acceptable data loss by application, in the event of a disaster. This can be from zero to minutes or hours, depending on the criticality of the data. For example, if you determine that you will have a backup schedule running at midnight each night, and you were to lose your systems at, say, 3pm the following day, all changes to that data would be lost. The RPO will identify how much data you believe you can afford to lose – in this instance it's a day's work.
- **Recovery time objective** (RTO) – defining the amount of acceptable downtime, from the initial disaster, to when each critical business process is available to users. For example, a company may be able to survive for days without its supplier's database, but only for hours without a printer or email system. The RTO is very dependent on the recovery processes the company chooses to employ, and how it implements them.

The lower the RPO and RTO, the more complex and expensive the backup policy will become. With an accurate definition of each, a backup strategy can be decided upon that is in line with the BIA, aiding the development of a recovery plan.

This should be defined as the business continuity plan; it should be an integral part of the company's IT strategy, and must include recovery of systems and data, but also what happens to staff if there is a denial of access or loss of office space.

Some form of alternative medium will be needed to store backups. It is preferable to use something removable and portable to allow backups to be stored away from the computer, such as a USB stick, external hard disk,

12

Figure 12.1 *Determining a continuity plan*

DVD-R, DVD+R, DVD-RW, another PC on the network, a web-based storage system, or a combination of any of these.

The backup process can be a manual one, which can be time-consuming, depending on the number of terminals and the amount of data being reviewed; or it can be automatic, using data backup software.

12.7   Digital information standards

When producing any information, it is essential to ensure that it is developed in a structured and documented way. This should allow a number of different users to work on the same information without affecting the format or the intention of the content. It is therefore essential to develop a 'standard' that encompasses the way information is to be created and developed. Such a standard will cover primarily the production of drawings, and will define a standard method and procedure used to develop and present all design information and documentation for projects; however, it may be expanded to cover presentations, reports and marketing information.

A standard:

- will ensure that all drawings created are to a consistent standard and format;
- will ensure that all drawings allow the efficient integration, production and communication of drawing data throughout the duration of a project, both internally and externally;
- should be flexible enough to adjust to changes in software and working processes;
- should be managed by a single source to ensure that decisions are amended and implemented, even while it may be driven and maintained by a group of users.

To ensure coordination with other consultants, and to ensure that best practice guidance is followed, any information standard should be based on the principles outlined within the following:

- BS 1192 – the British Standard that establishes the methodology for managing the production, distribution and quality of construction information, including that generated by CAD systems, and which draws extensively from the Code of Procedure for the Construction Industry, published by CPIC.

- PAS 1192-2:2013. Specification for information management for the capital/ delivery phase of construction projects using building information modelling. This specification develops the BS 1192 standard and is the first of two documents providing guidance about best practice implementation of BIM. It has been sponsored by the Construction Industry Council (CIC) and sets out the workflow and processes to create a BIM Level 2 model. The second document when completed will define the methodology for achieving a BIM Level 3 model.
- BS ISO 12006-2:2001. Building construction. Organization of information about construction works. Framework for classification of information. The implementation of BS ISO 12006-2 in the UK is published under the name Uniclass. It is intended for organising library materials and for structuring product literature and project information. A new edition of this standard is due to be published in 2014.
- AEC (UK) CAD and BIM Standards. A unified standard for the architectural, engineering and construction industry in the UK. AEC (UK) provides a number of best practice guidance documents for the production of CAD and BIM information.
- AVANTI ICT Collaborative Working: Toolkit documents.
- CPIC Production information: a code of procedure for the construction industry. This code has been revised and extended to cover the use of CAD, and to take into account the use of schedules of work. It provides pragmatic guidance on the use of drawings, specifications and schedules of work, and the methods used to coordinate the information contained within them. Key themes that appear in the code are standardisation, information reuse and information management.

Information standards should cover all the processes that occur throughout the design, construction and facility management work stages, as well as the coordination of the project information created by either internal or external design disciplines, including reports, specifications, schedules, model files (2D and 3D), drawings, programs, databases and quantities.

12.8   Software and information management

Current computer-aided design (CAD) software packages range from 2D vector-based drafting systems through to 3D solid and surface modellers, with or without metadata. However, all of the mainstream applications, whatever the basic system, are striving towards greater interoperability and the more efficient production of a single project BIM.

12

CAD requires a significant investment, and it is important to understand what application will best suit the type of work to be produced, both now and in the future. The choice of software will also be intrinsically linked to the choice of hardware and operating system, so it is important that all three are considered together. For example, powerful desktops are more suited to producing 3D images and designs using BIM techniques than are most laptops, which would struggle with the processing.

Understanding how software is utilised across a practice is also fundamental, and smaller practices may benefit from the sharing of software licences, whereas larger practices may consider investing in network licences. Software is generally licensed per number of users, but if different people are working on different applications at different stages of a project they will require the licence only when actually using the software. If there is a small server-controlled network, then installing the licence and applications to the server and allocating the rights to the software as it is opened on a terminal means that the number of licences required will be less than 100% of the workstations. Ensuring that staff close applications once they have completed a piece of work is difficult to manage, and can lead to a need for more licences per user than theoretically necessary.

Before reviewing the working requirements of any software it is worth understanding how the types and arrangements of software licensing are packaged for use. Software is continually developing, and new and better versions can be released annually, quickly outdating tools and the ability to communicate with others.

Licences can be assigned per user, per application; alternatively, developers can offer some form of annual membership or licence that enables each upgrade/development of the software that year to be received free of charge, based on a fee per user/workstation over and above the licence costs (which may be discounted in this instance).

It is important to ensure that software will be compatible before deciding on a mainstream application. Interoperability will avoid the more time-consuming and costly process of redrawing the design, and the potential loss of data each time impacts are assessed in different applications, as opposed to simply transferring a design from one to the other.

Programs that assess the environmental aspects of a design, for example, will work more effectively if they are compatible with the modelling software, and the development of the design will be less restricted if the software is compatible with programs that support the structural, mechanical, electrical, acoustics, lighting, and civil engineering disciplines.

Mainstream 2D and 3D packages may also offer 'light' versions with reduced functionality, which may suit both budget and aspirations, but again it is worth researching what the likely upgrade costs and the potential development of the software will be in the future. Furthermore, given the significant development and investment towards the production of a single project model utilising intelligent components, it is important to understand whether the software chosen, if not a BIM application, can and/or will be upgraded to offer a BIM solution.

Although special hardware is not required for 2D drafting and some 3D modelling, except perhaps a high-quality graphics card, if BIM is ultimately the preferred route then the software may be much more memory intensive and require faster, larger processors and graphics cards, which will impact on the workstations used.

In addition to CAD packages it is likely that the practice will be investing in desktop publishing software, database and scheduling software, programming and graphic/image manipulation, financial management and project management applications and many others. As with hardware, it is important to take into account compatibility, durability, flexibility and adaptability to the business, and the future of the business, when assessing which software package is the most appropriate.

References and further reading

BS 1192:2007. Collaborative production of architectural, engineering and construction information. Code of practice (London: BSI, 2007).

BS ISO 12006-2:2001. Building construction – Organization of information about construction works – Part 2: Framework for classification of information (London: BSI, 2001).

Hovestadt, L. and Danaher, T., *Beyond the Grid: Architecture and Information Technology* (Basel: Birkhäuser Verlag, 2009).

Kalay, Y.E. and Mitchell, W.J., *Architecture's New Media: Principles, Theories and Methods of Computer Aided Design* (Cambridge, MA: MIT Press, 2005).

Klaschka, R., *BIM in Small Practices* (London: RIBA Publishing, 2014 forthcoming).

Mosey, D., *BIM, the Law and the Way Forward for Construction* (London, RIBA Publishing, 2014 forthcoming).

PAS 1192-2:2013. Specification for information management for the capital/delivery phase of construction projects using building information modelling (London: BSI, 2013).

Race, S., *BIM Demystified*, 2nd edn (London: RIBA Publishing, 2013).

12

BIM

www.bimtaskgroup.org

CAD standards

http://aecuk.wordpress.com

CAD software

www.bentley.com
www.autodesk.com
www.graphisoft.com
www.nemetschek.net

Knowledge management

> **THIS CHAPTER:**
>
> - defines knowledge management and its uses;
> - describes how to establish a knowledge-based company;
> - introduces knowledge-led project processes.

13.1 Introduction

With the rising tide of information flooding across our desktops, it is more important than ever to filter out what we don't want – spam – and make sure we don't miss what is essential. But as critical as information management is knowledge management (KM). The means to share knowledge within a business community (that is, within a company and its supply chain) will give a practice a critical edge in an ever-more competitive marketplace. This is even more important with the advent of increasing levels of innovation, requiring the evolving knowledge to be assimilated at an ever faster rate.

There is a general realisation that companies must become more customer focused and create value, while at the same time staff functions and management structures are being rationalised and reduced to meet tighter financial margins. There is therefore a need to replace the informal knowledge management previously achieved through unplanned staff interaction with more formal means of communication and cross-fertilisation.

This is as important for the sole practitioner as for the medium or large practice, with increasing dependence on a network of associated companies or individuals to manage the design process and construction projects.

13.2 What is knowledge management?

People are valuable resources, and while the information they hold is useful, it is far more so if shared with others. Employees need to 'know what the company knows', and be able to make maximum use of the knowledge. This knowledge resides in many different places – in electronic databases and filing cabinets as well as in people's heads. All too often, even in a small company, one part of the business repeats the work of another simply because it is impossible to keep track of, and make use of, knowledge in other parts. Businesses need to know:

- what their knowledge assets are, and
- how to manage, access, and make use of these assets to get maximum return.

Knowledge assets are the knowledge regarding the market, the products, the technologies and the organisations that a business has or needs to have. KM is not only about managing these assets but also about the processes that act upon them. These processes include developing, preserving, using and sharing knowledge. Therefore KM involves the identification and analysis of available and required knowledge assets, and knowledge asset related processes, and the subsequent planning and control of actions to develop both the assets and the processes so as to fulfil organisational objectives. KM focuses on objectives such as:

- improved performance;
- innovation;
- the sharing of lessons learned;
- understanding best practice;
- continuous improvement;
- encouraging the sharing of knowledge.

It helps individuals and groups to:

- share insights;
- reduce redundant work or 'reinventing the wheel';
- reduce training time for new employees;
- retain knowledge as employees move to other companies;
- adapt to changing environments and markets.

Success depends in large part on the quality of knowledge that organisations apply to their business processes. In architecture this is typically expert knowledge of the building type – residential, commercial, industrial, and so on – as well as matters such as those covered in this book, relating to practice and project management.

KM as a specific process was established around 25 years ago, but is seldom discussed in the construction industry. Construction projects generate vast quantities of information (drawings, reports, specifications, correspondence, etc.) and there are well-established methods for storing and retrieving it. Important as this is, however, it is not the fundamental objective of KM. KM involves activities and processes to create, manage, retrieve and distribute information and the intellectual property of a company, including the insights and experiences of individuals and information embedded in the organisational processes of the company. For architects this is concerned primarily with the design process, and how to ensure the right knowledge is applied at the right time to deliver the best solution.

> **Continuous improvement**
>
> KM facilitates 'continuous improvement', a cornerstone of the lean design principles that originated in the motor industry and have been applied to construction by some of the most successful contractors and consultants. Lean thinking is focused on efficiency and the elimination of waste, and is based on five principles:
>
> • Specify what creates value from the customer's perspective.
> • Identify all steps across the whole value stream.
> • Make those actions that create value flow.
> • Only produce what is pulled (needed) by the customer, on a just-in-time basis.
> • Strive for perfection by continually removing successive layers of waste.
>
> Continuous improvement can be achieved only by measuring performance, and KM will facilitate this. For an explanation of these processes, refer to the Lean Construction Institute website: www.leanconstruction.org.

13.3   How is knowledge retained and communicated?

Knowledge is either 'tacit' or 'explicit'. Tacit knowledge is that which an individual may not be consciously aware of; explicit knowledge is knowledge that an individual holds consciously, in a form that can easily be communicated to others. Successful KM needs to convert internalised tacit knowledge into explicit knowledge in order for it to be shared.

Knowledge can also be considered as either the embedded knowledge of a system or the embodied knowledge representing a person's learned capability. Collaborative environments – 'communities of practice' as they are referred to – facilitate both knowledge creation and transfer, and this can be a model for an architectural practice.

Knowledge can be actively managed, or 'pushed', where individuals specifically feed knowledge into a shared facility or database for use by others. Alternatively, individuals can make knowledge requests of experts associated with a particular subject on an ad hoc basis (a 'pull' strategy). In such an instance, expert individuals can provide their insights to the particular person or people needing this (see Section 13.5).

At the strategic level the practice needs to be able to analyse and plan its business in terms of the knowledge it currently has, and the knowledge it needs for future business processes. At the tactical level a practice needs to be concerned with identifying and formalising existing knowledge, acquiring new knowledge for future use, archiving it, and creating systems that enable effective and efficient application of the knowledge within the organisation. At the operational level the knowledge is used in everyday practice by the staff of the business, who need access to the right knowledge, at the right time.

13.4   A plan of action

The following are matters to be considered in establishing a knowledge-based company.

- **Identifying what knowledge assets a company possesses**

  - Where is the knowledge asset?
  - What does it contain?
  - What is its use?
  - What form is it in?
  - How accessible is it?

The practice will need to assess what intellectual property it owns, and consider how best to use it – for example, a unique piece of R&D work that might give a commercial edge, or facilitate an introduction to a potential client or business partner. It should also organise its database to include:

- information on clients, consultants, contractors, suppliers and so on;
- information/benchmarking on best practice in the industry, as well as what tacit knowledge it has with the individuals within the practice and with business partners and collaborators, such that it is easily found and retrievable;
- internal news and information;
- practice information (staff, projects, etc.);
- the practice's standard forms;
- practice policies;
- practice manuals/procedures.

The practice should also consider development of new assets, tailored to its business development plan (see Sections 4.4, 5.2 and 5.3).

- **Analysing how the knowledge can add value**

  - What are the opportunities for using the knowledge asset?
  - What would be the effect of its use?
  - What are the current obstacles to its use?
  - What would be its increased value to the company?

Consider how to use the knowledge assets and optimise their commercial advantage. This might be either on projects, to improve the design, or

13

as part of a marketing initiative. Understand what it is aimed to achieve through this.

Assess whether there are any matters preventing or impeding its use such as copyright. Understand what measurable benefits it could bring.

- **Specifying what actions are necessary to achieve better usability and added value**

  - How to plan the actions to use the knowledge asset.
  - How to enact actions.
  - How to monitor actions.

Set out a programme for development and implementation of the assets. Continuous improvement can be achieved only through measurement. Plan proposed actions, and monitor their implementation.

- **Reviewing the use of the knowledge to ensure added value**

  - Did the use of it produce the desired added value?
  - How can the knowledge asset be maintained for this use?
  - Did the use create new opportunities?

Record how the assets are used, and which are the most valuable. Determine how best to manage and maintain them so that they remain up to date.

13.5 Knowledge management at the project level

Knowledge processes can be applied to great effect at a project level. The core principles that will make knowledge management work are:

- the establishment of 'coaches'; and
- the workshop as the place where design takes place.

Coaches are individuals with recognised skills and knowledge in the fields of concept design, technical and sustainable design, and in the principal sectors/building types operated in by the practice. They have a responsibility to maintain and develop knowledge in their field, and inject that knowledge into the project design process through the design workshop. In smaller practices one person may have more than one coaching role, although this should be avoided where possible. Where the practice has five people or fewer the process will occur more naturally, thanks to economies of scale, but the principles should be maintained nonetheless.

The design workshop provides an environment where all the knowledge necessary for the specific design activity can be located in one place. To derive the most benefit from the workshop, it is important that design is actually undertaken there, rather than it merely being a place to collate the data to be used in the design. This is a somewhat counterintuitive design methodology – architects' training involves working largely on their own, and evaluating their solution through critical review by peers after the design stage has been completed. The knowledge process needs to become part of the culture of the practice to work effectively, and thereby generate consistency of output. It is important to note that the coaches do not actually undertake the design, but – as their title denotes – facilitate it, and coach the design team using their expert knowledge and skills.

The aim of this approach is to ensure that the best expertise available within the practice is applied to every project, at the right times in the project cycle, and in the most effective ways possible.

In order to achieve this aim a practice will need to take the following steps:

- Identify core sectors and areas of expertise.
- Identify individuals with expertise, and exceptional experience and skill.
- Create coaching groups representing sector, technical, sustainability and concept areas, with a remit to increase skills and knowledge.
- Develop a workshop-based process involving coaching activity relative to project work.

Coaching activities should run in parallel with but be integral to project teamwork led by the project architect.

At project level, successful coaching continuously improves efficiency and the quality of design work. At practice level, successful coaching group activities have the ability to place the practice among the most knowledgeable practitioners in the chosen sector areas, among the most advanced in the understanding of new materials and construction techniques, and among the most skilled in the appreciation and realisation of finely crafted and coherent buildings.

The process must encompass all design activities, from inception through to post-project feedback, and should be based on the following key principles:

- Don't start designing until you are ready (i.e. have the necessary information with respect to brief, site and sector knowledge).
- Establish your design agenda (i.e. know what you want to achieve in terms of quality, cost and marketing value).
- Hold regular design workshops.
- Use your expertise.
- Don't change what you have fixed (i.e. use progressive fixity, and avoid revisiting decisions made during a previous design stage).

13

Key learning points

The following points will ensure consistent and efficient uptake of a knowledge-led approach to project work and delivering value:

- Ensure that the project architect and their team have ownership of the design, that the coaches are seen as advisers, and they do not take an executive role in the design process.
- Ensure that all members of staff buy in to the process, and use it consistently across the practice. It may be necessary to demonstrate its benefits to promote its use. The benefits are the delivery of better quality design, in terms both of creativity and of technical standards, and greater consistency of quality from project to project.
- Use design workshops right from the outset, and through to completion of the project. The degree of input of the different coaches may vary through the life of the project, but there is a role for all of them from start to finish. For example, the technical and sustainable design coaches may influence the orientation of the building at the first workshop, where initial design ideas are established. Concept coaches will ensure that the key design principles are maintained in the later, detailed design stages.
- As with all meetings, the design workshop should last no longer than is necessary – the project architect should set out an agenda beforehand, and make sure it is adhered to. Of course, the design process is not linear; it moves from broad issues to ones of detail, backwards and forwards, in an iterative manner. There will be some design sessions where the agenda is open, to allow this, but there should always be a goal to be reached at its conclusion.
- The attendees at workshops will vary and will be determined by the project architect based on the aims of that session. They do not necessarily have to include the full complement of coaches every time, but coaches should maintain an understanding of the status and content of the design, and be prepared to input where necessary.
- As coaches are unlikely to play their role full time, and will have projects of their own, they must get into the mindset that – within reason – they must make themselves available to participate in workshops.
- The process must be carefully managed so as to make the best use of the coaches' time. They are likely to be senior members of staff, and their efforts must therefore be carefully targeted so as to add value to the design process. For larger practices a knowledge manager should be given overall responsibility for coordinating the efforts of the coaches, and monitoring workshop implementation.

References and further reading

Anumba, C. J., Egbu, C. and Carrillo, P., *Knowledge Management in Construction* (Oxford: Blackwell Science, 2005).

Hyerle, D. N. and Alper, L., *Student Successes with Thinking Maps* (Thousand Oaks, CA: Corwin, 2011).

De Bono, E., *Six Thinking Hats* (London: Penguin, 2009).

Index